"Hailing frequencies open"

CRITICAL EXPLORATIONS IN SCIENCE FICTION AND FANTASY
(a series edited by Donald E. Palumbo and C.W. Sullivan III)
Earlier Works: www.mcfarlandpub.com
Recent Works: 42 *The Heritage of Heinlein* (Thomas D. Clareson and Joe Sanders, 2014)
43 *The Past That Might Have Been, the Future That May Come* (Lauren J. Lacey, 2014)
44 *Environments in Science Fiction: Essays* (ed. Susan M. Bernardo, 2014)
45 *Discworld and the Disciplines: Critical Approaches to the Terry Pratchett Works* (ed. Anne Hiebert Alton, William C. Spruiell, 2014)
46 *Nature and the Numinous in Mythopoeic Fantasy Literature* (Christopher Straw Brawley, 2014)
47 *J.R.R. Tolkien, Robert E. Howard and the Birth of Modern Fantasy* (Deke Parsons, 2014)
48 *The Monomyth in American Science Fiction Films* (Donald E. Palumbo, 2014)
49 *The Fantastic in Holocaust Literature and Film* (ed. Judith B. Kerman, John Edgar Browning, 2014)
50 *Star Wars in the Public Square* (Derek R. Sweet, 2016)
51 *An Asimov Companion* (Donald E. Palumbo, 2016)
52 *Michael Moorcock* (Mark Scroggins, 2016)
53 *The Last Midnight: Essays* (ed. Leisa A. Clark, Amanda Firestone, Mary F. Pharr, 2016)
54 *The Science Fiction Mythmakers: Religion, Science and Philosophy in Wells, Clarke, Dick and Herbert* (Jennifer Simkins, 2016)
55 *Gender and the Quest in British Science Fiction Television* (Tom Powers, 2016)
56 *Saving the World Through Science Fiction: James Gunn* (Michael R. Page, 2017)
57 *Wells Meets Deleuze* (Michael Starr, 2017)
58 *Science Fiction and Futurism: Their Terms and Ideas* (Ace G. Pilkington, 2017)
59 *Science Fiction in Classic Rock: Musical Explorations of Space, Technology and the Imagination, 1967–1982* (Robert McParland, 2017)
60 *Patricia A. McKillip and the Art of Fantasy World-Building* (Audrey Isabel Taylor, 2017)
61 *The Fabulous Journeys of* Alice *and* Pinocchio: *Exploring Their Parallel Worlds* (Laura Tosi with Peter Hunt, 2018)
62 *A* Dune *Companion: Characters, Places and Terms in Frank Herbert's Original Six Novels* (Donald E. Palumbo, 2018)
63 *Fantasy Literature and Christianity: A Study of the Mistborn, Coldfire, Fionavar Tapestry and Chronicles of Thomas Covenant Series* (Weronika Łaszkiewicz, 2018)
64 *The British Comic Invasion: Alan Moore, Warren Ellis, Grant Morrison and the Evolution of the American Style* (Jochen Ecke, 2019)
65 *The Archive Incarnate: The Embodiment and Transmission of Knowledge in Science Fiction* (Joseph Hurtgen, 2018)
66 *Women's Space: Essays on Female Characters in the 21st Century Science Fiction Western* (ed. Melanie A. Marotta, 2019)
67 *"Hailing frequencies open": Communication in* Star Trek: The Next Generation (Thomas D. Parham, III, 2019)
68 *The Global Vampire: Essays on the Undead in Popular Culture Around the World* (ed. Cait Coker, 2019)

"Hailing frequencies open"
Communication in *Star Trek: The Next Generation*

THOMAS D. PARHAM III

CRITICAL EXPLORATIONS IN
SCIENCE FICTION AND FANTASY, 67
Series Editors Donald E. Palumbo *and* C.W. Sullivan III

McFarland & Company, Inc., Publishers
Jefferson, North Carolina

ISBN (print) 978-1-4766-7668-5
ISBN (ebook) 978-1-4766-3657-3

LIBRARY OF CONGRESS AND BRITISH LIBRARY
CATALOGUING DATA ARE AVAILABLE

Library of Congress Control Number: 2019943095

© 2019 Thomas D. Parham III. All rights reserved

No part of this book may be reproduced or transmitted in any form or by any means, electronic or mechanical, including photocopying or recording, or by any information storage and retrieval system, without permission in writing from the publisher.

Front cover images © 2019 Shutterstock

Printed in the United States of America

*McFarland & Company, Inc., Publishers
Box 611, Jefferson, North Carolina 28640
www.mcfarlandpub.com*

To the memories of my parents, T. David Parham, Jr., and Marion Cordice Parham, who never quite understood my rabid fascination with a television show about space heroes but encouraged me nonetheless, and to the memory of Gene Roddenberry, who enticed generations of fans to dream of life in that "final frontier."

Acknowledgments

John Donne wrote, "No man is an island," which is certainly the case with this book.

First, I would like to acknowledge my graduate school mentors, Dr. Gillette Elvgren, Dr. Darlene Graves, Dr. Michael Graves, Dr. Terry Lindvall, Dr. Doug Tarpley, Dr. Elaine Waller, and Professor John Lawing, as well as three of my United States Naval Academy English professors who inspired me before each of them "shuffled off this mortal coil," Dr. Mary Howland, Dr. Nancy Wicker, and Dr. John Wooten.

Thanks to my dean, Dr. Stephen Johnson, and my chair, Professor Greg Michael, for sabbatical leave and release time to complete this project.

Special recognition to Wendy Mathias, for teaching me the "joy of lex" back in ninth grade. And a shout-out to my former colleagues at Viacom Consumer Products: Paula Block, Harry Lang, and Pam Newton.

I would be remiss if I did not mention Mark A. Altman, Ira Steven Behr, Kenneth Biller, David Gerrold, John Lemay, David Maddox, the late Richard Matheson, Jean Louise Matthias, Kevin Miller, Ronald D. Moore, Josh Rubinstein, P. K. Simonds, Jeri Taylor, and Ronald Wilkerson. Being able to interview people responsible for *Star Trek* and/or who share my love for it and other science fiction truly added depth and breadth to my research.

Many of my friends have helped me complete this task in one way or another: Thom and Lauri Deason, Erik and Jennifer Elvgren, Frank and Sheila Holley, Jim and Jill Lincoln, Ali Marie Matheson, Matt and Leslie Melton, Artie Terry, Alex and Judith Wainer, Tyler and Emily Welch, Julie and Jeremy Wieand, and Paul and Paula Williams.

Finally, I express appreciation to my family: Mae Pouget & Lane Thurmond, Evangeline Greene, Noel Cruz Adams, and my wife, Sarah Joy Adams. Thank you all for your love and encouragement.

Table of Contents

Acknowledgments — vi

Introduction — 1
   Launching *The Next Generation*   1
   The Twin Strains of Sci Fi   4

One—Background — 7
   Science Fiction from Shelley to Star Wars   7
   Growth of a Genre   11
   Star Trek*'s Generations*   15
   The New Voyages   24
   Contextual Communication Theories   32

Two—The Intrapersonal Context — 44
   Data and Symbolic Interactionism   44
   Gender Differences, Worf and Troi   52
   *Character Realization with Picard, Riker, Crusher
     and La Forge*   59
   Summary   63

Three—The Interpersonal Context — 65
   The Parent-Child Dyad   65
   The Mentor-Protégé Dyad   67
   The Friendship Dyad   70
   The Romance Dyad   74
   Summary   83

Four—The Group and Organizational Contexts — 85
   The Enterprise *Command Crew as a Group*   86
   Starfleet as an Organization   92
   Summary   98

viii   Table of Contents

Five—The Mass Communication Context, Part I   100
Intrapersonal Issues: Philosophy of The Next Generation   100
Interpersonal Issues: Parasocial Interactions   112

Six—The Mass Communication Context, Part II   116
Group/Organizational Issues: Fans and Texts   116

Seven—Next Frontiers for Communication Contexts   128
Intrapersonal Issues on Star Trek: Discovery—
   Michael Burnham and the Four Loves   128
Interpersonal Issues on Star Trek: Voyager   136
Group/Organizational Issues on Star Trek: Deep Space Nine—
   Organizational Dissent and the Maquis   142
Audience/Artifact Relationship with Star Trek: Enterprise—
   Reception Theory   145
Summary   149

Conclusion   150
Expanding the Universe   150
Trek Tech   151
The True Legacy   153
"The sky's the limit"   154

Appendix A: List of Star Trek: The Next Generation *Episodes*   157

Appendix B: Research Instrument for Star Trek *Survey*   160

Chapter Notes   163

Bibliography   169

Index   185

Introduction

On September 8, 2018, the Television Academy honored *Star Trek* with the prestigious Governors Award at the Creative Arts Emmy Awards ceremony. Bill Nye, "the Science Guy," led the proceedings and called Gene Roddenberry's creation "a social commentary on the state of humanity brilliantly disguised as science-fiction.... *Star Trek* may have started out as an entertainment series, but it changed the world. And I feel it changed the world for the better" (StarTrek.com). However, when the series debuted on NBC exactly 52 years earlier, the event transpired with little fanfare. Allan Asherman comments, "The September 14 issue of *Variety* contained a negative review of *Star Trek*, stating that the series 'won't work.' The reviewer called it dreary and confusing but conceded the leading performers were trying very hard to be credible. He concluded that *Star Trek* would be "better suited to the Saturday morning kidvid bloc" (31).[1]

In the five decades since its debut, *Star Trek* has developed from a short-lived network television series into a cultural phenomenon. Although the original series only lasted for 79 episodes, it has spawned an animated series, 13 successful motion pictures that grossed an aggregate of more than $1.4 billion, and five spin-off television shows (so far), not to mention countless novels, comic magazines, and other merchandise.

Launching The Next Generation

On October 10, 1986, Mel Harris, then-president of Paramount Television Group, held a studio press conference during which he announced, "Twenty years ago, the genius of one man brought to television a program that has transcended the medium. We are enormously pleased that the man, Gene Roddenberry, is going to do it again" (Nemecek 1). One reason why Harris' announcement came as a surprise was there was a whiff of *déjà vu*. Nine years earlier the studio had similarly announced—in *The New York Times*, no less—a new series, *Star Trek: Phase II*. This show was to launch a fourth television network formed by a consortium of independent stations (Engel 180–181). These plans never came to fruition because "Paramount [was] unable to sell enough advertising time to compete with established TV networks" (Gross 57). Preproduction plans for the *Phase II* pilot episode "In Thy Image" ultimately became the basis for *Star Trek: The Motion Picture* (Alexander 446). Although the history of the initial six *Star Trek* films is not this book's focus, the fact Gene Roddenberry was demoted to executive consultant for *Star Trek II: The Wrath of Khan* is both noteworthy and salient. Longtime fan Bjo Trimble opines, "It must have been a pang to see the child of his creation in the hands of others.... But *Star Trek* has grown far beyond any one person; perhaps even its creator" (46).

Roddenberry's involvement in the new series was an opportunity to disprove such thoughts. In a letter to Janet Quarton he wrote, "I am an independent artist to whom Paramount has laid down the challenge of a lifetime. They very carefully made it clear 'No one thinks it can be done again.' Could you turn your back on that? I certainly can't" (Alexander 501). Even ardent Trekkers were skeptical that lightning could strike again. *Starlog* publisher Kerry O'Quinn, writing before *Star Trek: The Next Generation*'s debut, speculates:

> Frankly, it will be a miracle if the new series succeeds. Nothing in TV History ever equalled [sic] *Star Trek*, and it will be impossible for people not to compare the new to the old—despite everything which is designed to separate the two shows. The *Star Trek* of the 1960s was of such outstanding quality that attempting to match it seems close to folly.
> The ingredient which prevents it from being folly is Gene Roddenberry [6].

Star Trek: The Next Generation premiered the week of September 28, 1987, on 150 television stations—including 108 network affiliates—throughout the United States (Alexander 501). Within six weeks, the show was picked up for a second season (529). In the July 23, 1988, issue of *TV Guide*, Gary D. Christenson compares the original and sequel series: "*Star Trek* depicted us in reckless youth, with a Starship captain who tamed space as vigorously as we laid claim to the future.... *Star Trek: The Next Generation* reveals the child grown—a little more polished, but also more complacent" (39). Reviewing the *Star Trek: The Next Generation—The*

Next Level Blu-ray sampler for *High-Def Digest*, Joshua Zyber opines the series "created a cultural sensation that would grow to eclipse its predecessor in popularity."

In 1994, *Star Trek: The Next Generation* completed a wildly successful, seven-year syndicated run. At the height of its popularity the program was "seen by 20 million people each week, making it second only to 'Wheel of Fortune' among syndicated shows" (Simpson 63). In addition, *Star Trek: The Next Generation* was the top-rated television show with men aged 18 to 49 and "grosse[d] $90 million in first-run ad revenue … and some $70 million in license-fee payments from stations rerunning [it] through the week" (Roush D1). Numerous people speculated as to why Paramount decided to stop production of *Star Trek: The Next Generation* while the show was so successful, but the film debut of the *Next Generation* cast in *Star Trek Generations* seemed to be the most logical explanation. The fifth sequel series *Star Trek: Discovery* premiered on the CBS All Access video-on-demand subscription service on September 24, 2017, and CBS renewed that show for a second season the following month (Goldberg).

Star Trek's impact on popular culture has earned it a prominent place in television history. David Gerrold, a writer for the original series, offers the following observation:

> It is clear that *Star Trek*—I am talking about the TV series and [the] movies here—has become a cultural artifact. The evidence is undeniable. You will find references to *Star Trek* everywhere you go. I've seen it pop up in comic strips, [television shows], murder mysteries, puzzle magazines, arcade games, [and] computer game[s]. *Star Trek* has been studied as a religious phenomenon, a psychological phenomenon, a cultural phenomenon, and even [as] a sexual phenomenon.
>
> I have particularly chosen these examples of the pervasiveness of *Star Trek* because they are "spontaneous." That is, neither Paramount Pictures, nor anyone else involved in merchandising, has created them. Rather, they have occurred as spontaneous expressions of individual affection for the show, its characters, the starship *Enterprise*, and the larger context of optimism that all of those elements represent. Truly *Star Trek* has transcended its origins as a 16-year-old TV series to become a larger expression of American culture [Nov. 82, 40].

Probably the most tangible sign of *Star Trek*'s emergence in American culture appeared in September 1976. NASA had received 400,000 letters from fans who requested that the first space shuttle be named the *Enterprise*. The space agency acquiesced to the fans' request, and the cast of *Star Trek* attended the unveiling of the *Enterprise* later that month. The September 21 edition of *The New York Times* carried the following full-page advertisement:

Introduction

WELCOME ABOARD ... SPACE SHUTTLE *ENTERPRISE* ...
Paramount Pictures and the thousands of loyal fans of "Star Trek" are happy that the United States of America's newest space shuttle has been named after "Star Trek's" starship, the *Enterprise*. (It's nice to know that sometimes science fiction becomes science fact.)[2] [Asherman 151].

The question remains: how and why did a failed 1960s television program transform into a cultural phenomenon and a multi-million dollar industry? To discover an answer, one must first consider the nature of the science-fiction genre.

The Twin Strains of Sci Fi

What is science fiction? Different people have different opinions. The editors of *The Science Fiction Encyclopedia* remark, "All in all, the sf label is so flexible in practice that it is not capable of clear definition.... A work of science fiction should be concerned with the extension of scientific knowledge and all manner of consequences thereof; and should be imaginatively and intellectually adventurous" (Anderson 1). In "Science as Fiction: Technology in Prime Time Television," Jane Banks and Jonathan David Tankel posit that the genre's function is societal. They write, "Science fiction becomes a forum where a particular society's concerns are fictionalized and futurized: *current* issues are reconfigured as speculation, fantasy, and entertainment" (27). The late author Robert A. Heinlein defined sci fi as "realistic speculation about possible future events, based solidly on adequate knowledge of the real world, past and present, and on a thorough understanding of the nature and significance of the scientific method" (22). Heinlein furthermore insisted that all sf writers maintain high scientific standards:

> [A] man whose writing shows that he knows nothing of ballistics nor of astronomy nor of any modern technology would do better not to attempt science fiction. Such things are not science fiction—entertainment they may be; serious speculation they cannot be. The obligation of the writer to his reader to know what he is talking about is even stronger in science fiction than elsewhere, because the ordinary reader has less chance to catch him out. It's not fair, it's cheating [30].

While one can appreciate Heinlein's demand for rigor on behalf of the sci-fi writer, his definition is too restrictive.

None of the above definitions by themselves is quite satisfactory, but author David Gerrold renders a proposal that achieves gestalt: "Science fiction is the contemporary fairy tale, it's the twentieth century morality play. At its worst, it's merely romantic escapism; but at its best, it is the postulation of an alternate reality with which to comment on this one" (*WoST* 13). Gerrold raises a salient point: there are two distinct schools of science fiction. In his book *Television Drama: Agency, Audience and Myth*, John Tulloch describes the "two historically dominant myths operating within the genre":

> (i) On the one hand, there is the SF genre's epistemologically realist potential to construct other worlds ("absent paradigms") which challenge the common-sense paradigms of our own....
> (ii) On the other hand, there was a different intellectual tendency, the mad "hero" of Romanticism, working beyond the *other* (distorted, unacceptable, anti-cultural) boundary of common sense. This was the central character of Victorian Gothic, the strangely experimenting outcast standing for the human spirit against the dull, "ordinary-everyday" and consensual state of social contingency [79–80].

Tulloch essentially points out that "serious" science fiction is based on the linear extrapolation that Heinlein advocated, while escapist space fantasy or space opera has roots in romantic literature. Despite many critics' presumptions that "realistic" sci fi and "escapist" sci fi are diametrically opposed, the genre as a whole is defined and broadened by the dialectical tension between the two traditions.

As the epitome of contemporary, popular science fiction, *Star Trek* has continually embodied this dialectic. The show has been grounded in carefully developed scientific extrapolation, yet at the same time it portrays the romantic aspects of space travel and the heroism of the space travelers. An example of this dialectic in action occurred during an exchange between Ira Steven Behr (executive producer of *Star Trek: Deep Space Nine*) and Kenneth Biller (then-executive story editor of *Star Trek: Voyager*) at a Writers Guild of America panel discussion on science fiction:

> BEHR: J. G. Ballard said, "Earth is the only alien planet." You can deal with aliens and their little gimmicks or with priests who have sex, but the most interesting stories deal with the human condition. The other stuff—transporters, for example—is all make-believe. They're like building blocks. You can have fun with them, but the intellectual pursuit is what's important.
> BILLER: The intellectual pursuits and ethical quandaries are fine, but my little brother—who is a big *Next Generation* fan—often reminds me that he and the other fans want action. They want to see our characters in jeopardy and fight their way out [30 Nov. 1994].

Panel member P. K. Simonds (co-producer of NBC's 1994–95 series *Earth 2*) appropriately added, "You can only get people to think about ideas when you get them to care" (30 Nov. 1994).

Aside from the financial success of the *Star Trek* franchise, creator Gene Roddenberry's other legacy was the union of "serious" science fiction (i.e., linear extrapolation) with space opera. In conjunction, these seemingly dissimilar elements allow *Star Trek* to appeal to a wide spectrum of fans. This researcher postulates that the writers and producers of the contemporary *Star Trek* series continue to exemplify this tension—between empirical sf and romantic sf—in their portrayals of the modes of communication used between and by the characters. The multilevel tapestry of communication contexts embedded within *Star Trek: The Next Generation* can help explain its appeal to viewers. These patterns serve as models for audience members whose sympathy with *Trek* characters on one or more levels often leads to empathy. As a result, *Star Trek* has inspired its audience to form parasocial interactions with the show as well as allowing them to transform mass culture into popular culture (Jenkins 87).

ONE

Background

Science Fiction from Shelley to Star Wars

Mary Shelley

Science fiction's roots are steeped in 19th-century romanticism. Mary Shelley's *Frankenstein* (1818) is regarded as a precursor to modern science fiction. Victor's quest to wield control over life (and death) made him the template for generations of fictional mad scientists who followed. In her introduction to the novel, Diane Johnson analyzes Shelley's dialogue: "As in Promethean legend, the creator has abandoned his creation, and has incurred his wrath; man is embittered and has turned away from God" (xv). Thomas D. Clareson adds to Johnson's analysis in describing the novel's climax:

> The scientist and his creature are locked in the chase across the Arctic ice, for Dr. Frankenstein has been overwhelmed by his sense of guilt at the outcome of his experiments—his creation of human life. As for the monster, he suffers as a result of what he regards as the injustice of a world he never made and lashes out after he has been ostracized by society (including his creator) [18].

Shelley's masterpiece, thus, is a precautionary tale about scientists who try to play God and "how terrible can be the world into which science may take an individual" (19).

Jules Verne

The next major forerunner of the science fiction genre was Jules Verne. Although Verne's novels were largely based on "pseudo-science,"[1] many of them proved to be prophetic. Biographer Lawrence Lynch comments on Verne's technique, "Using a modicum of scientific data as a point of departure, he added to and embellished it, included a few proper names and references for the sake of authenticity, and drew the rest of the material from his fertile imagination" (70). The *Nautilus* from *20,000 Leagues Under the Sea* is a typical example of Verne's creativity. Submersible boats had existed since the American Revolution but had never been deemed appropriate as warships. Though the combatants of the Battle of Hampton Roads—the USS *Monitor* and the CSS *Virginia*—during the U.S. Civil War were not submersibles, their lack of relative success combined with the failure of the *Hunley*, a Confederate submarine that sunk before returning to port, implied that an ironclad was not effective as a man-of-war. Verne's *Nautilus*, however, was an engineering marvel. A powerful warship powered by electricity, the *Nautilus* was also equipped with a library, an organ, a portrait gallery, and a collection of marine specimens.

An earlier Verne classic, *From the Earth to the Moon* (1865), is significant because of his predictions that Americans would be the first to go to the moon, that Florida would be the launch site, and that such a venture would be a vast engineering project. Lauds Lynch, "At a time when inventions like the railroad and steamboat were just coming into practical and reliable use, Verne was writing about space travel in realistic terms, and he was doing so 100 years before the project was actually accomplished" (43). The author's uncanny ability to predict the future is perhaps most evident in his "lost" novel, *Paris in the 20th Century*, which was written in 1863 but rejected by Verne's publisher Pierre-Jules Hetzel. In his rejection letter, he remarks, "You have undertaken an impossible task, and you have not executed it well" (Crumley 59). When the novel was discovered in 1994, reviewers were bemused that the "outlandish" descriptions in the novel include the fax machine, traffic jams on Paris streets illuminated by electric lights, elevated trains, the elevator, and Muzak— "200 pianos connected by electric current and played by a single musician" (59).

Verne, like Shelley, did not merely speculate about scientific invention in his writing but also related his insight into the human condition. Ray Bradbury groups Verne with Herman Melville and labels them both as ardent and "American" blasphemers: "'American' yes in their newness and their attack upon the universe and this world rolling through that universe" (1). He continues by contrasting the two authors:

> Melville's Whale resents inquiry. But Verne's "Nautilus" is the machine of curiousity ... prolonging a searchful blasphemy into construction and jigsawing the grand puzzle into a whole. Ahab orders God to reform Himself in a better image. Nemo asks mankind to reform in cleaner, higher-spirited, well-mannered ranks. Both men, being reformers, inevitably destroy for their purposes [9].

Many of Verne's novels focus on a reconstruction of society, but with a higher moral order than the original version (Lynch 63). Verne used science as a background for his works, but he always subordinated technology in favor of the technician. The author realized that despite how wondrous man's inventions might be, they would not be able to make "life one whit happier" (Crumley 59). Despite Verne's uncanny prescience, he has often been criticized for his lack of rigor in describing science. "Jules Verne had played with [scientific discovery], but his command of science and the scientific method was weak," comments David C. Smith. "[Verne's] books function best as adventure stories, even when scientifically plausible" (56).

H. G. Wells

The author credited with marrying "real" science with fiction was Herbert George Wells. Wells' novels often contained social commentary and emphasized "the linear extrapolation of present-day trends" (Canary 169). The author's concerns ran the gamut from post-catastrophic stories (*The War of The Worlds*), to the meaning of history (*The Time Machine*), to utopian literature (*A Modern Utopia*). In that latter novel Wells expresses "the hope that, under the leadership and intelligent planning of an elite group of persons, applying the most advanced and technological knowledge, man can build a progressively more ideal society" (King 249).[2] This conceit is diametrically opposed to the Judeo-Christian tenant of original sin, which is not surprising considering the cultural context of the author's era.

During Wells' time, new advances had been made in biology, geology, astronomy, and chemistry. Darwin's theory of evolution forever altered man's conception of his place in the universe and raised two major questions: "What more can be learned?" and "Can man replace the biblical God as creator?" (Smith 51–52). In challenging theology, science sought to answer questions concerning the nature of the universe and reality. Wells was the first science fiction writer to meet this challenge. Biographer David C. Smith remarks, "What Wells could do, which science usually resisted, was to posit ethical questions to be associated with the working out of the scientific method. Others could have posed these questions, but most had asked them within the context of Christianity, not realizing that answers could be sought outside the metaphysical realm" (53).

Wells' rejection of traditional theology is clearly shown in *The Island of Dr. Moreau.* Noted science fiction author and critic Brian W. Aldiss offers this analysis of the novel:

> Moreau is a nineteenth-century God—Mary Shelley's protagonist in his maturity—Frankenstein Unbound.... Blame for the wretched state of the Beasts is set firmly on Moreau. "Before they had been beasts, their instincts fitly adapted to their surroundings, and happy as living things may be. Now they stumbled in the shackles of humanity, lived in a fear that never died, fretted by a law they could not understand." At this moment, Wells is trying to create a synthesis between evolutionary and religious theory. Not to put too fine a gloss on it, he does not think highly of the Creator. Nor does he of the created. Moreau says it for Wells, declaring that he can "see into their very souls, and see there nothing but the souls of beasts, beasts that perish—anger, and the lusts to live and gratify themselves" [125].

Wells clearly subscribed to the Darwinistic view of man as an animal. The author, however, also favored the Nietzschean conception of the superman. "[A]lthough the future of man has in it the possibility for immortality and the other attributes of divinity," describes S. C. Fredericks, "the moral character of man as superman still seems less than satisfactory" (54).

Wells' first novel, *The Time Machine*, capsulizes the inherent dualism of these beliefs by showing the mutually parasitic world of the Morlock and the Eloi (Kagle 224–225). Man is both a pale, decadent, artistic people—the Eloi—as well as a dark, predatory creature—the Morlocks (Aldiss 118–119). The author's concern is teleological in nature: "Civilizations rise and fall, but man moves on to his destiny, which is God" (Canary 167). Wells sincerely believed in man's ability to transcend time (Warrick 188) but acknowledged human shortcomings as part of the inflexible catholicity of human nature (Delany 285). In his essay "Critical Methods: Speculative Fiction," Samuel R. Delany elaborates:

> Wells's "Romances of the Future" come from much the same impulse that produced his monumental multivolume *An Outline of History.* The future stories were an out growth of the perfectly viable fancy that history might well continue beyond the present. Both the historical work and the SF, however, [emerged] from the same Victorian views: man's knowledge, in general, and his technology, in particular, develop in a more or less orderly way; and also that, in a given situation, human behavior will always be more or less the same, no matter when, or where [283].

Thus, despite Wells' presumption that man could rise above his humanity and become godlike, he recognized that man's position in the natural order was precarious (Clareson 23). Wells is important to the legacy of science fiction because he married science and art, addressing "how and what the new and better world would be" (Smith 57).

Growth of a Genre

Over the years science fiction has grown from ill-regarded entertainment into a viable, accepted literary form. In his essay "On Science Fiction" C. S. Lewis observes, "There seems, in fact, to be a double paradox in its history: it began to be popular when it least deserved it, and to excite critical contempt as soon as it ceased to be wholly contemptible" (59). In particular Lewis is referring to the genre's early popularity in pulp magazines, which eventually did lead to a "Golden Age."

Pulp S-Fiction

EDGAR RICE BURROUGHS

Several early writers bridged the eras of Verne and Wells and the advent of pulp sf magazines in the early 20th century. Despite the contributions of writers such as Edgar Allan Poe, Sir Arthur Conan Doyle, and Robert Louis Stevenson, one of the most significant sf pioneers was Edgar Rice Burroughs. Burroughs' first story was a six-part serial, "Under the Moons of Mars," that debuted in an early pulp magazine, the *All-Story*. That tale eventually became the book *A Princess of Mars*, the first in the *John Carter, Warlord of Mars* series (Aldiss 156). The author's second story gave birth to one of the most popular heroes of all time—*Tarzan of the Apes*. Although not sci fi per se, Tarzan stories include fantastic elements such as lost civilizations, a motif borrowed from H. Rider Haggard (Clareson 128), and in one instance the Ape Man crossed over into Burroughs' *Pellucidar* series in *Tarzan at the Earth's Core*.

By the time he launched his fourth series (*Carson of Venus*), the author's formula was already well established. His protagonists were often inhabitants of new or lost worlds who were locked in a struggle with nature (21–22). Aldiss notes, "All Burroughs's novels are vaguely similar, wherever they are set, heroes and incidents being often transposable, as clips of crocodile fights were transposed from one Tarzan movie to the next" (161). This criticism and others—such as lack of characterization in Burroughs' novels—do not diminish his contributions to the genre. "His novels offer to a remarkable degree," continues Aldiss, "every facility for identifying with the hero and daydreaming through his triumphs" (162). More specifically, Clareson lauds Burroughs for his creativity: "[His] achievement lai[d] in his ability to infuse a new vitality into the conventions established by Haggard at a time when imitators of Haggard were beginning to voice their despair at the idea that soon there would be no unknown lands to discover" (135).

Hugo Gernsback

Hugo Gernsback is often credited with being the progenitor of modern science fiction. His importance was primarily to the escapist branch of sci fi. His magazine *Amazing Stories* (founded in 1926) played a part in popularizing the genre; early issues contained reprints of stories written by Verne, Wells, and their contemporaries. But as Gernsback gradually published original stories in *Amazing*, it became clear that his view of science fiction was severely limited. Samuel R. Delany elucidates, "Gernsback was solely interested in the wonderful things progress might bring. [His writing contains] none of the socially functional logic in which Wells indulged" (285). In short, Delany criticizes Gernsback's obsession with "thingness" and his focusing solely on technology and ignoring the sociological ramifications new inventions might cause. Sci fi writer and historian Brian W. Aldiss lambastes Gernsback as "one of the worst disasters ever to hit the science fiction field" (202). Aldiss cites Gernsback not only for his literary ineptitude, but also for "ghettoizing" science fiction: "Gernsback's segregation of what he liked to call 'scientification' into magazines designed to contain nothing else guaranteed the setting up of various narrow orthodoxies inimical to any thriving literature. A cultural chauvinism prevailed, with unfortunate consequences of which the field has yet to rid itself" (202). The glut of sf films and television programs that focus on special effects rather than plot and characterization demonstrates that Gernsback's limited view of science fiction is still subscribed to.

John W. Campbell

The true patron of modern sf was John W. Campbell. In 1937 Campbell became editor of *Astounding Science Fiction* (née *Astounding Stories*), a rival of *Amazing*. He is credited with taking early SF beyond its "space-opera" roots and imbuing it with credibility. Gernsback and his protégés started by focusing on technology alone. As other writers joined them, their approaches started to differ. "Slowly, intuitions of the way in which these objects might affect behavior began to appear in their stories," reveals Delany (287). "Editor Campbell was astute enough to see that this was perhaps the most powerful tool in the realization of these marvelous inventions. He encouraged writers to use this tool, to make the focus of the stories the juncture between the object and the behavior it causes" (287). Campbell's efforts were a logical extension of themes that H. G. Wells explored in his writing.

Campbell edited *Astounding*, which eventually changed its name to *Analog*, until 1950, but continued to be an active force in sci fi until his death in 1971. Because of his influence his tenure is often referred to as the Golden Age of science fiction. Stanley Schmidt explains, "Even after other magazines of comparable stature appeared in the 1950s,[3] a certain broad type of science fiction—usually quite sociological, but characteristically with a very solid scientific and technical foundation—continued to be referred to in such terms as 'the Campbell/*Analog* tradition'" (40). Numerous sci-fi luminaries such as Isaac Asimov, Arthur C. Clarke, and Robert A. Heinlein began their careers under Campbell's aegis. These men explored many of sci-fi's classical themes. Asimov developed comprehensive rules for the functioning of robots; Clarke often focused on the seeding of the universe by alien cultures or humans; and Heinlein explored encounters between humans and aliens. In 1955 C. S. Lewis noted, "[P]erhaps five or six years ago, there was an improvement [in science fiction]: not that very bad stories ceased to be the majority, but that the good ones became better and more numerous" (59). Campbell and his adherents were responsible for that increase of quality, and they forged the path for science fiction to become an accepted literary genre.

Cinemania

The medium that cemented science fiction's place in popular culture is film. Although early sci-fi classics like *Metropolis* (1927), *The Tunnel* (1935), and *Things to Come* (1936) were often eclipsed by the popularity of space-opera serials, including *Flash Gordon* and *Buck Rogers* (Aldiss 271), the advent of the atomic age brought forth a new spate of films in the 1950s. Unfortunately, many of them were B-movies about nuclear-mutated insects (*Them!*, 1954) or allegorical films about the communist "threat" (the original *Invasion of the Body Snatchers*, 1956). But amidst films that focused on fears and paranoia, there were a few gems that reflected the new approaches Campbell and his protégés were applying to science fiction. *The Day the Earth Stood Still* (1951), *Forbidden Planet* (1956), and *The Incredible Shrinking Man* (1957) are examples of such films with serious, thoughtful themes.

Kubrick's 2001: A Game Changer

The next major advance in science-fiction films occurred a decade later when *2001: A Space Odyssey* was released in 1968. Although based on a short story ("The Sentinel") by Arthur C. Clarke, *2001*'s screenplay was co-written by Stanley Kubrick and Clarke, and the film's vision is largely Kubrick's. "Whereas [other films were] anti-science in [their] pretense that there is sound, air, and normal gravity in the immense vacuum of outer space, *2001* scrupulously adheres to the scientific realities of space travel" (Suber i). Marc Mancini notes, "the [then-daring] spaceship interiors in *2001* came at a time when an aircraft cabin still looked like the inside of a culvert, with daisies pasted on" (12).

While many people were rightfully impressed with the film's production design, critics like Louis Gianetti and Roger Ebert noticed cinematic elements that were missing. "In Kubrick's *2001*," writes Gianetti, "[he] spends most of his time lovingly photographing the instruments of a spaceship, various space stations, and the enormous expanses of space itself. The few people in the movie seem almost incidental and certainly far less interesting than the real center of concern—the setting" (286–287). Though that grievance is in part warranted, Roger Ebert better understands Kubrick's real point:

> Kubrick's universe, and the spaceships he constructed to explore it, are simply out of scale with human concerns. The ships are perfect, impersonal machines which venture from one planet to another, and if men are tucked away somewhere inside them, then they get there, too. But the achievement belongs to the machine. And Kubrick's actors seem to sense this; they are lifelike but without emotion, like figures in a wax museum. Yet the machines are necessary because man himself is so helpless in the face of the universe [770].

2001: A Space Odyssey set new standards for the form and content of science-fiction films that followed.

The Seminal Space Opera

In May 1977—nine years after Kubrick's sf masterpiece—a low-budget science-fiction film by a relatively unknown director became a full-fledged phenomenon. That film was George Lucas' *Star Wars*. Purists like Harlan Ellison attacked the film and denigrated its effect on the genre: "[F]or all its vaunted SFX, the *Star Wars* trilogy has no more importance in the concern of the maturation of the sf cinema than does John Carpenter's odious and unnecessary remake of *The Thing* [1982] (as nasty a bit of filmic folly as has come our way of late)" ("Lurching" 12).[4] Others like Brian Aldiss could accept *Star Wars* for what it was—"a real gee-whiz movie." Writing in retrospect he lauds,

> It was apparent from [its release] that *Star Wars* was an outsize elephant with the brains of a gnat; what has become more evident is how beautiful it was filmed, how sharp the editing, how clear the storyline, how refreshingly open the sets. Moreover, since *Blade Runner* (1982) and *Dune* (1985), we see that the morality of the film was comparatively innocuous [271].

Ellison's criticism focuses on "Lucas' technique of assembling bits and pieces of well-worn sf elements to bring forth 'a new look'" rather than "fresh thinking" (12). But he fails to acknowledge that the derivative nature of Lucas' film series celebrated its space-opera antecedents. Moreover *Star Wars* reintroduced the heroic ideal, a concept missing from popular American culture in the wake of Vietnam and Watergate. The film's critical and financial success not only inspired two immediate sequels (and eventually a prequel trilogy, a sequel trilogy that concludes in December 2019 with *Episode IX*'s release, two anthology films, several animated television series, the forthcoming live-action series *The Mandalorian* for the Disney+ streaming service, and additional films in preproduction) but led to the contemporary release of numerous sci-fi films from various studios. Some of those films were creative disasters (e.g., *The Black Hole, Battlestar Galactica, Saturn 5*), but others (*Close Encounters of the Third Kind, E.T.: The Extra-Terrestrial,* and *Blade Runner*) were recognized by film critics as seminal works.

Star Trek's *Generations*

The Original Series

TELEGENESIS

Before the 1960s, science fiction was rare on television. Aside from an occasional space opera like *Captain Video* or *Tom Corbett, Space Cadet*, sci-fi television consisted of anthology programs like Rod Serling's *The Twilight Zone* and imitators like *The Outer Limits*. This situation changed because of a man named Eugene Wesley Roddenberry. A veteran B-17 bomber pilot, Gene Roddenberry had served first as an airline pilot and then as a policeman after World War II. His first love, yet, was writing. After a successful career moonlighting as a freelance scriptwriter on shows like *Naked City, Highway Patrol,* and *Dr. Kildare*, Roddenberry quit the police force in 1956 to focus on writing full time (Shatner with Kreski 13).

Inspired by the 1961 film *Master of the World*, the idea for a new science-fiction series began germinating in his mind. Biographer David Alexander explains, "Gene described his vision of a giant dirigible set in the late 1800's manned by a multiethnic crew traveling the world righting wrongs and doing good" (185). This series would not surface immediately because Roddenberry would first create and produce *The Lieutenant*, an acclaimed drama starring Gary Lockwood as the title character, Lt.

William Rice. "The program portrayed human drama in a military setting, examining social questions of the day" (186). Even though *The Lieutenant* was not renewed as expected after 29 episodes, the show allowed Roddenberry to establish working relationships with actors Lockwood, Leonard Nimoy, Nichelle Nichols, Walter Koenig, and Majel Barrett; directors Marc Daniels and Robert Butler; and a temporary secretary named Dorothy Fontana who aspired to be a writer (Shatner 17).

Before *The Lieutenant*'s demise, however, Roddenberry was hard at work developing a new series. Alexander relates:

> Gene had combined a number of his previous concepts—a ship as a "character" and integral to the story; the interaction between the ship's senior officers; the strong, heroic captain from C. S. Forester's Horatio Hornblower series; the multiracial crew with a strong, idealistic bond—the "band of brothers and sisters" from his dirigible series idea; and a number of other concepts he found in the literary genre of science fiction—to be dramatized and place on a starship two hundred years in the future.[5] Gene's series idea was something that had not been on television to date: adult drama with a continuing cast of characters in a science fiction setting. By March 11, 1964, he had the concept down in sixteen pages, enough to show industry buyers. He called it *Star Trek* [188].

Roddenberry first offered the series to MGM, which never responded to his correspondence. Subsequently he attempted to entice every major studio in Hollywood to help produce the series. Fortunately for him, Desilu Studios was in dire financial straits and was hard-pressed for a prestige series it could sell to a network. Oscar Katz, Desilu's executive vice president in charge of television production, read Roddenberry's proposal and envisioned *Star Trek* as the answer to his studio's problems. Within days, he arranged a pitching session between Roddenberry and CBS executives (Shatner 24–26).

PRELAUNCH

That meeting seemed to go well—at first. Several executives, including CBS president James Aubrey, attended the session. Shatner describes it:

> They listened to Gene's pitch with rapt attention, as opposed to the standard half-hearted, sleepy-eyed lassitude. They leaned forward in their chairs. They smiled at him. They praised Gene's ideas, and *then* they asked questions, extremely *specific* questions. "How can you do a show of this broad scope on a television-sized budget?" "How can you possibly create sets and other worlds that are cost-effective *and* realistic?" "How can you be sure that a series of this nature will appeal to a *large* audience?" "How will you create believable, budget-conscious optical effects?" [26].

After nearly three hours of questioning, the meeting abruptly stopped. Recounts Oscar Katz, "The CBS guys questioned us in such detail and for so long that I thought we had real interest from them about doing the series. They later passed on [it] and we found out that they had questioned us so thoroughly because they had a science fiction project called *Lost in Space* in development" (Alexander 195).[6] "Years later," according to Shatner, "Gene would still rail that CBS had raped him of his innovations without even paying him for his advice" (27).

Katz soon succeeded in attracting NBC's interest to *Star Trek*. Rather than immediately allocating the money to produce the pilot, Mort Werner (NBC's vice-president in charge of programming) gave Roddenberry $20,000 to develop three story ideas. Werner chose "The Cage" as the episode that would become *Star Trek*'s pilot (Asherman 10). Katz believed that decision had less to do with Roddenberry's script and more to do with Desilu's facilities:

> I think they selected this type of story to test Desilu on the hardest kind of story to produce because of the reputation Desilu had. Then, when they saw it they were satisfied that Desilu was able to produce quality material, but it was the wrong kind of episode to take around to advertising agencies and sell. It was too off the beaten path. They didn't see it as a typical episode [Alexander 224].

Roddenberry delivered "The Cage" to the network in February 1965, and it was promptly rejected. "The overall reason given for the rejection was that the pilot was just 'too cerebral.' NBC felt the show would go over the heads of most of the viewers, that it required too much thought on the part of the viewer to understand it" (Whitfield & Roddenberry 124).[7] This initial failure indicates that television audiences have not always embraced "serious" science fiction. "But *Star Trek* was not dead," writes Allan Asherman. "After spending $630,000 on 'The Cage,' NBC felt the series format deserved a second chance. For the first time in television history a second pilot was commissioned" (17).[8]

"If at first..."

The network's enthusiasm for *Star Trek* did carry a few stipulations. "[T]hey insisted that this second pilot should be filmed solely upon the basic preexisting sets built for 'The Cage,' emphasizing that they would by no means authorize *any* production costs exceeding $300,000" (Shatner 68). Another major problem was that NBC rejected most of the actors Roddenberry had chosen to man his starship. The network especially balked at the idea that a woman, Number One, was second-in-command of the *Enterprise*,[9] and also objected to the presence of Mr. Spock, a pointy-eared alien. Majel Barrett, who played Number One—and happened to be Roddenberry's then-mistress and eventually his wife—describes the situation:

> [Gene] explained to me that he figured he could probably fight to save one character, but not both. He told me about how badly he wanted to keep Spock, and about how important that character could become to the series. He tried to be very nice about it, and he also said, "We'll work you into it. Somehow or other, you'll be in the show."[10] [68].

Jeffrey Hunter, who played Captain Christopher Pike in "The Cage," was not one of the actors NBC objected to, but he nevertheless declined to participate in the second pilot. Previously Roddenberry had considered Lloyd Bridges for his captain; now, after Hunter's withdrawal from the role, Roddenberry considered Jack Lord but rejected his demand for 50 percent ownership of the series (Dillard 9). Ultimately the role of Captain James T. Kirk went to a Canadian actor, William Shatner.

Once again, NBC asked Roddenberry to develop three story ideas. Roddenberry enlisted the assistance of sf writers Stephen Kandel and Samuel A. Peeples to complete this task. The three men developed three scripts: Roddenberry's "The Omega Glory," Kandel's "Mudd's Women" (based on a story by Roddenberry), and Peeples' original "Where No Man Has Gone Before" (Asherman 17). NBC chose Peeples' script to be the second pilot. This time Roddenberry took no chances; he made sure that this episode had plenty of action. Though one could accuse Roddenberry of "selling out" by making the second pilot more of a space opera than its predecessor, the tension between intellectual stories and tales of action and adventure became a hallmark of the series. Describes Shatner: "Basically, Kirk's put in a trap. The fates have conspired to lock him into a situation where his own sense of responsibility and duty demand that he destroy a friend. It was a very simple story, and the dilemma was very clear: What is Kirk going to do? It was powerful, exciting and full of human drama" (76).

Leonard Nimoy, as Spock, was the only character who appeared in both pilots. Future *Trek* regulars who debuted in "Where No Man Has Gone Before" were George Takei as then-ship's biophysicist Hikaru Sulu and James Doohan as Chief Engineer Montgomery Scott. Filming was completed in July 1965, but since Roddenberry was overseeing two other pilots at the time (*Police Story* and *The Long Hunt of April Savage*) he did not deliver it to the network until January 1966 (Asherman 25).

The Five-Minus-Two-Year Mission

THE CAST

Pleased with the second pilot, NBC informed Desilu in mid–February that the show would be on the fall schedule. The final additions to the cast were DeForest Kelley as Dr. Leonard McCoy, Nichelle Nichols as communications officer Uhura, and Grace Lee Whitney as Yeoman Janice Rand. Kelley's casting occurred after turning down the role of Spock in "The Cage," being rejected by NBC for the doctor in the second pilot and being subsequently wooed by the network for the same position in the weekly series (Shatner 106–107).[11] Roddenberry cast Nichols, based on a guest-starring role from his earlier series *The Lieutenant*. Ironically, Whitney, who had been hyped as one of the main characters in network publicity, fulfilled her initial contract for seven of 13 episodes after which the character was dropped. True to his word, Roddenberry did find a new role for Majel Barrett—that of Nurse Christine Chapel, who appeared as a semi-regular throughout the series' run. In the second season, Walter Koenig was added as Ensign Pavel Chekhov, a cocky young Russian. Although Chekhov's inclusion in the crew responded to the Soviet Union's complaint that there were no Russians on the *Enterprise* (Whitfield & Roddenberry 250), Roddenberry was more interested in recruiting younger audience members by casting an actor resembling the lead singer of the Monkees (Shatner 224–225).

THE FANS

Though not always a media darling—as evidenced by a negative review in the entertainment trade publication *Daily Variety*—no one could deny that *Star Trek* was innovative television. While the civil rights struggle was being waged across the United States, Roddenberry's series postulated a future where man would overcome racial problems as evidenced by the *Enterprise*'s multi-ethnic crew. *Star Trek*, though, did often focus on interplanetary prejudices.[12] Stephen Whitfield writes:

> Roddenberry was determined to break through television's censorship barrier and do tales about important and meaningful things. He was certain television's audience was not the collection of nitwits that networks believed it to be. By using science fiction yarns on far-off planets, he was certain he could disguise the fact that he was actually talking about politics, sex, economics, the stupidity of war, and half a hundred other vital subjects usually prohibited on television [21–22].

The first group to embrace the show were attendees at the 24th Annual World Science Fiction Convention in Cleveland, Ohio. Roddenberry was there to promote the show five days before its network premiere. Author Allan Asherman, who attended the event, describes the audience's reaction to the second pilot:

> There was nothing childish about the episode, "Where No Man Has Gone Before." We waited for a kid or a wisecracking robot to enter the picture, but they never arrived. Even the music was somber, serious, and spectacular. We noticed people of varied races, genders, and planetary origins working together. Here was a future it did not hurt to imagine. Here was a constructive tomorrow for mankind, emphasizing exploration and expansion. This was the science fiction television series we all wanted to see [2].

Unfortunately, the American public was not as loyal as that group of fans. After the show's debut on September 8, 1966, its ratings steadily declined. As ratings decreased, though, the amount of fan mail increased. Dorothy (D. C.) Fontana (Roddenberry's former secretary who had become a writer and script consultant for *Star Trek*) recalls, "The first week after the show was on, a sack of mail began arriving, and I said, 'That's nice, that's really good.' And the second week, five sacks of mail came in. After that, they became so heavy we couldn't deal with it anymore" (Dillard 23). Despite the fact that legions of *Star Trek* fans emerged across the country—especially on college campuses—the show was in danger of cancellation. Roddenberry responded by asking author Harlan Ellison[13] if he would write letters to help save the show. The author subsequently contacted several colleagues, many of whom had written for *Trek*.[14] Led by Ellison, "The Committee" sent letters to publishers, magazines, and fan club presidents in December 1966. These letters encouraged viewers to write NBC in order to save the show.

THE LATTER YEARS

Ellison's preemptive strike appeared to pay off: NBC announced on March 14, 1967, that *Star Trek* had been renewed for the fall season (Asherman 67). Two months later Sheila Wolfe reported in the *Chicago Tribune*, "Reports that *Star Trek* was going to be grounded triggered a lot of mail but the writers needn't have bothered. NBC said it never planned to scrap the program in the first place" (Alexander 265). Wolfe's assessment aside, the publishing of the booklet "*Star Trek* Mail Call" by NBC in August 1967 was an overt acknowledgment of the show's large following. "The first page [of the booklet] acknowledged that the network received 29,000 pieces of mail from *Trek* fans during the show's first year," describes Asherman (67). Despite a few changes among the production staff, the series' second season nearly matched the creative success of the first. But toward the end of the year, rumors of *Trek*'s demise once again circulated. This time a group of fans, led by Bjo Trimble and her husband John, initiated a letter-writing campaign. As a result of their efforts, NBC received 115,893 letters, nearly half of which arrived during February 1968 (103).

"On Friday, March 1," reveals David Alexander, "NBC announced, *on the air*, that *Star Trek* was renewed and asked that no more letters be sent" (314). The network, however, placed the show in a 10 p.m. time slot—an hour normally considered a "graveyard slot" for a television show. Frustrated by his unsuccessful efforts to sway NBC's decision, Roddenberry quit the show (Dillard 41). Though he retained the title of executive producer, the day-to-day operations of *Star Trek* were left to newcomer Fred Freiberger. He replaced producer Gene L. Coon, who left to work on another show. While Freiberger's producing skills may have been unfairly maligned over the years,[15] most viewers generally agree that the show's third year was consistently abysmal. Symptomatic of the dearth of quality are such episodes as "Spock's Brain," in which the Vulcan's brain is kidnapped by aliens, and "The Way to Eden," which focused on a band of space hippies.

Aside from the show's creative problems, NBC frequently preempted the show. Sensing the show was again in danger of cancellation, fans waged another letter campaign to the network. Their attempts were fruitless. In mid-February NBC released the list of shows that had been ordered for another season: *Star Trek* was not on the list (Alexander 365). Allan Asherman reports, "No first-run episodes were aired from March 21 to June 3, 1969—when the last first-run show, 'Turnabout Intruder,' was televised. The five-year mission of the *Enterprise* had apparently come to a premature end" (104). William Shatner opines that the show's untimely demise was actually beneficial: "NBC actually did *Star Trek* a favor by canceling it. With declining ratings and freefalling creative content, the show was mercifully yanked from the airwaves before it had the chance to alienate its legions of fans" (*Star Trek Movie Memories* 20).

Trekkus Interruptus

RUMBLINGS OF A RETURN

Several curious phenomena occurred after *Star Trek*'s cancellation. In October 1969, Paramount Pictures, which had absorbed Desilu Studios during the show's run, began syndicating *Trek* (Alexander 377). And the show's popularity increased dramatically:

> The show's audience is vastly wider now [1975] in reruns than it ever was in its first-run days. Its reruns compete very successfully with new prime-time shows, and with the network news—years after it was expected to die. The syndicated reruns have become such a gold mine for the producers that they have been reluctant to undercut that market by reviving the show—despite the letters which continue to pour in to Paramount and NBC urging revival [Lichtenberg et al. 3].

The first national *Star Trek* convention was held on the weekend of January 21–23, 1972, in New York City. "Five hundred fans were expected," remarks J. M. Dillard. "Well over three thousand people packed inside the Statler-Hilton to listen to guest of honor Gene Roddenberry" (49). In his book *Star Trek Movie Memories* (1994), William Shatner discloses that Roddenberry himself delayed the imminent return of the show: "As early as 1972, Paramount came to Roddenberry, asking him to return to the lot and start thinking about bringing *Star Trek* back, either as a TV movie or perhaps a very-low-budget big-screener. Gene turned them down immediately" (22). Roddenberry, apparently, was more intent on pursuing other projects than returning to *Trek*.

TOONED IN

He did agree later that year, though, to Filmation Associates' proposal for an animated *Star Trek* series. After fighting for—and winning—creative control of the show, NBC aired it for two seasons starting on September 8, 1973, exactly seven years after the premiere of the original series (Alexander 406). By this time, even NBC executives acknowledged they had probably canceled *Star Trek* too soon (397). The animated series was a means for the network to atone for its mistake. Under Roddenberry's auspices, animated *Trek* was a triumph. With the exception of Walter Koenig, all of the original cast provided voices for their characters.[16] Many writers who provided scripts for the original series, including Samuel A. Peeples, David Gerrold, and D. C. Fontana (who also served as associate producer and story editor), also wrote for this new incarnation (Asherman 143). *Los Angeles Times* reviewer Cecil Smith thought *Star Trek* was out of place on Saturday mornings and compared it with "a Mercedes in a soapbox derby" (Alexander 408–409). Shortly after winning an Emmy in 1975 for children's programming, *Star Trek* was canceled (again) by NBC.

Progress and Retrogression

FALSE STARTS

During the next five years, *Star Trek* underwent numerous attempts at revival. For simplicity's sake, David Alexander's synopsis forms a useful sequence of events. In the spring of 1975, Paramount decided to make a medium budget *Star Trek* film and entered into a preliminary agreement with Roddenberry (445). "Gene was given back his old office and hired to write a low-budget, feature-length *Star Trek* movie script that would cost the studio, start to finish, somewhere between two and three million dollars," comments William Shatner (36). Unfortunately Paramount hated that script ("The God Thing"), "and other attempts at scripts by other writers met with no success" (Alexander 445). Paramount also doubted the film's ability to attract an audience. When fans discover this, they "bombard Paramount with letters." By this time a model of the *Enterprise* hung near the *Spirit of St. Louis* in the Smithsonian Institution in Washington, D.C. (Lichtenberg 2), and in September 1976 NASA responded to public pressure and named the first space shuttle *Enterprise*.

Star Trek: The Lost Generation

Finally convinced that there was a healthy audience for a *Star Trek* film, Paramount decided to greenlight it. But on June 7, 1977, *The San Francisco Chronicle* reported that after nine months of pre-production and $500,000, the project was canceled (Alexander 436). Evidently it suffered from creative anarchy. In an interview with Susan Sackett, Roddenberry reflects:

> Paramount went about the movie in exactly the wrong way to accomplish something artistic. They decided to make it a committee effort, and have no one really in charge. They told me that I had creative control—then told Jerry Isenberg that he had it, and then without his knowing it they also told the director [Philip Kaufman] that *he* had creative control. You can't make a worthwhile movie that way. Good movies are made almost invariably by one person carrying the enthusiasm and the vision of it into completion ["Ménage à Troi" 25].

Roddenberry pointed out an additional factor that got the film canceled. Eleven days after the previous decision, Paramount Pictures made a stunning announcement in *The New York Times*: *Star Trek* was to return to television as a weekly series. Under the direction of chairman Barry Diller and president Michael Eisner, Paramount Pictures had decided to create a fourth TV network out of independent stations using a new *Trek* series as a launch pad. It was scheduled to air 8:00–9:00 p.m. Saturday nights and would be followed by a movie of the week (Engel 180–181).

With *Star Trek* as its flagship show, Paramount executives thought they had the bait to lure stations across the country to join the fledgling network. Michael Eisner explains, "There just seemed to be an undercurrent of attention to *Star Trek*. We wanted to get a nice strong base on which to build the night. It was a cult, and it seemed to me at the time that the cult was large enough to start a fourth network" (181). *Star Trek— Phase II* was the official series' title. The pilot episode, "In Thy Image," was to reunite the original crew (except for Spock) and introduce three new characters: Commander William Decker, second-in-command; Lieutenant Ilia, a sensual navigator; and Lt. Xon, a Vulcan science officer (Gross "*Star Trek II*" 45).[17] Aside from Nimoy, all the original actors had agreed to reprise their roles, and the new characters had been cast (Asherman 152). Sets were constructed, 20 scripts were in various stages of development, and production was set to begin on November 30, 1977. Paramount executives slowly became aware, however, that their plans were in trouble. Edward Gross relates, "Paramount [was] unable to sell enough advertising time to compete with established TV networks" (57). The *Star Trek* project was once again placed in stasis, albeit for a short time.

The New Voyages

The Motionless Picture

After the plug was pulled on the Paramount Network, executives decided to increase the budget of "In Thy Image" and release it theatrically rather than on television. Production was postponed until spring 1978. Then, on March 28, all of the original *Enterprise* crew (including Nimoy) and creator Gene Roddenberry attended a historic press conference. Michael Eisner announced the production of *Star Trek: The Motion Picture*. Robert Wise would direct; Roddenberry would produce; and all of the original cast would appear (Alexander 446).[18] The still-growing success of *Star Wars* as well as the critical and financial achievement of Steven Spielberg's *Close Encounters of the Third Kind* swayed Paramount's decision to give the *Star Trek* film a substantial ($15 million) budget. Aside from a few changes, the film was based on the pilot script ("In Thy Image") for the abandoned television series. Several production delays ensued because of difficulties with special effects as well as troublesome script rewrites.

The April 7, 1979, release date was eventually pushed back to December 7. Although *Star Trek: The Motion Picture* grossed $180 million worldwide, numerous critics savaged it. In *Science Fiction Films of the Seventies*, Craig Anderson observes, "The film is obviously a product of fear: afraid of being too different, too changed from the beloved television series, *The Motion Picture* warps along the middle ground and, while attempting to please everyone, satisfies few" (237). David Gerrold, author of the classic *Star Trek* episode "The Trouble with Tribbles," gave his critique in his monthly *Starlog* column:

> The film's philosophical statement is identical to the statements the TV series made 10 years ago. As a TV series, *Star Trek* may have been right for the 60s—and there was much in it that spoke to the 70s too. But, as we enter the 80s, perhaps it is time to ask the next questions. We know the simple answers already. They're the obvious ones. Yes, humanity is going to go [to] the stars. And yes—and perhaps this is the most important point the film does make—there is a very logical and *valuable* reason for the existence of human emotions. But if *Star Trek* fails to excite a mystic sense in the viewer, it is because it has not yet advanced beyond those statements to consider the implications, nor to ask, "And then what do we do? Where do we go next?" "Out there. Thataway," isn't quite the right answer ["Spock-alypse Now" 70].

Gerrold implied the film captured the typical metaphysical concerns of *Star Trek*, but failed to balance those with *Trek*'s space-opera sensibilities. Harlan Ellison's review was less kind:

> It is not that *Star Trek—The Motion Picture* is a bad film; it isn't. Clearly, it is also not a good film. The saddening reality is simply that it is a dull film: an often boring film, a stultifyingly predictable film, a tragically *average* film. With a two-million-dollar production pricetag one could do no other than applaud it. Bearing a freight-load cost of something in excess of $44 million and the unbounded expectations held for it, the timid creation that crawled across premiere movie screens on December 7, 1979, deserves little more than regrets and a weary shake of the head ["Ellison Reviews *Trek*" 61].

In defense of the film's producers, the $44 million price tag was misleading. Alexander posits, "Part of that huge expense was the [special effects] debacle, but part of it was that all the development costs for all the previous movie and TV projects were dumped into the movie budget barrel" (450). Despite the film's gross earnings, Paramount sought ways to minimize production costs of future *Trek* films, thereby maximizing their profit. Their solution was to hold Roddenberry accountable for the cost overruns and to hire a new producer.

Khan-frontations

Shortly after starting a new position at Paramount, veteran television producer Harve Bennett was summoned to meet with his bosses, including Michael Eisner, Jeffrey Katzenberg, Barry Diller, and Charlie Bluhdorn. Bluhdorn bluntly asked Bennett his opinion of *STTMP*. He cautiously responded, "Well, I thought it was boring" (Engel 205). Next, Bluhdorn queried, "Can you make a *Star Trek II* for less than forty-five million dollars?" to which Bennett prophetically replied, "Where I come from, I could make four or five movies for that" (Dillard 72). At that point Bennett was appointed the producer of the *Star Trek* films, a position he retained until after the release of *Star Trek VI: The Undiscovered Country*. Roddenberry's role was defined as "executive consultant," an innocuous title that tangentially associated him with the film series. Much has been written about the ongoing conflicts between Bennett and Roddenberry concerning the films' production.[19] But the fact remains that Paramount's decision was proper for the franchise. In a June 1982 *Starlog* article, Bjo Trimble gives her assessment of the situation: "Gene, it seemed, was not working on the film at all, except in the capacity of advisor. It must have been a pang to see the child of his creation in the hands of others, and as a fellow Leo who dislikes delegating authority, I can appreciate how he must have felt. But *Star Trek* has grown far beyond any one person; perhaps even its creator" (46). Even *Star Trek* lovers suspected that the franchise might benefit from a new approach.

Having never seen the original series, Bennett viewed all 79 episodes and determined that one, "Space Seed," contained a character (Khan Noonian Singh) that would be a worthy adversary for Kirk and the *Enterprise* crew. Working closely with screenwriter Jack B. Sowards and director Nicholas Meyer, the trio crafted *Star Trek II: The Wrath of Khan*. Publicly Roddenberry lent his support to Bennett's approach: "Nothing will please me more than to have Harve Bennett and the other people involved come back and make *Star Trek* as relevant to the 80s as our show was to the 60s and have a fine new *Star Trek* better than the first" (Szalay 60).

Privately, though, the two men often strived to reach a middle ground. Martha J. Bonds interviewed Bennett and discussed this issue:

> Bennett indicates that he and *Trek* creator Gene Roddenberry were able to achieve a good working relationship. Director Nicholas Meyer's interest in things nautical led him to view Kirk as Horatio Hornblower in space—the same perception spoken of by Roddenberry in early treatments for the show. "Now, Gene has drifted from that concept and, confronted with our first draft script, his comments noted that 'Starfleet is *not* the navy.' And I argued back by memo, saying, 'It used to be!'" [48].

Despite these disputes, the finished product is arguably the finest *Star Trek* film. David Gerrold highly praised it in his November 1982 *Starlog* column: "There is a sense of joyousness throughout [*Star Trek II*]. It is the joy of life that we are feeling—we are alive because we love solving problems. We love adventure and confrontation with the unknown—in ourselves, as well as out in the Universe" (42). Even Roddenberry conceded in a letter to Janet Quarton (dated July 3, 1982), "I think they did a pretty good job in making *Star Trek* work in a motion picture" (Alexander 465). Bennett, thus, had found the proper balance between high and low science fiction in his first *Trek* enterprise.

Something Old, Something New

Under Bennett's aegis, the *Star Trek* film franchise proceeded smoothly—and profitably—with the release of *Star Trek III: The Search for Spock* in 1984 and *Star Trek IV: The Voyage Home* in 1986. As the latter film was being produced, Paramount executives began to reexamine the viability of a new *Star Trek* television series. Marta Houske, a close friend of Roddenberry, recalls:

> To the best of my memory, Paramount asked Gene to do a new *Star Trek* series. He told them, "No way, I owe it to the fans to maintain the integrity of the series, etc." So, a while later he and I were having a drink at Nuclear Nuances on Melrose and he said, "You won't believe it. They're doing it on their own." I didn't know Gene's legal position and said, "They can't." To which Gene replied, "Yes, they can and they are." He was disgusted [Alexander 498].

In September 1986, John Pike, president of Paramount Television sent Roddenberry an overview of preliminary concepts for the series. The veteran producer took exception to the manning of the *Enterprise* by Starfleet cadets and to an increased emphasis on militarism. Moreover he feared the proposed "Animal House in outer space" format would damage the *Trek* franchise (500). On October 10, 1986, Mel Harris, then President of Paramount Television Group, made a stunning announcement at a studio press conference: "Twenty years ago, the genius of one man brought to television a program that has transcended the medium. We are enormously pleased that that man, Gene Roddenberry, is going to do it again. Just as public demand kept the original series on the air, this new series is also a result of grass roots support for Gene and his vision" (Nemecek 1).

Roddenberry's appointment to helm *Star Trek: The Next Generation* was significant on many levels. Despite earlier reluctance to return to *Trek*, Roddenberry seized the opportunity to prove he was responsible for its success. Widespread opposition to *Next Generation* only made him more determined. He wrote Janet Quarton, "I am an independent artist to whom Paramount has laid down the challenge of a lifetime. They very carefully made it clear 'No one thinks it can be done again.' Could you turn your back on that? I certainly can't" (Alexander 501).[20] Moreover, despite their treatment of Roddenberry with regard to the film series, Paramount executives acknowledged his involvement was crucial. At a June 1989 *Star Trek* convention in Los Angeles, he informed the audience, "Paramount still owns the basic copyright on *Star Trek*. The reason that I have some say [on *Star Trek*] is that Paramount is a little afraid that all of you would commit revolution" (Engel 221–222). Most important, even skeptical Trekkers knew there was a possibility that lightning could strike again. Writing before *Star Trek: The Next Generation*'s debut, *Starlog* publisher Kerry O'Quinn opined:

> Frankly, it will be a miracle if the new series succeeds. Nothing in TV history ever equalled [sic] *Star Trek*, and it will be impossible for people not to compare the new to the old—despite everything which is designed to separate the two shows. The *Star Trek* of the 1960s was of such outstanding quality that attempting to match it seems close to folly. The ingredient which prevents it from *being* folly is Gene Roddenberry [6].

The series debuted the week of September 28, 1987, on 150 stations (including 108 network affiliates) throughout the country. Alexander observes, "For an hour a week, Paramount had a fifth network and could sell national advertising time" (501). Despite conventional wisdom, the show was an instant success. Reviewing the show in the July 23, 1988, issue of *TV Guide*, Gary D. Christenson wrote: "*Star Trek* depicted us in reckless youth, with a Starship captain who tamed space as vigorously as we laid claim to the future…. *Star Trek: The Next Generation* reveals the child grown—a little more polished, but also more complacent. And if there's a bit of gray and a wrinkle or two, so much the better" (39). Within six weeks of its debut, the show was picked up for another year (Alexander 529). *Star Trek: The Next Generation* was well on its way to a 178-episode run that would span seven years.

The Next Generation of Spinoffs

Deep Space Nine

In 1991, Brandon Tartikoff left his job as NBC network president to become chairman of Paramount Pictures. One of his first actions was to call *Star Trek: The Next Generation*'s showrunner Rick Berman. He recalls the meeting:

> I went up to his office and he said to me, "I want to do a new series. I want you to do it, and I want it to start next year. My idea is The Rifleman in space … a father and son in space." He didn't know anything about *Star Trek*. So, I got together with Michael Piller and we started thinking about a father and a son in space. That was the beginning of *Deep Space Nine* [Altman & Gross 413].

Judith and Garfield Reeves-Stevens explain, "Since the new show would most likely appear on television while *The Next Generation* was still running, that ruled out a Starship-based show" (59). Berman and fellow co-creator Michael Piller decide to set the show on a space station near an alien planet and chose Bajor, a world created for the *Next Generation* episode "Ensign Ro." Berman elaborates, "We had structured a conflict between the people living near this wormhole, the Cardassians and the Bajorans; the Bajorans being the kind of sweet, good people and the Cardassians being the militaristic creeps" (Altman & Gross 416). While developing the series, Berman and Piller decided the space station "would be a darker and grittier environment than fans of both the original series and *The Next Generation* were used to seeing" Erdmann 4).

By introducing a cast of characters that included non–Starfleet personnel, *Deep Space Nine* could adhere to Roddenberry's ideology for enlightened 24th-century human beings yet still have, as Berman elucidates, "conflict amongst the non–Starfleet people and between the Starfleet people and non–Starfleet people" (4). Ira Steven Behr, a veteran *Star Trek: The Next Generation* writer, describes himself as "shocked" when Piller approached him to work on the new show because his TNG experience had ended with frustration. "I went back home and I read the bible and I saw certain things in it that could speak to me: the captain who had suffered a great defeat and a great loss. The isolated shapeshifter sheriff; the young doctor" (Altman & Gross 418). As the series solidified, Berman and Piller selected Avery Brooks—an African American actor best known for *Spenser: For Hire* and its spinoff *A Man Called Hawk*—to play station commander Benjamin Sisko. He applauds the color-blind casting: "It's about time it should be easy for us to accept that kind of reality, that we are able to get past this notion of the black and white of it and look at the 'human' of it" (Reeves-Stevens 178). In addition, Colm Meaney's character Chief Miles O'Brien—who appeared in 52 episodes of *Star Trek: The Next Generation*—and his family would transfer from the *U.S.S. Enterprise*-D to station *Deep Space 9*. Daniel Holloway and Joe Otterson acknowledge in a 25th anniversary tribute, "'DS9' never matched the viewership success of 'TNG,'" but has aged well because of eventual showrunner Behr's foray into serial storytelling, which allows DS9 to "lend itself more to binge viewing than most other dramas of its era" (*Variety*). Some Trekkers like *Medium*'s Alexander Chavers and *io9*'s Beth Elderkin go so far as to posit that *Deep Space Nine* is the finest of all the *Star Trek* series.

VOYAGER

As aforementioned, in 1977 Paramount planned to establish a fourth television network by gathering a consortium of independent stations (Engel 180–181). Those plans were shelved because of difficulty booking advertisers. By the time Paramount revisited the idea and allied itself with Chris-Craft Industries to form the United Paramount Network (UPN), Newscorp had already started a fourth broadcasting network—Fox—and Warner Bros. would launch a fifth network (The WB) mere days before *Star Trek: Voyager* premiered on January 16, 1995, as UPN's flagship series (Ruditis 1). Tom Mazza (Paramount's executive vice president of creative affairs) admits, "To be honest, I don't believe necessarily that *Voyager* tonally was the right show for UPN, but it was a platform from which the network could jump off" (Altman & Gross 553). Since *Star Trek: The Next Generation* had completed its run, *Voyager* could be set on a spaceship. Paul Ruditis explains, "More than just putting another group of people on a ship visiting familiar territory or choosing a central location around which stories could revolve, the new series needed a hook, something that brought it back to the heart of Star Trek and exploration" (1). After a brief visit to station *Deep Space 9* in the pilot episode "Caretaker," *Starship Voyager* would be flung across the galaxy into the uncharted territory of the Delta Quadrant.

This show sought to distinguish itself from its forebears in a few ways. First off, 30 years after network executives rejected a female second-in-command in the original series first pilot "The Cage," Captain Kathryn Janeway would command *U.S.S. Voyager*. Next, the crew would be composed of Starfleet personnel and Maquis rebels. Co-Creator/Executive Producer Rick Berman discloses the reasons why:

> Without breaking Gene's rules, we were always trying to find ways of creating conflict. This show featured the inherent conflict between Captain Janeway's crew and that of the Maquis vessel. The Maquis became provisional Starfleet officers, but there will always be conflict between them and that gave us something new and unique [Altman & Gross 554].

Finally, since the starship was essentially "lost in space" (to borrow a phrase from another sci-fi franchise), Janeway and her crew have an overriding goal. Fellow co-creator/executive producer Michael Piller illuminates the premise's genesis:

> You know [when] Q sends the *Enterprise* off to some strange quadrant and we meet the Borg, but we solve everything in an hour and get back home? Well, what if we *don't*? What if we get stuck there in space and it is completely unknown to us and this is the story of that journey back and of our trying to find our way back? [Altman & Gross 555].

Co-creator/executive producer Jeri Taylor admits, "The challenge of staying fresh and original is the main reason that we took the very risky move of throwing our people to the opposite end of the galaxy and cutting ties with everything that's familiar" (555). Like *The Next Generation* and *Deep Space Nine*, *Voyager* would complete seven seasons, and the starship returned to Earth in the series finale "Endgame."

The Prequel Series

ENTERPRISE

Star Trek: Voyager would be the last of the franchise's series to be set in the 24th century. Wary of potential franchise fatigue, Rick Berman wanted to let *Star Trek* rest awhile before launching a new show, but Paramount was determined. He reminisces, "In fact, they wanted it to start before *Voyager* ended and I managed to get them to at least wait until *Voyager* went off the air" (Altman & Gross 644). Berman recruited *Next Generation* and *Voyager* veteran Brannon Braga to co-create the new series, which they made a prequel to take it out of the 24th century. He clarifies, "We wanted to show what happened in the period in *Star Trek* history between *Star Trek: First Contact* and Kirk" (646). This idea may have worked in concept, but the execution did not deliver upon the series' potential. Darren Mooney comments, "*Star Trek: Enterprise* will always be the first *Star Trek* spin-off to be cancelled rather than retired, the first live-action spin-off to run less than seven seasons" (*the m0vie blog*). Even James L. Conway who helmed the pilot "Broken Bow" admits, "The pilot of *Enterprise* was terrific. But then the first season was very repetitive and it felt like it was written by people who were burned out" (Altman & Gross 676). Berman and Braga instituted a mid-course correction in the second season finale to energize the series, but it proved controversial. As *Wired's* Graeme McMillan equivocates, "The third [season] is ... well, it depends how you feel about what was intended to be a new direction for the show." (See Chapter 7 for more details.) By the time new showrunner Manny Coto took charge in season four and told stories that resonated with hardcore Trekkers, UPN had already canceled *Enterprise*.

DISCOVERY

Enterprise's finale aired in May 2005, and UPN itself ultimately merged with The WB to form The CW Television Network in September 2006. A few years later, Paramount Pictures tapped prolific writer/director/producer J. J. Abrams to reboot the movie franchise; the eleventh feature film—simply entitled *Star Trek*—created an alternate timeline that reset five decades of continuity.[21] Two sequels followed; a third has been postponed indefinitely (Mendelson). But *Star Trek* on television was not finished yet. "On November 2, 2015," reports Ian Spelling, "CBS Television Studios announced that it was developing a totally new *Star Trek* television series—only not for television" (DISC:OCE 6). He clarifies this seeming oxymoron:

> Since Star Trek last graced TV screens, network television has seen a huge slice of the broadcasting pie taken by on-demand streaming content providers like Netflix, Hulu, and Amazon, and CBS decided to move with the times. Launching their own streaming platform CBS All Access, this would be the home of the new *Star Trek*.

On February 9, 2016, CBS announced Bryan Fuller would return to the *Star Trek* universe to co-create the new show. Fuller started his career on *Deep Space Nine* and *Voyager* before creating Emmy Award-winner *Pushing Daisies* among other acclaimed series. In the press release, CBS Television Studios president David Stapf said, "When we began discussions about [*Star Trek*] returning to television, we immediately knew that Bryan Fuller would be the ideal person to work alongside Alex Kurtzman to create a fresh and authentic take on this classic and timeless series." No stranger to *Star Trek* himself, Kurtzman had written the first two J. J. Abrams-helmed films. That July at San Diego Comic-Con, Fuller hosted a special panel and revealed the title of the series and its lead ship, "I couldn't think of a more *Star Trek*-themed name for a ship than *Discovery*" (8). Other details included the following: the setting would be the "Prime" universe (not Abrams' alternate timeline), the era would be ten years before Captain Kirk's *Enterprise*, the protagonist would be female but not *Discovery*'s captain, and the crew would include a gay character (8). Fuller departed the series shortly after writing the pilot, which led to development and production delays. Yet when CBS aired the first hour on September 24, 2017, the show's potential was undeniable, causing Maureen Ryan to opine, "'Discovery' could provide viewers with the kind of character-driven, space-set sci-fi narrative that has long been missing from the television scene" (*Variety*).

Contextual Communication Theories

This book examines the 178 episodes of *Star Trek: The Next Generation* as a metanarrative. In *Rhetorical Criticism* (1989), Sonja Foss defines

"Narrative [as] a way of ordering and presenting a view of the world through a description of a situation involving characters, actions, and settings that changes over time" (229). "Metafiction," according to Didier Coste, is a "system of polyreference that incites [the reader] textually to raise polyreference to the power of 2 or more" (125). By regarding *Star Trek: The Next Generation* as a metanarrative, each episode will be considered as a segment of an organic whole. Or as Henry Jenkins, III, describes in his essay "*Star Trek* Rerun, Reread, Rewritten" (1988), "[F]ans perceive the individual episodes as contributing to one great program text" (95). Specific communication contexts exhibited within the *Star Trek: The Next Generation* metanarrative will be scrutinized. Those levels will include intrapersonal, interpersonal, group and organizational. Since the mass communication context is not an inherent aspect of this television series, the focus will instead be placed on the audience-artifact relationship.

Intrapersonal

Intrapersonal communication focuses "on the inner dialogue going on within the individual" (Griffin 11). Two theories of intrapersonal communication will be used to analyze main characters from *Star Trek: The Next Generation*.

THEORIES

Symbolic Interactionism. George Herbert Mead was a social psychologist who viewed previous analyses of human behavior as simplistic and reductionistic. He believed human beings were much too complex to be merely quantified and explained with stock theories. Though Mead never formally gathered his theories and findings prior to his death, his followers at the University of Chicago published them in several volumes. One of those works, *Mind, Self, & Society: From the Standpoint of a Social Behaviorist*, became the foundation for symbolic interactionism. The crux of symbolic interactionism is the social act—the fusion of the troika of society, self, and mind. Mead labels the social act as "a dynamic whole, no part of which can be considered or understood by itself—a complex organic process implied by each individual stimulus and response involved in it" (7). Stated concisely, a social act consists of (1) an initial gesture by one person, (2) a response to that gesture by another person, and (3) the result of the act or its meaning as perceived by the two parties (Littlejohn 171).

Mead differentiates the society in which humans abide from that of other animals in three ways. First, humans possess highly developed central nervous systems that imbue them with self-awareness (sentience), thus elevating them above the rest of nature (236–237). The next concept could be called reflexivity. Mead writes:

> The principle which I have suggested as basic to human social organization is that of communication involving participation in the other. This requires the appearance of the other in the self, the identification of the other in the self, the reaching of self-consciousness through the other. It is through taking this role of the other that he is able to come back on himself and so direct his own process of communication [253–254].

Use of significant symbols is the final trait that separates human societies from those of other animals. Mead defines a significant symbol as "that part of the act which serves as a gesture to call out the other part of the process, the response of the other, in the experience of the form that makes the gesture" (268).

As aforementioned, the ability to assume the role of the other is crucial to communication. Mead theorizes that self, the second component of the social act troika, is dependent on "the generalized other," "the organized community or social group which gives to the individual his unity of self" (154). Furthermore, self is the combination of "I" and "Me." He posits, "The 'I' is the response of the organism to the attitudes of the others; the 'me' is the organized set of attitudes of others which one assumes. The attitudes of the others constitute the organized 'me,' and then one reacts toward that as an 'I'" (175). Littlejohn elucidates Mead's supposition:

> The *I* is the impulsive, unorganized, undirected, unpredictable part of the person. The *me* is the generalized other, made up of the organized and consistent patterns shared with others. Every act begins with an impulse from the I and quickly becomes controlled by the me. The I is the driving force in action, whereas the me provides direction and guidance [173].

The dialectic between the I and the me, then, provides the basis for Mead's concept of self.

Mind is the final element of the social act process. "Meaning," writes Mead, "arises and lies within the field of the relation between the gesture of a given human organism and the subsequent behavior of this organism as indicated to another organism by that gesture" (76). In short, if a person's gesture indicates to another person the resultant behavior of the first person, then the gesture has meaning. Moreover, humans have the capacity to use language to symbolize gestures, situations, or objects. Mead calls this procedure "symbolization." He iterates:

> Symbolization constitutes objects not constituted before, objects which would not exist except for the context of social relationships wherein symbolization occurs.

Language does not simply symbolize a situation or object which is already there in advance; it makes possible the existence or the appearance of that situation or object, for it is a part of the mechanism whereby that situation or object is created [78].

Defining physical objects as those that cannot socially respond to an individual, Mead highlights that they are abstractions "which we make from the social response to nature" (184). Em Griffin, in *A First Look at Communication Theory*, emphasizes the importance of this process: "Mead believed that symbolic naming is the basis for society. The biblical book of Genesis states that Adam's first job was to name the animals—the dawn of civilization" (74). It is important, however, to point out that Mead is not advocating the social construction of reality. He and the interactionists believe, rather, "the extent of knowing is the extent of naming" and that "intelligence is the ability to symbolically label everything we encounter" (Griffin 74).

Gender Differences. Carol Gilligan's seminal book *In a Different Voice* is based on research she undertook as a direct result to psychological studies conducted by Lawrence Kohlberg, who built on research by Erik Erikson and Jean Piaget to produce a theory of moral growth. The problem Gilligan identified with Kohlberg's research is that he and his predecessors failed to include females in their test group. "Piaget referred to 'the child,' but only male children were involved in [his] research," chides Melanie M. Bloom in "Sex Differences in Ethical Systems: A Useful Framework for Interpreting Communication Research." She continues:

> Kohlberg's research into moral development also exclusively used males and resulted in a hierarchical development ladder that placed principles and concepts of fairness at the top in the "most mature" position and relationships and concepts of caring and responsibility in the middle. Once again, the male response had become the norm. When women's responses grouped in the middle of the hierarchy, women were defined as morally "arrested" in their development [245].

As a colleague of Kohlberg's for more than years, Gilligan had the opportunity to hear other subjects respond to his hypothetical dilemmas.

She theorizes, "the interpersonal dynamics of gender identity formation are different for boys and girls" (7). Since the mother is primary caretaker for children, girls identify with their mothers and form a continuing attachment. Boys, on the other hand, see their mothers as different from themselves and perceive a need to separate from the primary caretaker in order to assert their own identity. Gilligan concludes:

> Consequently, relationships, and particularly issues of dependency, are experienced differently by women and men.... Since masculinity is defined through separation while femininity is defined through attachment, male gender identity is threatened

by intimacy while female gender identity is threatened by separation. Thus males tend to have difficulty with relationships, while females tend to have problems with individuation [8].

As a result of the differences in the development of their gender identities, men and women form different concepts of ethics. Citing Piaget's observation, which was corroborated by Northwestern University sociologist Janet Lever, Gilligan posits, "boys in their games are more concerned with rules while girls are more concerned with relationships, often at the expense of the game itself" (16). Bloom succinctly elucidates, "Men develop an ethical system concerned with fairness and based on universal principles, rules, and laws. Women form an ethical system concerned with responsibility based on caring, empathy, and inclusion" (246). Gilligan is careful, however, not to favor either the male ethic of justice or the female ethic of care. She concludes her final chapter with the following statement:

> While an ethic of justice proceeds from the premise of equality, an ethic of care rests on the premise of nonviolence. In the representation of maturity, both perspectives converge in the realization that just as inequality adversely affects both parties in an unequal relationship, so too violence is destructive for everyone involved. This dialogue between fairness and care not only provides a better understanding of relations between the sexes but also gives rise to a more comprehensive portrayal of adult work and family relationships [174].

In short, neither ethic is superior; they are merely different.

APPLICATION

Data will be examined by using aspects of Mead's theory of symbolic interactionism. Gender differences as described in Gilligan's *In a Different Voice* will be explored by contrasting Worf and Troi. Harvey R. Greenberg's "In Search of Spock: A Psychoanalytic Inquiry" will serve as a structural template for this section, but the researcher will also consider Marsha F. Cassidy's "*Dallas* Refigured" (1989) and feminist critiques of the original series—Karin Blair's "Sex and *Star Trek*" and Anne Cranny-Francis' "Sexuality and Sex-Role Stereotyping in *Star Trek*." Cassidy's discussion of "character realization" will be especially useful to trace how the *Star Trek* characters were developed during the series' run.

Interpersonal

DYADIC THEORY

William W. Wilmot defines dyadic communication as "any face-to-face transaction between two people" (4). Dyadic theory builds upon the precepts of the interactionists. "Because each participant is affected in a dyadic transaction," Wilmot explains, "dyadic communication is *not* a linear, one-way event" (11). He characterizes dyads as sharing three traits— "uniqueness, completeness, and distinctiveness from larger groups" (14). Dyads are unique because no two are exactly alike. No person's relationship with another will be exactly similar to that possessed by another dyad. Wilmot remarks that a dyad is complete because it "functions as a completed unit [and] cannot be subdivided" (16). The final aspect, distinctiveness, acknowledges that dyads are the building blocks of the three subsequent communication contexts.

In moving from intrapersonal communication to dyadic communication, there is a fundamental shift of focus. Whereas the former theory centers on self-perception, the latter focuses on perception of the other. Wilmot emphasizes two perceptual regularities that occur in dyadic contexts. First, since a person often has to act on the basis of incomplete information, he makes sense of another person's behavior by imposing structure on it (63). The problem inherent in this process is that the observer can only interpret the other person's behavior as it relates back to her own experience.[22] Attribution of causality and responsibility is the other perceptual regularity. Wilmot points out, "From the general view that events are caused, we view human behavior as being caused" (65). The amount of responsibility attributed to the other person depends on whether the suspected causes are external or internal.

Perhaps the most useful elements of dyadic theory focus on its more practical aspects, such as identifying the elements of interpersonal attraction. Wilmot cites propinquity, similarity, and behavior as being "inextricably tied to the attraction [a person] feels toward another" (70). By propinquity, he refers to proximity or physical closeness. In other words, to develop a relationship the two parties should be able to physically interact. The precept of similarity raises the familiar adages "Do birds of a feather flock together?" or "Do opposites attract?"

Although Wilmot treads the middle ground between the two extremes, he concludes that a successful relationship will include a blend of similarities and differences. Behavior, the final element, is the outward manifestation of both participants' internal perceptions. Each person's other-perception (and subsequent behavior) is continually affected during the dyadic transaction. Borrowing from Altman and Taylor's social penetration theory, Wilmot enumerates the stages of a relationship as initiation, stabilization, and dissolution (143). Increasing levels of self-disclosure guide a dyad through these first two stages. He explains though relational dissolution is often traumatic, it is often caused by "conflict in the core areas," such as sex, values, or goals (156).

APPLICATION

Four types of dyadic relationships will be scrutinized: parent-child relationships, mentor-protégé relationships, friendships, and romances. Journal articles that will serve as overlays for this section will include Jane Elizabeth Ellington and Joseph W. Critelli's "Analysis of a Modern Myth," and April Selly's "'I Have Been, and Ever Shall Be, Your Friend.'"

Group and Organizational

THEORIES

Group. Group communication focuses on the interaction of people in small groups, especially in relation to the decision making process (Littlejohn 17). By definition, the group context necessitates understanding of interpersonal and intrapersonal theories, but its uniqueness gives it special qualities. One such quality is "synergy," which Em Griffin defines as "the recurrent finding that the whole is more than the sum of the parts" (206). For most of the 20th century, John Dewey's "reflective thinking" model was the dominant paradigm for the decision-making process. It consists of six stages:

1. Recognize the problem.
2. Diagnose the problem's cause.
3. Analyze the problem's cause.
4. Consider possible solutions.
5. Test to learn which solutions will work.
6. Implement the best solution [Griffin 209, Fisher 131].

Acknowledging this process was effective for individuals—as Dewey originally intended—but ill-suited for groups, B. Aubrey Fisher concluded, "[G]roups do not *make* decisions. Decisions *emerge* from group interaction" (139).

Fisher's interact system model of decision emergence is based on the premise that "a group is a collection of individuals whose communicative behaviors—specifically, acts, interacts, and double interacts—become interstructured and repetitive in the form of predictable patterns" (26–27). The notion of "interacts," sequences of two adjacent acts performed by group members, is crucial to the theory (248). Using interaction analysis, "a form of content analysis applied to human communicative behaviors" (235), Fisher analyzed groups by classifying their interacts into 12 categories: four levels of interpretation, ranging from favorable to neutrally ambiguous; four levels of substantiation, with the aforementioned range; clarification; modification; agreement; and disagreement (239). Stephen W. Littlejohn elucidates:

> In observing a group, Fisher [would] create a matrix with twelve rows and twelve columns, corresponding to the twelve categories in his system. This matrix thus contains 144 cells, one for each potential type of interact. In other words, the observer will classify the first act and the second act, placing a mark in the appropriate cell between the two. In this way the researcher can actually see the character and frequency of act pairs in a group discussion [306].

From his observations, Fisher discovered "four distinct phases of group decision making, each characterized by a different pattern of interaction" (140). The phases are orientation, conflict, emergence, and reinforcement. During the orientation phase, group members typically demonstrate high levels of clarification and agreement. Clarification tends to reduce uncertainty group members feel at the outset of their task. It also allows for a way to express disagreement in a positive manner (Griffin 213).[23] Overall, orientation "is a period of forming opinions, not rocking the boat, and getting rid of social inhibitions" (Fisher 141). As its name implies, the conflict phase begins as ambiguity lessens and fervor for or against a specific proposal emerges. Littlejohn notes, "As people group together according to their common stands on the issues, polarization grows" (306).

Dissent and social conflict subside during the emergence phase, as members soften their positions and reformulate their attitudes. Fisher cites the "recurrence of ambiguity" as the hallmark of the emergence phase (142). Unlike during orientation, ambiguity in the third stage reflects "muted disapproval" rather than tentative agreement (Griffin 214). This ambiguity allows a forceful dissenter from the conflict phase to gradually "[change] his opinion from disfavor to favor through the mediating step of expressing ambiguous opinions" (Fisher 143). Since the third phase is where the group's ultimate decision becomes apparent, it typically lasts longer than the other stages. Reinforcement, the final stage, is terse compared to its antecedents, but it is vital because here is where a "spirit of unity" pervades the decision-making process (144). Littlejohn adds, "Comments are almost uniformly positive and favorable, and more interaction occurs on matters of interpretation. The ambiguity that marked the third phase tends to disappear" (307).

Organizational. Organizational communication takes place in sizable collective systems and encompasses aspects of group, interpersonal, and intrapersonal theories (Littlejohn 17). Previously, systems theorists viewed living organisms as appropriate metaphors for organizations. Karl Weick discarded that approach because he felt it was too restrictive. He chose instead to describe organizations as a lively *process* and developed what is known as the information systems approach to organizations (Griffin 244). Weick's central premise is that the purpose of organizing is to remove equivocality from the informational environment. He describes, "The activities of organizing are directed toward the establishment of a workable level of certainty. An organization attempts to transform equivocal information into a degree of unequivocality with which it can work and to which it is accustomed" (245). In other words, Weick recognizes that to act effectively, organizations must reduce uncertainty or ambiguity in their environments.

In *The Social Psychology of Organizing*, he posits: "Interlocked behaviors are the basic elements that constitute any organization. They consist of repetitive, reciprocal contingent behaviors that develop and are maintained by two or more actors. Each actor uses and is used by the other person for the accomplishment of activities that neither alone could accomplish" (91).

Weick further theorizes that these interlocking behaviors occur in a system of three separate processes—enactment, selection, and retention. "The enactment process," he writes, "creates the information that the system adapts to, and in doing so removes a small amount of equivocality" (91).

Em Griffin interprets this by saying, "In the terms of open systems theory, the environment is as much an output as it is an input. Through enactment, people organizing together invent their environment rather than merely discovering it" (249). The next process, selection, consists of "[sorting] through the variety present in the equivocal information, [admitting] those portions which satisfy the criteria, thereby [putting] the equivocal information into orderly form" (Weick 92). These first two steps are grounded in the premise that some form of action will be taken during enactment. Weick cannot overemphasize his contention that failure to act causes ineffective organizations; he clearly states, "Chaotic action is preferable to orderly inaction" (107). Selection, then, becomes a means of interpreting the previous action, which Griffin likens to "retrospective sense making" (249). Finally, though retention is essentially a storage process, "it also removes some equivocality by integrating newer items with items previously retained" (Weick 92). During this final stage, Weick encourages leaders to challenge previously held assumptions, thereby gaining the flexibility of not relying too much on the past.

APPLICATION

This section has a split emphasis. First, it will focus on the *Enterprise* command crew, a small group, led by Captain Picard. The decision-making process will be explored by using B. Aubrey Fisher's interact system model of decision emergence. Thomas Schatz's essay "*St. Elsewhere* and the Evolution of the Ensemble Series" (1985) is also a useful model for examining the core of characters; it discusses how the late '70s brought forth shows with larger casts that allowed for realism and reinforced patriarchal roles. Second, the role that the organization Starfleet plays on *Star Trek: The Next Generation* will be explored. Starfleet, as exemplified by the *Enterprise* command structure, will be examined with regard to Karl Weick's information systems approach to organizations. Rick Worland's "Captain Kirk: Cold Warrior" raises some interesting secondary issues concerning Starfleet as a political organization paralleling NATO. This view will lead to analyses of *Star Trek*'s portrayal of encounters with alien cultures. The hallmark of the show has always been the "Prime Directive," a laissez-faire policy that forbids Starfleet personnel to interfere with emerging cultures. During the original series, Kirk and crew seemed to violate that decree on a regular basis. On *Star Trek: The Next Generation*, however, Picard and his staff only transgressed that boundary on nine occasions. A thorough examination of those aberrations, as well as examinations of futuristic diplomacy, will reveal whether the series upheld Roddenberry's precept of "Infinite Diversity in Infinite Combinations."

The Audience-Artifact Relationship

Mass communication is generally regarded as the final communication context. Because mass media play no significant part in the *Star Trek* universe, focus will be placed on the relationship between the artifact as a mass-communication text and its audience. Three distinct relationships exist between the *Star Trek* phenomenon and its adherents. Accordingly, these associations parallel the four previous communication contexts—intrapersonal, interpersonal, group and organizational.

INTRAPERSONAL ISSUES

As aforementioned, intrapersonal communication focuses "on the inner dialogue going on within the individual" (Griffin 11). In their introduction to *An Approach to Literature*, Cleanth Brooks, John Thibaut Purser, and Robert Penn Warren posit:

> Literature appeals to us because it enlarges our experience of the world and of ourselves—for insofar as literature opens a new world for us, and a new view of the old world we have lived in, it also indicates new kinds of response to the world. The study of literature is one of the things that can lead to the discovery of new dimensions of the self [1].

Though science fiction was not initially taken seriously as literature, it "became the vehicle for social criticism" during its golden age (Bloch 102). *Star Trek*, the paradigm of popular sci fi, has continually stimulated viewers to reexamine not only the world around them, but their individual thought processes as well. The creators of *Star Trek: The Next Generation* regularly emphasized this intrapersonal approach, as exemplified by the episodes "Darmok," "Ship in a Bottle," and "Ethics," which respectively focused on epistemology, ontology, and axiology. Captain Picard's nemesis Q epitomizes this aspect of the show's intent in the series finale, "All Good Things...":

> [The Q Continuum] wanted to see if you had the ability to expand your mind to new horizons. And for one brief moment you did. For that one fraction of a second you were open to options you had never considered. *That* is the exploration that awaits you—not mapping stars and studying nebulae, but charting the unknown possibilities of existence.

Q highlights that though technology is advanced in the 24th century, the human equation is still vital. This segment will explore episodes that contain intrapersonal motifs to discover the messages the show's creators hoped to impart.

Interpersonal Issues

A parasocial interaction is a "one-sided interpersonal relationship that television viewers establish with media characters" (Rubin & McHugh 280). Donald Horton and R. Richard Wohl pioneered this concept in their 1956 *Psychiatry* article "Mass Communication and Para-Social Interaction: Observations on Intimacy at a Distance." They argue that a viewer can develop a bond of intimacy with a media personality through "shared experiences existing only through viewing of the personality or persona over time" (Rubin & McHugh 280). As continued viewings occur, the audience member and the character develop a pseudo-interpersonal relationship. Since the character is reliable, the viewer becomes a loyal "friend." This section will explore parasocial interactions between *The Next Generation* and its audience. Crucial to this discussion is a 1992 survey of *Star*

Trek fans who attended a convention in Virginia Beach. Researchers Thom Parham and Alex Wainer theorized that causal links exist between *Star Trek*'s appeal and its portrayal of strong mentor-protégé couplings. Though they initially hoped to differentiate between how men and women perceive those dyads, the researchers discovered that both sexes are attracted to the show because of the variety of dyadic relationships.

Group and Organizational Issues

In his article "The Concept of Artistic Matrices" (1978), John G. Cawelti thoroughly discusses how the relationship between audience, critic-interpreters, and creators mediates and defines popular culture. He develops four models—communal, mythical, professional, and reflexive— to explain how art emerges from patterns within the larger culture. The *Star Trek* phenomenon aligns with Cawelti's mythical matrix. He explains:

> The crucial feature of this matrix is the special authority which is granted by participants in the matrix to the creator-performers, the genres they employ and possibly, in some cases, the medium that is used. In addition, the mythical matrix is characterized by a symbolic system consisting of an integrated body of narrative.... Because the creator-performer is given a special authority, he is somewhat distanced from the audience and tends to become more so as the culture develops.... [T]he mythical texts, though, have an existence apart from the performer and are usually conceived of as having been created by some special authority figure in the past. [298–299].

Here Cawelti identifies factors that define the *Trek* phenomenon. The late Gene Roddenberry, revered by some fans as the "Great Bird of the Galaxy," created *Star Trek* five-plus decades ago. Loyal viewers organized campaigns to keep the original series on the air its second and third years. Their demand for more product eventually spawned five additional series and the film franchise. In this final segment, the researcher will explore how *Star Trek* has enticed fans—loyal fans—to form a sub-culture, which has taken a life of its own. To echo an earlier quote from Bjo Trimble ("My Part" 46), the phenomenon transcended its creator while he was alive and continues to do so after his demise.

Two

The Intrapersonal Context

In *A First Look at Communication Theory*, Em Griffin defines intrapersonal communication as focusing "on the inner dialogue going on within the individual" (11). The depth of characterization on *Star Trek* has been a factor that distinguishes it from mere space operas like *Buck Rogers* or *Flash Gordon*. Though not all of *Star Trek: The Next Generation* characters received the same amount of development during the series' run, several perspectives can be used to analyze characters' "inner journeys."

Data and Symbolic Interactionism

In each *Star Trek* series, there has been at least one character whose purpose was to gauge the human experience. In classic *Trek*, that character was Commander Spock, the *Enterprise*'s half-human and half-Vulcan science officer. When creating *Next Generation*, Roddenberry and company set out not to duplicate the original characters per se. Rather than to have another half-breed alien fulfill that need, they decided instead to have an android, an artificial life-form.[1] Like Leonard Nimoy's Spock from the original series, Brent Spiner's Data became the "breakout" character of the new show. As the resident non-humans, both roles gave viewers a perspective to explore the nature of humanity. Their inner journeys differed, however. Whereas Spock sought to exorcise his human half to render his Vulcan heritage's dominance, the synthetic being Data sought to become more human.

Background

The concept of an artificial life-form has been a staple in science-fiction literature and has roots in medieval alchemy. In *Tools for Convivi-*

ality, Ivan Illich relates, "The alchemist's dream of making a homunculus in the test tube slowly took the shape of creating robots to *work* for man, and to educate men to *work* alongside them" (30). Karel Čapek coined the term "robot" in his 1921 play *R.U.R.*, which stood for "Rossum's Universal Robots." Pop culture pundit Camille Paglia notes:

> Robots have come a long way in the history of science fiction. Ever since the rough, uncouth monster of Mary Shelley's *Frankenstein* (1818), artificial beings have symbolized both the creativity and the danger of Western intellect, which exploded from the 17th century rebirth of science into the machine age of the Industrial Revolution. The comical, clunky Robby the Robot in the film *Forbidden Planet* (1956) was the obedient servant of the strong-willed Dr. Morbius (Walter Pidgeon), but HAL, the sinister rebel computer of Stanley Kubrick's *2001: A Space Odyssey* (1968), turned on his masters and seemed about to enslave mankind [46].

Literary antecedents aside, Data's spiritual grandfather was Questor, the android hero of a 1974 Roddenberry pilot (Alexander 402–403).

In "Encounter at Farpoint," *Star Trek: The Next Generation*'s series' premiere, the *Enterprise*'s second-in-command, Cmdr. Will Riker, calls Data "Pinocchio," a sobriquet that encapsulates the android's aspirations. The writers and producers would fully explore that motif during the series' 178 episodes and the subsequent feature films. Symbolic interactionism, which emerged from the writings of George Herbert Mead, is a useful theoretical framework from which to examine the Data character. Mead's troika of mind, self, and society is aptly applied to the character's development during *Next Generation*'s tenure.

Mind

In *Mind, Self, & Society: From the Standpoint of a Social Behaviorist*, Mead theorizes that humans derive meaning from an individual's gesture and subsequent behavior toward another based on that gesture (76). Mead clearly believes that one's concept of "mind" is interwoven with a continuing interpersonal dialogue between one and an "other." (Though the theorist also believes symbolic naming or symbolization is integral to the mind's process [74], this researcher will explore that theme under the topic of society, in which Mead also finds it crucial.) Five episodes that focus on Data's unique, interpersonal dialogue with another person outside the regular crew are "Legacy" (#406), "In Theory" (#425), "Hero Worship" (#511), "The Most Toys" (#322), and "Silicon Avatar" (#504).

"Legacy" is a milestone because it was *Star Trek: The Next Generation*'s 80th episode—significant because classic *Trek* only lasted 79 episodes.

To celebrate, the producers evoked the memory of Tasha Yar, the first-season security officer killed in the line of duty. Visiting the failed colony where Yar was born, the *Enterprise* crew encounters a woman who claims to be her sister, Ishara. Data is intrigued because of his sexual liaison with Tasha during the series' second episode, "The Naked Now." Because of that fact, he forms an attachment to Ishara, which she manipulates to her advantage. Mark Altman analyzes, "[T]hough some of its contemporary gang allegory falls flat, the betrayal of the crew by Ishara is poignant and well–played, particularly the ambiguities seen in her character when Data bids Yar farewell in the episode's coda" (EG, Oct. 1991, 27). Michael Piller agrees by saying, "There's nothing as poignant as seeing the betrayal of an innocent, as Data is" (27).

The elusive concept of romance is the topic of "In Theory," a logical extension of concepts explored in "The Ensigns of Command" (#302). Rather than the earlier episode's subplot of flirtation, this show comprises a full-blown love story. Jenna D'Sora, a crew member on the rebound from a failed relationship, falls for Data. Puzzled by her infatuation, he consults Guinan—Whoopi Goldberg's enigmatic bartender—and attempts to reciprocate Jenna's affections. The results are disastrous, but the episode highlights that affairs of the heart transcend pure logic. Data encounters a different form of interpersonal bonding in "Hero Worship," when an orphaned youth embraces the android as a father figure. Staff writer Brannon Braga notes, "It's always nice when you have a new twist. Data [confronts] someone who wants to be an android as opposed to him wanting to be human. [T]he scene where Data confesses to wishing he knew what the taste of a malted was like is very touching" (Altman, EG, Oct. 1992, 62).

The aforementioned episodes focus on Data's positive, interpersonal, mind-defining experiences. "The Most Toys" and "Silicon Avatar," however, detail negative aspects. The former episode is a variation of a clichéd science-fiction plot—a malevolent alien captures one of our heroes as a specimen for a personal collection. The interesting aspect of this episode is that Data is "pushed to the brink of murder for a logical reason"—his adversary, Fajo, is morally repugnant (Nemecek 125). Data's misstatement about a weapon being fired while he is beamed away is likewise intriguing. Mark Altman describes, "It's a step forward in the evolution of a character, and a fascinating issue for Star Trek to deal with. And it's the only thing that elevates this episode above your average *Space: 1999*" (EG, Sept. 1990, 49).[2]

"Silicon Avatar" is the second episode to follow-up "Datalore" (#113), which had introduced Data's "bad seed," older brother Lore. Loosely inspired by *Moby Dick*, "Avatar" reintroduces the Crystalline Entity as the elusive and destructive quarry of Dr. Kila Marr, who fulfills the role as Captain Ahab. Her attitude toward Data changes when she learns he possesses the memories of the colonists, including her deceased son, but she betrays this newfound bond by shattering the entity. Teleplay writer Jeri Taylor recalls, "I wanted to [write] it because I felt being a mother and a woman I could identify with what would have to be the worst kind of loss anyone could suffer, the death of a child. I was really able to tap into those feelings and tell a story about a woman whose vendetta over the loss of her son ruined her" (Altman, EG, Oct. 1992, 45). After Dr. Marr has enacted her revenge, the dispassionate android informs the doctor that her son would regret that she ruined her career for his sake.

Self

Mead defines self as being dependent on the generalized other. He elucidates by remarking that self is dependent on the dialectic between the "I" and the "Me," defining "I" as one's response to the attitudes of others and "Me" as the organized attitudes of others. This conceit complements Martin Buber's position in *I & Thou* (1923) that the key differentiation between the "I–It" and "I–Thou" relationships is that in the former, people treat each other as objects while in the latter, people engage in a true, interrelating dialogue (Grenz & Olson 80). In addition to considering the "I–Me" dialectic, one must also examine the concept of family, since a person's self-concept is often drawn from his or her family relationship.

OTHER

One of the first episodes focusing on a particular aspect of Data's personality was "The Outrageous Okona" (#204) in which he explores the concept of comedy. Despite coaching from a holodeck comedian played by Joe Piscopo and help from Guinan, the android never manages to grasp the elusive concept. This theme recurs throughout the series and is essential to Data's sub-plot in *Star Trek Generations*. Attempting to simulate humor, he spontaneously pushes Dr. Crusher off a sailing ship during a holodeck simulation. Geordi's reprimand of that behavior causes Data to have his friend install the emotion chip Dr. Soong bequeathed him. Though he learns that possessing emotions subjects him to the realm of irrationality, Data learns they are an essential facet of being human.

A third-season episode, "The Ensigns of Command" (#302) focuses on a weightier concern. Data learns about leadership when he is given his first command assignment and must confront the stubborn colony leader and circumvent colonists' prejudice against his android nature. He ultimately persuades the colonists to leave by using a measured display of force. Episode scribe Melinda Snodgrass laments,

> I wish you could have seen my version. I wanted to take Data one step further in his development as a human being. I wanted to stress him and have him face a situation where logic isn't enough, to show that in order to command you have to have charisma. You have to learn to wave your [manhood] and hope your[s] is bigger than the other guy's [Altman, EG, Sept. 1990, 40].

Data confronts similar prejudices in "Redemption, Part II" (#501), when he is given temporary command of a starship and encounters prejudice from his subordinates. He again learns that forcefulness and simulated anger can be effective leadership tools.

In a less successful effort, "Thine Own Self" (#716), the writing staff returns to a *Frankenstein* motif, Mary Shelley's seminal tale of artificial man. Stranded on a developing planet with amnesia and a container of radioactive metal, Data befriends a young girl. The one-note premise leads nowhere, though it does exhaust *Frankenstein*-type imagery, including angry villagers who surround "the creature." Even scripter Ron Moore confesses, "I could never figure out what this show was about or what I was trying to do with this episode. And it shows" (Kutzera 79).[3]

Family

Data was initially conceived to be a unique being—a veritable orphan. By the end of the series, however, his uniqueness was challenged. His evil brother Lore is introduced in "Datalore" (#113), returns to torment Data in "Brothers" (#403), and meets his fate at the end of "Descent" (#626/701). Having learned in "The Most Toys" (#322) that killing is sometimes necessary, Data has no qualms about dispatching his brother. Jeri Taylor reveals, "All the episodes Lore was in clearly [indicated he] was out of control and was never going to change. So, in a sense, from the first time he appeared in 'Datalore' over the seasons, Data had time to assess this" (personal interview). Data also meets his "grandfather," Dr. Ira Graves, who was Dr. Soong's mentor in "The Schizoid Man" (#206) and eventually Dr. Soong himself in "Brothers." Those encounters with male family members always seemed to end with the tragedy of betrayal.

The two instances with Data's female relatives were more heartfelt.

Desiring the need to procreate, he creates Lal in "The Offspring" (#316). Data explains to a flustered Picard: "I have observed that in most species, there is a primal instinct to perpetuate themselves. Until now, I have been the last of my kind. If I were to be damaged or destroyed, I would be lost forever.

But if I am successful, with the creation of Lal, my continuance is assured." "Although Starfleet's plans to take control of the new android bear an annoying resemblance to 'The Measure of a Man,' the story is sufficiently original and engaging," critiques Altman (EG, Sept. 1990, 46). In *Star Trek: The Next Generation*'s final year, Data encounters Juliana Soong, his "mother" in "Inheritance" (#710). By this point in the series, the writers had probably shown viewers far too much about him, spoiling his mystique. The revelation that Juliana herself is an android is "a plot-twist that's an old science fiction chestnut," as Dale Kutzera points out (60). But Data's agonizing decision not to tell Juliana elevates him to a new understanding of humanity, and the inclusion of the Lal backstory from "The Offspring" helps make this an emotionally-satisfying tale (Altman "Seventh Season" 35).

Society

Society is the final element of Mead's troika. He theorized, in turn, that three influences combine to define one's role in society: the central nervous system, which imbues humans with sentience; reflexivity, or the taking on the role of the other; and the use of significant symbols.

SENTIENCE

One of the recurring themes of *Star Trek: The Next Generation* is Data's quest to become human. Sentience, or self-awareness, is one of the traits scientists use to classify a being as alive. Though Data has no central nervous system per se, he does possess a complex system of neural nets. From the series premiere forward, none of the *Enterprise* crew doubt that Data is self-aware.[4] The first episode to focus on the android's status as a sentient being is "The Measure of a Man" (#209). Cmdr. Bruce Maddox, a cyberneticist, intends to disassemble Data in order to replicate other androids. Starfleet, at Data's behest, convenes a hearing to determine whether he is property or a living creature. "Writer Melinda Snodgrass," describes Larry Nemecek in *The Star Trek: The Next Generation Companion*, "drew on her own experience as an attorney to craft this timeless tale of personal rights" (77).[5]

Another type of challenge for Data comes in the form of Sherlock Holmes' arch-enemy Moriarty, who first appears in the second-season episode "Elementary, Dear Data" (#203). Having easily beaten holodeck scenarios based on Conan Doyle's stories, Data meets his match when Geordi inadvertently creates a sentient Moriarty, who knows he is a simulation. This episode suffers, however, "as a result of Gene Roddenberry's decision to delete the episode's original ending in which Picard deceives Moriarty into believing he can never leave the Holodeck" (Altman, EG, Sept. 1990, 33). Four years later, Data gets a rematch when Moriarty is accidentally "freed" by Lt. Barclay in "Ship in a Bottle" (#612). Highly annoyed that he has been kept in limbo for so many years, Moriarty enacts his revenge by trapping Data, Picard, and Barclay in his "ship in a bottle"—a holodeck within a holodeck. The plot evolves like a chess game between the two artificially-created, sentient beings until the *Enterprise* crew members outwit their captor by trapping him in an isolated memory cube. Aside from tackling the notion of imbued sentience, this episode also questions the nature of reality. Picard dryly offers in the episode's coda, "Who knows, our reality may be very much like theirs and all this may be an elaborate simulation running inside a little device" ("Ship in a Bottle").

REFLEXIVITY

Mead posits that the ability to take on the role of another is crucial to the construction of society. As a student of human nature, Data constantly attempts to place himself in other's roles. An outward manifestation of this desire is evidenced by his willingness to study acting. In three episodes—"The Defector" (#310), "Frame of Mind" (#621), and "Emergence" (#723)—the android performs scenes from plays. The first and last instances are noteworthy because the respective plays are Shakespeare's *Henry V* and *The Tempest*. Although both scenes reflect events in the episodes, Data learns from Picard how to better interpret his character's motivations:

> Data, you're here to learn about the human condition, and there is no better way of doing that than by embracing Shakespeare. But you must discover it through your own performance, not by imitating others.... Listen to what Shakespeare is telling you about the man [Henry V], Data. A king who had true feeling for his soldiers would wish to share their fears with them on the eve of battle ["The Defector"].

After they exit the holodeck, Data asks when he will be ready for a real audience and is told not to be in a hurry. Evidently by season six, Beverly is impressed enough with the android's acting ability to cast him in the play "Frame of Mind" with Riker in the lead (Landis, *TNG Episode Guide*, computer software, 1994).

Symbols

The use of significant symbols is Mead's final societal element. Probably the most astonishing development in Data's "human" development is the ability to dream, which he gains in "Birthright, Part I" (#616). After receiving a plasma shock, Data collapses and has a vision of Dr. Soong. Encouraged by Worf to seek his "father" (which mirrors the Klingon's own quest), Data eventually succeeds and learns that he has gained a new ability—to dream. Director Winrich Kolbe's surreal style accurately renders writer Brannon Braga's vision of delving into Jungian archetypes and dream images. Kolbe does a stunning job "in visualizing Data's dream," lauds Mark A. Altman, "as the android encounters Dr. Soong forging a bird's wing on an anvil that turns real when immersed in water and flies away" ("The Making of Birthright" 72). Unfortunately the follow-up episode "Phantasms" (#706) fails to fulfill its promising premise of Data's first nightmares. Dale Kutzera chastises, "Director Patrick Stewart does what he can with this incomprehensible script, using wide–angle lenses to create some intriguing dream imagery, most notably Troi as a cake, and Crusher sucking out Riker's brains through a straw" (54).

Summary

In describing the android, second-season story editor Melinda Snodgrass says it best: "I've always used Data as the child. More so than Wesley, who is very competent and capable, Data is exploring what it means to be human, which is what any child does as they [sic] grow up" (Altman "The Importance" 36). Snodgrass' comments echo psychiatrist Harvey R. Greenberg's analysis of the classic *Trek*'s Spock in "In Search of Spock: A Psychoanalytic Inquiry." Like his antecedent, Data "embodies the central virtues and dilemmas of the pubertal years" and reflects "many a Terran youngster's search for a viable identity" (54). David Gerrold, working on TNG's preproduction phase describes, "What is most appealing about Data as a character is he would like to know if it's possible for an android to not simply *simulate* humanity, but to actually achieve it" ("*Star Trek* Report" 20). Data's quest for humanity frequently serves as a dramatic foil for other characters, who grapple with similar concerns. This pursuit, enlivened by Brent Spiner's acting prowess, explains why Data has become the *Next Generation*'s standout character.

Gender Differences, Worf and Troi

Background

The original *Star Trek* series included two female characters, Lt. Uhura, the communications officer, and Nurse Chapel; neither role was exactly trend setting. Although Uhura shared television's first interracial kiss with Captain Kirk in the episode "Plato's Stepchildren," her duties generally consisted of hailing approaching vessels. Similarly, though a medical professional, Chapel was limited to pining over the stoic Mr. Spock, who could never reciprocate her affections. Feminist criticism like Karin Blair's "Sex and *Star Trek*" (1983) and Anne Cranny-Francis' "Sexuality and Sex-Role Stereotyping in *Star Trek*" (1985) often attribute these stereotypical portrayals to Roddenberry's limited view of 23rd-century women. To such feminists, *Star Trek* exemplifies a future where man is free to fulfill wild, sexual fantasies at the expense of women. Though Captain Kirk's incessant trysts with female aliens can be blamed on *Trek*'s creator, it is unfair to hold him accountable for Starfleet's implicit "glass ceiling." After all, the first pilot included a female second-in-command for Captain Christopher Pike. But Number One was replaced with a male counterpart in the second pilot since network executives balked at placing a woman in such a position of authority (Alexander 230).

When the feature film franchise began with the 1979 release of *Star Trek: The Motion Picture*, Uhura and Chapel were both promoted to higher ranks, though their positions within the *Trek* cast remained much the same. The creation of new characters for *Star Trek: The Next Generation* posed new challenges for that series' producers with regards to portrayals of gender. Jeri Taylor, a former executive producer of *Star Trek: The Next Generation* and co-creator of *Star Trek: Voyager*, discusses the gender issue in depth:

> I can say with pride that I made a conscious effort—and I think to some extent achieved—giving the women of *Next Generation* more important roles. One of the problems was that Gene Roddenberry, with all of his good intentions and enlightened thinking, nonetheless put the women into very traditional, nurturing, caregiving roles. In his defense, he created Tasha Yar also, who was head of security, [but] she left. Denise [Crosby], the actress left. And so that left us with a doctor and a psychologist—the people who sort of help the guys out with their problems. So I thought that it was really right and that Gene would applaud the effort to break them out of those roles. And so [I] looked for ways to get them into more mainstream kinds of stories. To get them into action. To get them in situations of com-

mand. To get them in situations of jeopardy and let their intelligence and cunning and shrewdness and bravery shine with all the heroism that the men were allowed to shine [personal interview].

Despite the female *Star Trek: The Next Generation* characters' initial adherence to traditional gender roles, Carol Gilligan suggests in her book *In a Different Voice* that those stereotypes are not necessarily detrimental. Gilligan acknowledges fundamental differences between the sexes but promotes unity through diversity. Contrasting two *Next Generation* characters, Counselor Deanna Troi and Security Officer Worf, from Gilligan's perspective will prove useful in determining their intrapersonal issues.

Gender Identity Formation

Boys and girls develop their gender identities separately, according to Gilligan. Girls identify with their primary caregivers, usually their mothers, and form continuing attachments. Boys, on the other hand, feel a need to separate from their primary caregivers in order to form a sense of identity (7).

Deanna and Lwaxana

The first episode of *Star Trek: The Next Generation* to focus on Deanna is "Haven" (#111), which introduces her flamboyant mother, Lwaxana Troi. Bearing Gilligan's theories in mind, the writers' choice to define Deanna Troi in relation to her mother is not surprising. Though the daughter-mother conflict is typical situation comedy fodder regarding an arranged marriage, the actors' performances make the episode appealing. Mark Altman revels, "Have fun watching Counselor Troi and her mother at odds as Marina Sirtis plays straightwoman to Majel Barrett's campy Lwaxana Troi" (EG, Sept. 1990, 27). Lwaxana returns in five additional episodes: "Manhunt" (#219), "Ménage à Troi" (#324), "Half a Life" (#422), "Cost of Living" (#520), and "Dark Page" (#707). While the earlier episodes are intended to be mostly humorous,[6] the later installments highlight serious aspects of Lwaxana's personality.

In "Half a Life" (#422) she falls in love with an alien scientist who is fated to euthanize himself on his 60th birthday. "It showed a whole new side to Majel Barrett as an actress," resounds director Les Landau. "She's usually this flimsy, whimsical Auntie Mame character, but in this episode she's a very sensitive, warm and caring individual" (Altman, EG, Oct. 1991, 46). This trend continues in "Cost of Living." To take her mind off her impending marriage to a man she's never met, Lwaxana takes Alexander

Rozhenko under her wing, much to the consternation of his father Worf and Deanna Troi. Lwaxana's final appearance on *Star Trek: The Next Generation* in "Dark Page" helps explain the character's motivations. After contact with the Cairn—another telepathic race—endangers her mother's psyche, Deanna must enter Lwaxana's mind. There the counselor discovers her mother has long suppressed the memory of Kestra, a daughter who died in a tragic, childhood accident. Deanna's journey leads to healing for her mother and strengthens the bond between the women.

Worf: Son of Mogh

Unlike girls, boys establish their identity by separating themselves from their primary caregivers (Gilligan 7). Worf, the *Enterprise*'s security officer, had an atypical time establishing his identity. The first-season episode "Heart of Glory" (#120) lays the groundwork for the series arc affectionately known as the "Klingon saga." Worf's family was killed on Khitomer in a Romulan attack, and he was rescued by Starfleet officers.[7] Raised by human foster parents—Sergey and Helena Rozhenko—on the farming colony of Gault, he attended Starfleet Academy with his foster brother, Nikolai, who abandoned school and returned home.[8] Worf's de facto expatriation initially leaves him unable to satisfy the demands of his Klingon heritage. He is only able to commemorate the tenth anniversary of his Age of Ascension (a Klingon *bar mitzvah*) with the help of his human friends who set up a special holodeck program for him. His true initiation into the ways of his people and his journey of identity would not begin until the series' third season.

Ethics

Gilligan defines the development of ethics as another key difference between men and women. Boys at an early age are more concerned with the rules of a game, while girls place a higher priority on their relationships, even at the expense of the game (16). She acknowledges the male ethic of justice may lead to violence whereas the female ethic of care "rests on the premise of non–violence" (174).

Worf and the Justice Ethic

Worf learns he has a younger brother in "Sins of the Father" (#317). Left behind by their parents, Kurn was fostered by a family friend after the Khitomer massacre. Now he has come to enlist his older brother's help; their father has been posthumously accused of betraying the Khitomer outpost. Entangled in the machinations of Klingon politics, Worf learns that if the true traitor—the late father of Duras, a member of the High Council—is revealed then the Empire will plunge into civil war. To preserve peace, Worf honorably sacrifices his family name. "The episode ends on a powerful note as the assembled Klingon contingent turns their backs on Worf as he leaves, now a pariah," relates Mark Altman. "It's a major step for Star Trek with important implications for the series" (EG, Sept. 1990, 46).

Those implications arrive in "Reunion" (#407). Larry Nemecek denotes, "And what a time for Worf! In one fell swoop he learns he has a son, his mate is killed, and he in turn kills her murderer and his family's accuser; he then sends his newfound son off to live with his own foster parents" (146).[9] The civil war Worf sought to avoid with his discommendation erupts in "Redemption" (#426/501). Duras' sisters conspire with Romulans to take over the Klingon Empire. Mark Altman posits, "The show works best in its exploration of the Picard/Worf command dynamic even if it misses the epic Shakespearean quality of its *King Lear–like* premise" (EG, Oct. 1991, 51). David Landis elucidates:

> It seems clear that Picard pushed Worf into resigning his commission for political reasons. He knew that a Starfleet officer playing a pivotal role in the Klingon Civil War would not be tolerated by either the Klingons or the Federation. In ordering Worf to return to duty, he forced Worf to choose his place, either on the Enterprise, or with Gowron. Worf chose Gowron, believing rightly that the fate of his people was at stake [*TNG Episode Guide*, computer software, 1994].

Unfortunately, the second half of "Redemption" is overburdened with subplots. Worf's plight is given short shrift as Data assumes temporary command of a starship, and Romulan Commander Sela is revealed to be the daughter of the alternate timeline Tasha Yar (from "Yesterday's Enterprise" [#315]). Michael Dorn, who portrays Worf, admits, "They packed a lot of things into one episode ... a lot of things. It was too much" (Altman, EG, Oct. 1992, 36–37). Nevertheless, Worf reclaims his family honor and identity in the process.

Troi and the Care Ethic

In the first two seasons of *Star Trek: The Next Generation*, the writers seemed not to know what to do with Troi's character. Being half Betazoid, she possesses the ability to sense emotions (rather than full telepathy like her mother). Oft times she was merely used as a human tricorder.[10] Year three marks a new approach for the counselor; she gets to counsel people. She comforts young Jeremy Aster regarding the death of his mother in

"The Bonding" (#305) and deduces Roga Danar is a victim of government mind control in "The Hunted" (#311). "[A]fter three years in space, and on the air, we finally get to see Counselor Troi counsel someone in 'Hollow Pursuits' (#321)," grouses Altman (EG, Sept. 1990, 49). That someone is Reginald Barclay, a junior officer addicted to holodeck fantasies.

Troi's challenge as ship's counselor is to help integrate the socially maladjusted "Broccoli" (as his detractors call him) into the crew's mainstream. Despite Larry Nemecek's assertions that "those involved in this show deny they intended to make a comment aimed at Trek's more obsessive fans" (125), Mark Altman sees Barclay as a surrogate for *Trek* fans who need to "turn off the tube, take off the 'Make It So' button and go outside and have some real fun" (49). In any case, "it was refreshing to see that everyone in [Starfleet] was not strong-willed and confident. Reg Barclay was more of an 'everyman' than any other character in the series so far" (Landis, *TNG Episode Guide*, computer software, 1994). By this time the writers comprehend that a counselor is, as David Gerrold describes, a "chaplainlike character whose job is to tend to the crewmen's inner life" (Alexander 226–227).[11] Troi's counseling sessions would become a frequent motif in forthcoming episodes.

Syncretism: Putting It Together

At the end of *In a Different Voice*, Carol Gilligan concludes by suggesting an open dialogue between the "feminine" and "masculine" ethics. By extension, a logical solution for the *Trek* producers regarding Troi and Worf would be to incorporate atypical gender roles into those characters' normal patterns. For Troi, this approach would entail learning to assert a justice ethic; for Worf, incorporating a care ethic. The writers and producers accomplished these tasks by giving each character a long-range story arc during the series' latter years.

TROI'S EMPOWERMENT

Aside from not knowing how to portray Troi, the writers often placed her in a stereotypical female role—that of victim. Marina Sirtis, the actress who portrays Troi, was troubled by this fact. She said, "The women on this show are very non-threatening. I don't think it's realistic. It's not realistic for the 20th century, so it's definitely not realistic for the 24th century" (Altman, EG, Oct. 1991, 39). Sirtis was responding to the numerous times her character was portrayed as a woman in jeopardy. For example, in "Skin of Evil" (#123) and "Who Watches the Watchers" (#304), Troi is kidnapped; in "The Child" (#201), she is impregnated by an unknown force[12]; and in "Power Play" (#515) and "Man of the People" (#603), her mind is taken over by aliens. The first "Troi in jeop" episode that stands out is "The Loss" (#410), in which the counselor temporarily loses her empathic powers. Larry Nemecek applauds,

> This episode gave Marina Sirtis a rarer chance to stretch and shine as Troi—and made those weeks of being written out of the series in season one seem very far away indeed. Riker here calls Troi a "blue-blooded Betazoid" who's always had a unique means of control to fall back on, giving her character a subtext that was sadly lacking in the early years [150].

Mark Altman agrees with Nemecek that the TNG writers learned to create conflict among their cast by using an external catalyst, in this case a cloud of two-dimensional creatures. He writes, "In Gene Roddenberry's rose-colored universe where everyone gets along, it's hard to believe Troi turns into a superbitch. But it's fun" (EG, Oct. 1991, 29).[13] Though early in the series she has a token stint as leader of an Away team on a female-dominated planet in "Angel One" (#114), the counselor's empowerment would not take place for years.

When "Disaster" (#505) strikes the *Enterprise*, Troi takes command, since she is senior officer on the bridge. She clashes with the newly arrived Ensign Ro Laren, who is also on the bridge and lacks faith in the counselor's command abilities. Sirtis was upset that the script left her in command, "but having to take instructions from an ensign" (Landis, *TNG Episode Guide*, computer software, 1994). She felt as a lieutenant commander and a graduate of Starfleet Academy, Troi should have received training in ship operations. The next episode where she flouts convention is "A Fistful of Datas" (#608). Posing as "Durango," a mysterious stranger, Troi joins Worf on a holodeck adventure in the "ancient American West." Her crowning achievement, however, emerges that season in "Face of the Enemy" (#614). Mark Altman synopsizes: "In the episode, Troi awakens aboard a Romulan warbird where she has been physically transformed into a member of the dreaded Tal Shiar, the most feared branch of the Romulan secret service. Confused, the counselor finds out that she is on a covert mission to transport Romulan defectors to the Federation" ("Marina Sirtis, Betazoid Beauty" 65). Marina Sirtis' strong performance is accented by Carolyn Seymour's portrayal of the Romulan Commander. The co-executive producer at the time, Jeri Taylor admits, "When those two women tee off against each other, it's great because we don't get that much conflict among our people, but between those two it's just spit and vinegar and they were dynamic" (66).

Troi completes her journey of empowerment in "Thine Own Self" (#716) when she takes the bridge officer's test for promotion to commander. The counselor breezes through every section except the engineering exam, which she fails by repeatedly destroying the ship in simulation. Only when she is willing to sacrifice the life of a simulated Geordi La Forge does she pass. Setting aside her care ethic, Troi learns the *Enterprise*'s safety is more important than any one life. To quote *Star Trek II: The Wrath of Khan*, "The needs of the many outweigh the needs of the few ... or the one."

Papa Worf

During Worf's journey the final three years of *Star Trek: The Next Generation*, he reconciles his gender identity by becoming primary caregiver to his own progeny. In the episode "New Ground" (#510), the security officer receives an unexpected family visit: foster mother Helena Rozhenko informs Worf she and her husband can no longer give Alexander the attention he deserves and leaves the child with Worf. Story editor Ron Moore defends the decision to keep Alexander aboard the *Enterprise* in light of negative response from numerous fans:

> I thought it was a good decision to give Worf a son. Worf is more Klingon than the Klingons are. He doesn't have a real good sense of humor; he doesn't laugh a lot. The Klingons are these boisterous Vikings in space and his whole relationship with his son is geared towards making him the perfect little warrior. The fact that Alexander's mother (K'Ehleyr) didn't share any of those ideas immediately put the two into conflict. That's the essence of drama and it's built into stories of the two of them knocking heads [Altman, EG, Oct. 1992, 54].

Despite viewers' fears the character's presence could turn the series into "Romper Room: The Next Generation," Alexander only appeared in four additional episodes—"Ethics" (#516), "Cost of Living" (#520), "A Fistful of Datas" (#608), and "Firstborn" (#721).

The writers are also careful not to reiterate the "problem child" motif in those episodes. "Ethics" focuses on Worf's desire to commit ritual suicide after an accident paralyzes him. An irate Riker refuses to help the Klingon, reminding him it is tradition for the oldest son to assist in such a procedure.[14] Rather than traumatizing Alexander, Worf successfully undergoes a risky medical procedure. "Cost of Living," four episodes later, returns to the father-son conflict as a theme, this time adding a new variable—Lwaxana Troi. "This is a show that was promised as Auntie Mame arriving aboard and taking Worf's son under her wing to bring him out of his shell in her own flamboyant way," remarks executive producer Rick

Berman. "It's delightful, funny and wonderful" (Altman, EG, Oct. 1992, 86). The aforementioned "A Fistful of Datas" is an inspired holodeck romp with Worf, Alexander, and Troi having a rousing adventure in the "ancient American west." Unfortunately, Alexander's final appearance in "Firstborn" exhausts the trope of Worf's attempts to turn his reluctant son into a warrior. In the episode, a mysterious family friend who arrives to assist with that goal turns out to be a future Alexander, who has traveled to the past to prevent his father's death. Despite the episode's convoluted logic, Worf ultimately realizes Alexander must adopt the Klingon cultural ways at his own pace. Actor Michael Dorn comments on the episode's nebulous ending, "We don't really know what happens now. Just that the future is uncertain. It's just like real life, but Worf is still a terrible father. He hasn't got a clue" (Altman "Seventh Season" 42).

Summary

Aside from Data, Worf and Troi are arguably the two *Star Trek: The Next Generation* crew members whose characters have progressed the most during the 178 episodes of the series. Ironically, as their characters became more defined through reconciliation of gender identities, their destinies became intermingled. The introduction of Alexander as a recurring character during season five led to increased roles for both Worf and Troi. Not surprisingly, the writers planted seeds for a romance between the two characters—an arc explored during the series' final season.

Character Realization with Picard, Riker, Crusher and La Forge

This researcher posits that the four remaining *Star Trek: The Next Generation* characters—Picard, Riker, Crusher, and La Forge—never received the depth of character development as Data, Worf, and Troi. The opening credits of the show clearly identify Picard and Riker, played, respectively, by Patrick Stewart and Jonathan Frakes as the stars. Likewise, no one can dispute that many episodes focus on these two characters.[15] The problem remains, however, that after 178 episodes and four feature films Picard and Riker are virtual ciphers to the audience. The paucity of episodes devoted to Crusher and La Forge indicate a similar problem. Despite the familiarity the actors gained with their characters over time, none seemed to develop much beyond their initial portrayals in the series pilot.

Background

Marsha F. Cassidy discusses such "character realization" in her essay "*Dallas* Refigured" (1989). "The extended plot of the series becomes character descriptive, circumscribing in the main characters the ethical boundaries for each personality. Through repetition, characters express the possible variations of behavior innate to their psychological makeup, incrementally changing but also remaining true to themselves" (51). The relative predictability of these *Star Trek: The Next Generation* characters made them less realized than their counterparts. Diane Werts further charges, "The dazzling guest stars made the TNG regulars look dull in comparison. Stripped of the original series' simplistic physical compulsions [i.e., preoccupation with dalliances], these folks also seemed drained of passion" (23). Though her case is perhaps overstated, Werts' point remains valid. Not surprisingly, all four actors pushed to give their characters more to do, but the results often did not match expectations.

Capt. Picard

As commanding officer of the *Enterprise*, Jean-Luc Picard clearly sets the tone for the crew. He is a 24th-century version of Plato's philosopher-king and is described in "Skin of Evil" (#123) as having "the heart of an explorer and the soul of a poet." Yet many of the early *Star Trek: The Next Generation* episodes focused on Picard's ethereal side, with too much time devoted to philosophy and too little to action. In an interview with Mark A. Altman, Michael Piller recalled:

> Patrick [Stewart] came to me in the middle of the [third] season and said, "I'm bored. You haven't given me anything interesting to do." He was upset with the way Picard was being treated and he had every right to be. Third season we were basically just trying to keep our head above water, because we didn't have anything in development. I think if you look back at this fourth season. I don't think Patrick's had one complaint. He's gotten to die, been Borgified, all kinds of things [EG, Oct. 1991, 22].

Though the writers made a conscious effort to give Stewart more to do—such as going on a secret mission to the planet Romulus in "Unification" (#507/8) or combating terrorists in "Starship Mine" (#618)—relatively few stories focused on Picard's inner struggles.

One of the events that cause him to reexamine his life is his encounter with a mysterious probe in "The Inner Light" (#525). The probe allows Picard to live an entire lifetime—during the span of the episode—as "Kamin" on the doomed planet Kataan. David Landis recounts, "This episode gave Picard the chance to experience a life he could never have, one with a home, a wife, and children. It was a simple yet profound story, with Stewart's acting ability making it all believable" (*TNG Episode Guide*, computer software, 1994). Picard's newfound insight to relationships (and music) is revisited in "Lessons" (#619), but it never becomes prominent in the series again. The feature film *Generations*, in fact, shows Picard once again reevaluating his decision not to have a family in the wake of his brother and nephew's deaths. This subplot would have been unnecessary had the series writers given proper attention to similar themes that were already posited.

Cmdr. Riker

Cmdr. William T. Riker was clearly created to be reminiscent of James T. Kirk, another *Trek* character "with an action-oriented command style and a healthy libido" (Nemecek 14). Aside from a clichéd feud with his demanding father in "The Icarus Factor" (#214), Riker's personality did not develop much beyond the above description. That situation changed in "The Best of Both Worlds" (#326/401). Facing a crisis of confidence, Riker is thrust into the spotlight first when an ambitious Starfleet officer sets her sights on his job and then when he must assume command and outwit Picard, who has been captured and altered by the fearsome Borg. Michael Piller, who wrote the highly-acclaimed episodes, illuminates:

> [Riker] comes to the realization that ambition isn't everything. If you're happy and comfortable and find the rewards in the people you work with, that's something that counts for a great deal. We push ourselves and push ourselves and sometimes it is good to do that. It has certainly been healthy for my career. But there are also times when you sit back and enjoy your success and being with the people you love. That was really me speaking through Riker [Altman "The Making of 'The Best'" 49].

Unfortunately, not much happened for the character after that. Actor Jonathan Frakes joked at the sixth-season press conference that Riker was like the *Enterprise*'s vice-president, whose most significant tasks were to carry out the instructions of his commander. He quipped, "I'd like to think of myself more like Al Gore than Dan Quayle" (Altman "Will Riker" 58). The most overt sign the character was not progressing was that while developing "Second Chances" (#624), several writers conspired to kill Will Riker and replace him with his transporter-cloned brother, Thomas (58). Berman and Piller quashed the movement on the grounds that it would undermine the character's growth in "The Best of Both Worlds."[16] Sadly, the failure to develop the character further limited Riker's growth.

Dr. Crusher

Of all the *Star Trek: The Next Generation* characters, Crusher almost has a built-in excuse for being so sketchily drawn: she was written out of the series during the second season as part of a "chemistry experiment" with the doctors (Nemecek 64).[17] That, though, does not justify that out of 178 episodes, only ten focus on Crusher. Staff writer Brannon Braga freely admitted:

> I feel that [Crusher is] somewhat neglected. We try to service all the characters. I think Ron [Moore] and I have written her more than anyone else. We utilize her whenever we can. We like the character. Gates [McFadden] has a great sense of humor. The problem I have with Crusher is that she has no sense of humor. My favorite Crusher scene was [fourth season's] "Data's Day," where she's teaching him how to dance. Gates is a great dancer. It's a delightful scene that had pep and humor. But frequently Crusher is too serious. Sometimes I try to write her upbeat and she still comes out very serious [Altman, Oct. 1992, EG, 86].[18]

Jeri Taylor, former *Star Trek: The Next Generation* executive producer, speculated that Crusher's lack of humor arose from Gates McFadden's desire to portray a "very serious, dedicated professional" (personal interview).

To McFadden's credit, that side of Crusher is clearly drawn, as evidenced by her clash with a colleague in "Ethics" (#516). After Lt. Worf survives a risky surgical experiment, Crusher admonishes Dr. Russell for taking shortcuts and risking his patients' lives. During seventh season, Crusher did manage to loosen up. "Eventually with episodes like 'Sub Rosa' (#714), we tapped into [Crusher's] sexuality and in 'Attached' (#708) with Picard, she was playful and that was very engaging," describes Taylor. "With time, maybe we could have taken her in some other directions" (personal interview).

Lt. Cmdr. La Forge

Without a doubt, this researcher postulates the Geordi La Forge character is the least realized and arguably least interesting of *Star Trek: The*

Next Generation's characters. A tribute to George La Forge, an enthusiastic *Star Trek* fan who died from muscular dystrophy, the role of the blind officer who sees with prosthetic eyes was meant to inspire viewers with physical disabilities (Alexander 536). But aside from being blind (and African American), Geordi is a bit dull. His second-season promotion to chief engineer does little to heighten his personality. Actor LeVar Burton observed, "I don't think we've really seen Geordi develop in the last year or two. I'd like to see a member of his family or see him have a real relationship with a woman, not a Holodeck fantasy" (Altman, EG, Oct. 1992, 91).[19] Here Burton refers to his character's ineptness in affairs of the heart. David Landis notes, "Geordi simply does not seem to be that lucky with women, which is probably best, since his first love must undoubtedly be the *Enterprise*" (*TNG Episode Guide*, computer software, 1994). That assessment makes La Forge a spiritual heir to Montgomery Scott ("Scotty"), the original *Enterprise*'s engineer; the two characters even meet and work side by side in the sixth-season episode "Relics" (#604). Their encounter truly highlights, though, the contrast between Scotty's charming personality and La Forge's relative banality.

Summary

Though the seven main characters of *Star Trek: The Next Generation* are not explored equally during the show's tenure, they all demonstrate Roddenberry's tenet that man is ascending the evolutionary ladder, albeit each character at his or her own pace. Jean-Luc Picard, especially, epitomizes the future of enlightened man. Gender identity reconciliation in the Worf and Troi characters is fascinating when one considers that in classic *Star Trek*'s final episode, "Turnabout Intruder," one of Kirk's former girlfriends trades bodies with him so she can command a starship. Clearly, *Star Trek: The Next Generation*'s writers affirm a future where gender is no longer an obstacle in a person's quest for fulfillment.

Data's quest to become human is likewise intriguing because it reverses conventional wisdom regarding technology. Modern philosophers like Jacques Ellul feared that man should never relinquish control to technology or be manipulated by it and become "a kind of machine" (383). The synthetic humanoid Data, in contrast, is the apex of technology but yearns for the fullness of human life. Roddenberry's characters consistently manage "to balance the material wonders of technology with the spiritual demands of [their] human nature," an admonition given by John Naisbitt in his 1982 book *Megatrends* (36). In doing so, the *Star Trek: The Next Generation* characters embody a heroic ideal and set standards that audience members admire and can hope to achieve. The desire for exploration is not limited to the physical universe but includes the inner reaches of the human mind (Isrig 45).

The journey of self-perception, though, is but the first step Roddenberry's characters take in the evolutionary process. Aside from exploring one's psyche, the next most important measure is knowing one's surroundings. From a communication standpoint, this involves transactional interactions with other people on the interpersonal level.

Three

The Interpersonal Context

Dyadic theory is the crux of interpersonal communication because it involves "any face-to-face transaction between two people" (Wilmot 4). In his book *Dyadic Communication*, William W. Wilmot notes the non-linear nature of dyadic communication makes each pairing unique, complete, and distinctive from larger groups (11, 14). Unlike intrapersonal communication, which focuses on self-perception, dyadic theory centers on other-perception, giving it a unique transactional quality. Part of the allure of any television show, especially the *Star Trek* series, is the richness of characters' interactions.

Jeri Taylor, an executive producer of *Star Trek: The Next Generation* and co-creator of *Star Trek: Voyager*, contrasts the development of dyads in those two shows:

> It has really been in the evolution of the stories that these pairings, and there are many permutations of the pairings that seem to be happening. We sort of just observe all these possible combinations of relationships that are set in motion and that we can explore. And [on *Voyager*] I think that's something that is unlike *Next Generation*. There were not as many obvious pairings. There were the failed love affairs—Picard & Crusher and Riker & Troi—which was more of a problem than anything else, but other than that people didn't seem to pair up as quickly as these [*Voyager* characters] have [personal interview].

Taylor clearly implies that characters eventually seem to take on lives of their own, which the writers tap into. Despite the paucity of developed dyadic relationships on *Star Trek: The Next Generation*, four types of them will be scrutinized: parent-child relationships, mentor-protégé relationships, friendships, and romances.

The Parent-Child Dyad

Three parent-child relationships receive significant attention during the run of *Next Generation*: Dr. Beverly Crusher and her son Wesley;

Counselor Deanna Troi and her mother Lwaxana; and Security Officer Worf and his son Alexander.[1] Because the latter dyads are discussed in the previous chapter, this researcher will focus on the Crushers. In his May 1987 report on the series' preproduction phase, David Gerrold revealed:

> The new [*Enterprise*] is twice as large as the original and carries a complement of 907 Starfleet officers and their families. (Yes, there are children aboard the [ship]— no, they are *not* the heroes of the series. They are simply the children of the crew.) Because of the length of the mission, and because many of our crew have made Starfleet their career, Starfleet has expanded the capabilities of this starship to allow these officers to bring their families with them ["Generations" 14].

This arrangement was to be emphasized by the fact that the ship's doctor, a widow, would be raising a 16-year-old daughter, *Leslie* Crusher. An addendum to that article noted that at press time, the daughter was changed to a son, Wesley (Gerrold 15). Robert Justman, the show's first producer, recalls, "I thought, Jeez, anybody and everybody has had boy teenagers; let's do a girl. Let's explore the problems that female adolescents go through. Then Gene switched it back to Wesley because he felt there would be a wider range of stories if [the character] were male instead of female" (Nemecek 14).

The facility with which the younger Crusher's sex was changed signified the superficial nature of the characters' inceptions. "Beverly Crusher at first was referred to only in relation to Wesley, and didn't rate her own page of background notes until the final writers' guide edition," reveals Larry Nemecek (15). This revelation is salient in retrospect considering that of the seven main characters, Beverly is the least developed by the series' end. Part of the problem is that early on, the decision was made to deemphasize her attachment with Wesley by giving him a bridge assignment.[2] Former *Star Trek: The Next Generation* writer-producer Ronald D. Moore explains:

> When you look at the pilot, the implication is that you're gonna play a lot of Wesley and Beverly. He's set up as a young boy. It seems like he's going to be part of the *Enterprise*'s life—part of the unofficial life of the *Enterprise*, the below decks stuff. Then what seemed to happen over the course of the first season was [the writers] turned him into "Wesley the wonder boy." Once he moved to the bridge and started sitting Conn all the time, that really took him out of the domestic scene with his mother [telephone interview].

Gates McFadden, who portrayed Dr. Crusher, disagrees with the results of that shift:

> I didn't like the way my relationship with my son was going. I felt like Donna Reed, worrying about his lunchbox. I think every time Wesley was in trouble or needed

guidance he went to a male figure, which I found a bit insulting, considering how many single parents there are in the world now. I can't imagine that Chelsea [Clinton] would only talk to Bill and never to Hillary if she had a problem [Altman "These Were the Voyages" 43].

Though the mother-son relationship occasionally took center stage, such as in "Family" (#402), in which Beverly gives her son a prerecorded message from his late father, or in "Remember Me" (#405), where Wes accidentally traps his mother in a "warp bubble," the producers' initial attempt to portray a parent-child dyad was essentially abandoned in order to focus on another type of relationship.[3]

The Mentor-Protégé Dyad

The role of a mentor is a concept explored from several vantage points during *TNG*'s run. The origin of the word "mentor" hearkens back to Greek mythology: "In Homer's *Odyssey*, Mentor (which means 'advisor') was an Ithacan nobleman to whom Ulysses entrusted the management of his household while he was away fighting in the Trojan Wars. Mentor, or the virgin goddess Athena in his likeness, gave advice to Ulysses' son, Telemachus, and roused him to action" (Harding 28).

Robert Bly, a leading proponent of the early 1990s men's movement, posits, "In the ancient tradition, the male who grows is one who is able to contact the energy coming from older males—and from women as well, but especially male spiritual teachers who transmit positive male energy" (Thompson 191). Since antiquity, young men like Telemachus "[u]nsure of their own fathers [have searched] for older, more senior men who will help them solidify a fragile masculine identity, which is usually of the brittle, instrumental sort that emphasizes career achievement and public demonstration of power and strength" (Osherson 46). On *Next Generation*, Capt. Picard mentors three of his subordinates who have lost their fathers—Wesley Crusher, Lt. Worf, and Lt. Cmdr. Data.

Picard and Wesley Crusher

Larry Nemecek notes this dyad was one of "the first real character dynamics to emerge in this early memo-writing phase [of *Star Trek: The Next Generation*]" (14). Part of the initial bond between the two characters is the fact Wesley's father, Jack, died under Picard's command. In a sense, Picard feels a moral obligation to shepherd the youth. That commitment becomes overt in the early episode "Where No One Has Gone Before" (#106). A mysterious traveler from another dimension advises Picard that Wes has the potential to become a "Mozart of engineering" if he receives the proper encouragement. By story's end, the captain has assigned young Mr. Crusher to "learn this ship," which he does by serving as an acting ensign. Despite the fact that too many first-season episodes hinge on Wesley's ability to be a prodigious *deus ex machina*,[4] his bridge position places him under the captain's aegis. In "Coming Of Age" (#119), Wesley takes the entrance examination for Starfleet Academy but loses the coveted spot to another entrant with a higher score. After asking him if he did his best, Picard consoles the lad by confiding, "I failed the first time, too. And you may not tell anyone."

A similar moment occurs next season in "Samaritan Snare" (#217). En route to take another battery of Starfleet Academy exams, Wesley shares a shuttle ride with the captain, who is scheduled for cardiac replacement. Crusher's anxiety abates as the captain recounts a youthful barroom brawl, which caused him to need an artificial heart. Though a portent of conflict in the relationship appears in "The Bonding" (#305), when Wesley discloses he initially blamed Picard for his father's death, that issue is perfunctorily resolved. Toward the end of the season he is given a field promotion to ensign in "Ménage à Troi" (#324) because he missed the Academy entrance exams by helping rescue the kidnapped Riker, Deanna Troi and Lwaxana Troi. In "Final Mission" (#409) early the next season, young Mr. Crusher finally gains admission to Starfleet Academy.[5] The show marks Wil Wheaton's last performance as a *Star Trek: The Next Generation* series lead. Instead of saving the whole ship, he must only save the captain's life after their shuttlecraft crashes on a desert planet. Though the situation is "somewhat clichéd," as Altman points out, the episode is "redeemed by strong writing" and performances (EG, Oct. 1991, 28). Wheaton returns as Wesley two times apiece during seasons five and seven; his second and fourth appearances mark new directions for the character.[6]

In "The First Duty" (#519), Wesley's "squeaky-clean" image is tarnished as he becomes part of a cover-up at Starfleet Academy. His complicity leads him into a direct confrontation with Picard. Ron Moore, who co-wrote the episode, initially resisted the notion of Wesley "ratting his friends out." He explains, "It isn't that I wanted Wesley to get away with it so much. He was gonna have to go down, too. But I didn't really want him to have to turn on his friends, because that seemed unattractive at the time" (telephone interview). In retrospect, Moore is comfortable with the produced episode, which emphasized Wesley was not so much betraying his friends as accepting culpability for the consequences of their collective action, the flight maneuver that caused a comrade's death.

Wesley's final appearance on the series, "Journey's End" (#720), pays off the cryptic comments the Traveler makes about him in "Where No One Has Gone Before." On leave from Starfleet Academy, Wesley reconsiders his future after undergoing a "vision quest."[7] Ron Moore, who also wrote this episode, had a personal investment in the character's fate:

> I was eager to do "First Duty" and then I was eager to do "Journey's End" because to me the Wesley character had never really crystallized in the series. He was this super, smart-ass kid. And it didn't seem believable that they put this kid in the pilot seat of the *Enterprise*, and I thought it was kind of a slap that the kid got to wear the uniform and didn't go through the Academy. And I just never bought any of it.... And then after ["First Duty"], as we looked back at the character, and what we had been saying about the character since day one, we've got "Mozart" pushing buttons on a console, which seemed kind of silly. And everything about the Wesley character seemed to point him in another direction. We kept saying the kid's a mathematical genius. He has this instinct for physics and quantum-level mechanics that no one else can touch, and the kid is just going through the standard things— going to Starfleet Academy and he's gonna be a bridge officer. And it just seemed like he was telling himself to do something for the wrong reasons. It was a dilemma that I could identify with, because when I was in college I went through the same thing[8] [telephone interview].

Wesley's story intertwines with a colony of Native American Indians who are forced to relocate because of a new treaty with the Cardassians. After warning the colonists, young Mr. Crusher is berated by his mentor, Capt. Picard, and resigns from Starfleet Academy. At the height of tensions between all parties, Wesley manages to extricate himself from the normal space-time continuum where it is revealed that the Traveler is ready to embark with Wes on a new journey. Though the two halves of the story are an uneasy fit[9] the episode does logically wrap up Wesley's character. Executive producer Jeri Taylor explains this was a conscious effort since "we felt certain we would not use him in the feature [films]" (Kutzera 87). Ironically, this episode does contain poignant mother-son moments, which are woefully missing from the majority of episodes where Beverly and Wesley appear together.

Picard, Data and Worf

Though the Picard-Wesley Crusher dyad is the prominent mentor-protégé relationship during *Star Trek: The Next Generation*'s run, the captain also guides two other subordinates—Worf and Data. Ron Moore elucidated:

There is a bond between Worf and Picard and between Picard and Data. The Data-Picard relationship was something we played quite a bit. Picard was, in essence, his mentor without coming out and being his mentor. He was always down at the holodeck looking at Data's plays, listening to him talk about this and that. And they always had some interesting scenes together talking about humanity and emotions and Shakespeare. And Worf, to a certain extent, the same way. I mean, Worf brought Picard into the whole Klingon saga, and that interest was always kept alive. Any time there was a Klingon thing going on, Picard was always sort of drawn into it and shared some insight in to Worf. I don't know how much they even told the rest of the *Enterprise* crew of the things they went off and did together [telephone interview].

The emphasis on mentor-protégé relationships within the series is intriguing because it acknowledges "the presence of mentors [is] central to men's career success and to their maturation as people" (Osherson 45). Picard's willingness to "stimulate curiosity, provide information and share experiences" by stepping into the mentor role is evidence of his strength as both a leader and as a self-actualized, 24th-century man (Lee 126).

The Friendship Dyad

Data and Geordi La Forge

One of the hallmarks of Gene Roddenberry's *Star Trek* universe is the fact that virtually all Starfleet personnel get along with each other. Though all of the *Enterprise* crew is cordial, few strong friendships between crew members are portrayed. The exemplar is the rapport between Data and Geordi La Forge. Their association is delineated in the series' initial *Writers/Directors Guide*. Series creator Roddenberry described: "[Geordi's] closest friend is Data, and the two of them are particularly efficient when working together on Away missions. Because of his 'eyes,' [the VISOR, a prosthetic device that allows the blind officer to see the electromagnetic spectrum] Geordi can also perform some of the functions of a tricorder" (7).

The rationale is that Data, a "walking library," complements Geordi, a "human tricorder" (28). In *Dyadic Communication*, Wilmot cites propinquity and similarity as two of the factors that bind people together (70). During the first season, La Forge and Data's bridge posts are side by side at Conn and Ops, which satisfies the propinquity requirement. As for similarity, Roddenberry remarks, "The fact both want to be 'fully human' (their private term) is something that strengthens their relationship" (34). Though Data's quest for humanity remains an ongoing theme, La Forge's desire for "normal vision" was abandoned once actor LeVar Burton realized his character had become "a role model for handicapped people" (Nemecek 73).[10]

Though Geordi's promotion to chief engineer—at the start of the second season—removes him from his bridge position next to Data, the officers' friendship is frequently highlighted. "Elementary, Dear Data" (#203) establishes that they spend leisure time together, in this case on the holodeck. Because both are uniquely gifted with scientific prowess, they frequently solve technical problems together, and in "Interface" (#703), the logical Data violates the captain's orders by aiding Geordi's futile attempt to find his missing mother. When the android ponders having a relationship with Jenna D'Sora ("In Theory" [#425]), the engineer wisely advises "find someone else to give you advice."[11] The seventh-season "Force of Nature" (#709), ostensibly an environmental show, also focuses on the duo. Dale Kutzera observes, "The early scenes regarding Data's cat nicely display LeVar Burton's comedic timing and point out what a strength the friendship between Data and Geordi has been to this series. But these scenes merely pad out the early acts of what is a thin story" (59).

In her essay "'I Have Been, and Ever Shall Be, Your Friend': *Star Trek, The Deerslayer* and the American Romance" (1986), April Selly posits that Kirk and Spock's friendship (classic *Star Trek*) descends from a long line of fraternal relationships portrayed in American literature (89). Antecedents she lists include Natty Bumppo and Chingachgook from *Deerslayer*, Ishmael and QueeQueg from *Moby Dick*, and Huck and Jim from *Huckleberry Finn*. In that same vein, one can ironically note that rather than being composed of a white male and an "other," La Forge and Data's friendship entails a handicapped, non-white male and a synthetic "other." Such extrapolation of literary conceits is perhaps one of the qualities that endears *Star Trek: The Next Generation* to its devout followers.

Beverly Crusher and Deanna Troi

An ideal counterpart to the Data-La Forge friendship would have been Dr. Beverly Crusher's camaraderie with Counselor Deanna Troi. In fact, Mary Fan lauds the sequel series for highlighting female friendships.

> *Star Trek* has been doing it right since *Star Trek: The Next Generation*. Female friendships are incredibly important in real life, providing women and girls with solidarity, comfort, confidence, joy and candor in a world that, unfortunately, still treats them as second-class citizens in many cases and certainly places more pressures on them. So, when the women of *Star Trek* bond, help each other, and experi-

ence joy in each other's company, they're providing a positive example to those at home watching [*The Verge*].

However, out of the 178 installments of the series, very few episodes highlight the Crusher-Troi friendship. More problematic is the fact those few episodes include scenes of the two female senior officers engaged in conversations about men.

A 1985 comic strip by Alison Bechdel inspired the Bechdel Test and denotes three basic requirements for a movie (or television show): "it has to have at least two women in it, they have to talk to each other, and they have to discuss something besides a man" (Liao). Although never designed to serve as the "be-all and end-all" regarding female representation, this test can be useful for describing how mass media often exclude and/or marginalize women. The three *Star Trek: The Next Generation* episodes with memorable Crusher-Troi conversations are "The Price" (#308), "Second Chances" (#624), and "Sub Rosa" (#714). In the first episode, the women prepare for a gymnastics session and discuss Deanna's potential romance with Devinoni Ral, a visiting negotiator; in the next episode, Beverly supports Deanna rekindling her relationship with Lt. Thomas Riker, Will Riker's transporter-created "twin." And in the last installment, Troi counsels Crusher regarding Ronin, her literal "dream lover." Needless to say, these conversations fail the Bechdel Test because each centers on a man. Thus, though Beverly and Deanna work out together, "attend to each other's emotional needs, lean on each other, and confide in one another," their "generally positive and drama-free relationship" (Fan) is often depicted as stereotypical "girl talk."

Jean-Luc Picard and Guinan

One of the more unique friendships depicted on *Star Trek: The Next Generation* is that of Captain Picard and enigmatic Ten Forward host Guinan. While advising Riker who is trying to determine how to rescue a kidnapped Picard from the Borg ("The Best of Both Worlds, Part II" #401), she discloses that her relationship with Jean-Luc goes "beyond friendship and beyond family." She also teases how they met, which is depicted in the fifth-season finale/sixth-season premiere, "Time's Arrow" (#526/601). Guinan often serves as a confidante to Picard, a unique role only she can fulfill since she is outside of the starship's chain of command. As William Shakespeare wrote in *Henry IV, Part II*, "Uneasy lies the head that wears a crown." In three significant episodes Guinan gives Picard particularly sage advice.

When Data's rights as an individual are challenged in "The Measure of a Man" (#209), Picard represents the android in a hearing. Realizing that he's losing, the captain turns to her for counsel.

> GUINAN: Consider that in the history of many worlds there have always been disposable creatures. They do the dirty work. They do the work that no one else wants to do, because it's too difficult or too hazardous. And an army of Datas, all disposable? You don't have to think about their welfare; you don't think about how they feel. Whole generations of disposable people.
> PICARD: You're talking about slavery.
> GUINAN: I think that's a little harsh.
> PICARD: I don't think that's a little harsh, I think that's the truth. But that's a truth that we have obscured behind a … comfortable, easy euphemism. "Property." But that's not the issue at all, is it?

This argument proves persuasive since the United Federation of Planets does not condone slavery. In "The Best of Both Worlds," a visibly shaken Picard tours Ten Forward, and Guinan reassures him humanity will prevail against the Borg by surviving, just as her own people did despite the loss of their homeworld.

Perhaps the most fascinating portrayal of Guinan as Picard's confidante appears in "I, Borg" (#523). She initially questions his decision to render aid to the lone Borg drone, Third of Five. During a fencing match with the captain, she feigns an injury only to beat him and cautions, "You felt sorry for me. Look what it got you." But after La Forge convinces her to meet "Hugh," as the drone now calls himself, she changes her mind and lobbies Picard to *not* use the invasive program:

> GUINAN: If you are going to use this person—
> PICARD: It's not a person, dammit! It's a Borg!

Picard ultimately decides not to install the weaponized program. (See Chapter Four for a thorough discussion of this decision.) Guinan's input, undoubtedly, carries considerable influence with the Captain. The aforementioned "Time's Arrow" two-parter depicts how the characters "meet." Although the emotional depth of their relationship is never explained, Dany Roth advances an interesting, yet dubious theory:

> My favorite Guinan moment is from "Time's Arrow Part 2" when she and Picard are trapped in a cave together. Now, keep in mind, for Guinan, this is the first time she and Picard meet. And that moment, while not the best, is very hot. Like, Picard gives Guinan some crazy bedroom eyes and that was when I was like, "Oh, snap, that's what Guinan meant about being closer than friends and family and whatnot." They've been a secret couple this WHOLE. TIME. [*SyFy Wire*].

Though Roth's theory is far fetched, it could help elucidate Guinan's otherwise, never-explained comment that she and Picard are "beyond friendship and beyond family" ("Best of Both Worlds, Part II").

The Romance Dyad

Feminist critics have long denounced the original *Star Trek* for its stereotypical treatment of women. Diane Werts states, "Rarely were the women of the original *Star Trek* series that well-respected. More often than not, they were good-time playthings, obsequious helpmates, or dangerously seductive Mata Haris strewn weekly in the path of our (male) heroes like so many lethal land mines" (22). In "Sex and *Star Trek*" (1983), Karin Blair particularly reviles the captain's incessant trysts with alien women:

> Captain Kirk, commander of the starship *Enterprise*, acts in most cases as the agent of male fantasies, and becomes involved with the "disposable female," [who] often functions as an instrument for the resolution of a dramatic situaion [*sic*]. This involvement often has an ulterior motive—e.g., is cultivated to elicit from her crucial information [292].

When *Star Trek: The Next Generation* was conceived, Cmdr. Riker was designated as the heir to Kirk's machismo. Larry Nemecek notes, "Along with an action-oriented command style and a healthy libido, Riker also shares with [his] predecessor the middle initial T" (14). Despite that character's early womanizing, the *Trek* powers-that-be eventually decided that all of the characters would occasionally engage in dalliances.

In *The Nitpicker's Guide for Next Generation Trekkers* (1993), Phil Farrand enumerates a "romance tote board," which is accurate through season six:

1. Number of women who kiss Picard: seven
2. Number of women who have intimate interludes with Riker: four
3. Number of women who fall for Data: three
4. Number of men who make a pass at Troi: six
5. Number of women who make a pass at Crusher: one
6. Number of women who give La Forge the brush-off: two
7. Number of women snarled at by Worf: three
8. Number of girlfriends for Wesley: three
9. Number of fantasy women in the series: at least thirteen
10. Number of fantasy men: none [171].

While Farrand's final two items suggest *Star Trek: The Next Generation* is as sexist as the classic series, its producers clearly approached romance in a more adult manner. Diane Werts, for example, commends that Capt. Picard's "occasional trysts were with clever, accomplished women who shared his love of music or enthusiasm for exploration" (23). There are three types of romantic dyads worthy of investigation: the doomed relationships of various characters, the two failed romances (Picard-Crusher and Riker-Troi), and the unlikely relationship between Worf and Troi that developed during the series' last three years.

The Doomed Relationships

WORF AND K'EHLEYR

Worf is the first *Star Trek: The Next Generation* character to have an ill-fated relationship. In the second season, he is reunited with K'Ehleyr, his former love in "The Emissary" (#220). They consummate their passion after an arousing holodeck simulation, but she disembarks without taking the Klingon marriage oath. When K'Ehleyr returns a season and a half later in "Reunion" (#407), she brings a surprise—their son, Alexander. Worf's arch-rival Duras murders her after she discovers he is responsible for Worf's "dishonor" ("Sins of the Father" #317); in turn, he kills Duras. The decision to kill K'Ehleyr was controversial among fans. In his TNG *Episode Guide*, David R. Landis even suggests, "Worf's killing of Duras could have still happened, then he could have found that Dr. Crusher managed to save his mate. The *Enterprise* is designed to have families on board, so there was no reason to get rid of her" (computer software, 1994). Such a solution, however, would have been a cop-out according to Ron Moore:

> There really is no reason for [Worf] to go kill Duras unless you get to that point. You would need something that's gonna really inspire murderous fury in Worf. And, at the time, there were no plans to bring K'Ehleyr aboard or to use her very much. We only brought her back in that episode because she made an interesting impression in the second season as Worf's paramour. We could plausibly say that she had a child, and she just happened to fit some interesting elements. It wasn't until after she was dead that we started getting all of this fan mail about how much people loved her. It was very surprising [telephone interview].

Though K'Ehleyr dies, the addition of Alexander as a recurring character the next season is a legacy to her "life."

CRUSHER AND ODAN

Aside from her questionable relationship with the captain, which will be explored shortly, Dr. Crusher's consequential love affair during the series was with Odan, a Trillian ambassador, in "The Host" (#423). After he is mortally wounded, Beverly learns Odan is a symbiote who lives in different host bodies, and she is nonplused when the new host body arrives—that of a young woman. The first episode to serve as an allegory for homosexuality (or asexuality, as Nemecek points out), some viewers felt its resolution was inconsistent with the rest of the story (165). Mark Altman critiques:

> The issues raised, albeit extremely subtley [sic], about gay rights, are as daring as the show has ever gotten in addressing contemporary social issues. The show cops out at the end when Crusher rebuffs Odan who gets transplanted into the body of a woman, even though Crusher was clearly in love with the entity, regardless of the forms it has taken. "Perhaps someday our ability to love won't be so limited," Crusher says in the episode's coda [EG, Oct. 1991, 46].

Those issues would be explored again, but more explicitly, in the next season.

RIKER AND SOREN

"The Outcast" (#517) deals with homosexuality, "which many fans had been asking for, in typical Science Fiction style," remarks David R. Landis.¹² He explains:

> It put the traits to be examined onto an alien species, and twisted the perspective a bit. This resulted in the J'naii race, where neuter asexuality was the norm, and heterosexuality was considered deviant behavior. It gave the viewers a chance to hear many of the arguments used against gays and lesbians in our own society applied against someone we would consider "normal" [*TNG Episode Guide*, computer software, 1994].

Cmdr. Riker falls in love with the androgynous Soren, who reciprocates as he/she begins to explore forbidden female tendencies. This episode generated more mail than any other in *Trek* history. Although most feedback was "very, very positive," episode author Taylor concedes:

> I did get some letters from GLAAD (a gay and lesbian organization), who believed that at the end—Riker goes down to rescue [Soren] and she had been brainwashed and couldn't even remember why she had the feelings for him that she had—they had the feeling that we were saying that's what should happen. And that it was in violation of everything that they would believe—that gay people should be altered so that they are straight. And I wrote back saying that that was the opposite of what we were trying to say. This was a tragedy. It was a terrible tragedy; it was an awful thing [the J'naii] did, and it was Riker's great loss, as it was Soren's great loss that that happened. But I was able to see in hindsight that people who wanted to interpret [the episode's ending] in that way would do so, and in that case, it might have done a slight disservice. But I think the overwhelming message of the piece was so clearly in favor of tolerance that it would be pretty hard to get away from that [personal interview].

Despite the controversy, Jonathan Frakes, who portrays Riker, opines, "I didn't think [the producers] were gutsy enough to take it where they should have. Soren should have been obviously more male" (Altman, EG, Oct. 1992, 78).[13]

PICARD AND NELLA DAREN

Unlike Crusher's and Riker's relationships, Picard's tragic love affair in "Lessons" (#619) has no gender-bending overtones. The captain falls in love with Nella Daren, the new chief of the *Enterprise*'s Stellar Sciences department. "This episode built on the changes in Picard's outlook on having a family that were started in the episode 'Inner Light' (#525)," describes Landis (*TNG Episode Guide*, computer software, 1994).[14] Though the romance could have been "potentially mundane and maudlin," the casting of Wendy Hughes as Daren helped avoid that (Altman, EG, Oct. 1993, 70). Story editor René Echevarria explains:

> We cast a woman who's closer to Picard's age than the women we've seen him with in the past like Jennifer Hetrick and Michelle Phillips. We wanted somebody who had weight as opposed to it being purely sexual. It also deals with those issues of how difficult it is to go out with someone you work with, especially someone who is your underling [70, 75].

Patrick Stewart's chemistry with Hughes makes the relationship believable, as the couple, initially bonded by a love of music, discover they have more in common. After Daren survives a potentially fatal mission that Picard sends her on, however, she requests a transfer and the affair abruptly ends.[15]

The Failed Relationships

The two most notorious dyadic relationships on *Star Trek: The Next Generation* are probably the two failed love affairs—Picard and Crusher, and Riker and Troi. Jeri Taylor admits those pairings were "more of a problem than anything else" (personal interview).

PICARD AND CRUSHER

The relationship between the captain and the doctor is ambiguous in the series' premiere "Encounter at Farpoint," although there is a subtextual hint that Beverly perhaps blames Jean-Luc for her late husband's death. In the next episode "The Naked Now" (#103), however, the characters are quickly paired off when a mysterious virus intoxicates the crew, releasing their inhibitions. Throughout the rest of the first season, there is sexual tension between Picard and Crusher; they share a holodeck adventure together in "The Big Goodbye" (#112) and are stranded in a ditch together in "The Arsenal of Freedom" (#121). The latter episode "started out as a vastly different show," reveals then-writer and producer Robert Lewin. He continues: "It was originally going to be a love story in which Picard was dying and Beverly [Crusher] was going to reveal how she really felt about him. I tried to deal with that in a very sensitive and moving way, but it gradually changed because Gene Roddenberry did not want to do a love story" (Altman, EG, Sept. 1990, 30).

Instead the show became an "action-adventure yarn/morality tale about arms merchants" (Nemecek 53). During the second season, the relationship became a moot point because Gates McFadden's Dr. Crusher character was replaced by Diana Muldaur's Dr. Pulaski. The change of doctors was part of the great "chemistry experiment." Executive producer Rick Berman explains, "There were those who believed at the end of the first season that they didn't like the way the character was developing, vis-à-vis Gates's performance, and managed to convince Mr. Roddenberry of that. I was not a fan of that decision" (Nemecek 64).

Fan reaction to the new doctor was extremely negative and Roddenberry and Berman agreed "the Pulaski character was not working out" (99). The producers asked McFadden to consider coming back, which she "graciously did" (99). Rather than plunging back into the Picard-Crusher romance, the writers decided to continue an ongoing tease based on an incident from "The Arsenal of Freedom." In that episode, Crusher tells Picard, "Jean-Luc ... there's something I've been wanting to tell you." Unfortunately, her disclosure is interrupted by a crisis. This pattern continues in "The High Ground" (#312), where they are captured by terrorists; "Allegiance" (#318), where a Picard impostor woos then drops Beverly; and "Remember Me" (#405), when Beverly is trapped in a warp bubble. Though the situations are all different, she still never manages to complete her thought.[16] "Qpid" (#420) later in the fourth season hints how Picard and Crusher see each other. Vash, a mercenary archaeologist with whom Picard had a dalliance with in "Captain's Holiday" (#319), returns and is dismayed to learn he wants to keep their relationship platonic. She and Beverly are likewise surprised to learn that Picard told neither woman about the other. The next two seasons virtually ignored the relationship, which disappointed both actors. In an interview at the end of season six, Patrick Stewart comments:

> At the beginning there was more than a suggestion that there was romance in the air, but it died in the cradle and the good Doctor and the good Captain are

extremely fond of one another and very, very good and loyal friends. I think there's little chance of it going any further, but who knows what might happen next year [Altman "The Acting Ensemble" 45].

Despite being declared a "dead issue" by interviewer Altman, fans and actors received a pleasant surprise the next season.

In "Attached" (#708), "the long-simmering romance between Captain Picard and Dr. Crusher is tackled head on when the two are captured by warring aliens and equipped with gadgets that link them telepathically" (Kutzera 47). The startling revelation is that Jean-Luc has been in love with Beverly since before she married his best friend, Jack. Director Jonathan Frakes remarks, "We finally saw Picard and Crusher together and I thought it was great. I particularly liked the long scene of them together by the campfire, where they really explored their relationship and their attraction to each other" (Altman "Seventh Season Episode Guide" 34). Some fans felt betrayed by the ambiguous ending, in which Crusher abruptly ends a date and Picard quietly blows out candles. Gates McFadden defends the ambiguity: "I wanted it to be open ended and so did Patrick. [W]hen Crusher walked out the door I was not playing it like it was over by any means. Some people were just disappointed that we didn't fall right into bed, but I think it makes it interesting that there is obviously chemistry" (Kutzera 48). Executive producer Jeri Taylor adds, "We didn't consciously want to wrap up arcs or bring things to neat conclusions because, of course, the feature films will continue" (personal interview). The series' finale, "All Good Things..." (#725/726), continues this subtext by revealing that in one possible future Picard and Crusher marry but eventually divorce.

RIKER AND TROI

Curiously, the Riker-Troi love affair has roots in the stillborn 1970s television series *Star Trek: Phase II*, whose Will Decker and Ilia characters are the spiritual antecedents to Will Riker and Troi. Though the former duo appear in *Star Trek: The Motion Picture*, they are transformed with V'ger into a new entity by the film's conclusion. Series creator Roddenberry clearly delineated Riker and Troi's relationship in the TNG *Writers/Directors Guide*:

> Troi and Number One [Riker] have met before; they both felt a strong mutual attraction then, and they still feel it now; but their relationship remains unconsummated.[17] Number One is now hesitating over this intimacy since Troi is under his command and he fears that this will affect his judgment. Yet, there is no doubt that the affair was meaningful and pleasant to both and he finds it difficult to end it [31].

After the above information is set up in the pilot, "Encounter at Farpoint," nothing much happens between the pair the first two seasons. Riker shows jealousy in "Haven" (#111) when Troi almost marries Wyatt Miller; she is likewise annoyed by Mistress Beata's seduction of him in "Angel One" (#114). The couple comfort each other after Tasha Yar's death later that year in "Skin of Evil" (#123). Despite romantic inactivity during season two, Riker is distressed by Troi's pregnancy in "The Child" (#201) and snipes, "I don't mean to be indelicate, but who's the father?" Though the season finale, "Shades of Gray" (#222), is a dreadful clip show, Troi stands vigil over the comatose Riker, her "imzadi."

At the end of season three, the romance heats up in "Ménage à Troi" (#324), when they spend shore leave together on Betazed. Their pleasure is cut short when they and Deanna's mother are kidnapped by Ferengi. The next season, however, the writers again deemphasize the love affair. Complained Jonathan Frakes:

> I still wish I understood why they dropped the Riker/Troi relationship. Marina [Sirtis] and I have been fighting to keep that alive for years. The writers have told us that they've swept that relationship under the carpet so that Riker and Troi would be available for alien relationships, but I wonder if there isn't some value in having a relationship between us [Altman "Jonathan Frakes" 47].

"The Loss" (#410) does reveal, though, an interesting facet to their relationship. After she loses her powers, "Riker calls Troi a 'blue-blooded Betazoid' who's always had a unique means of control to fall back on" (Nemecek 150). This revelation shows unacknowledged tension in the relationship. An episode the next season, "Violations" (#512), contains a flashback showing that Troi decided to cool the relationship once both learned of their assignments to the *Enterprise*. The only element that redeems "Conundrum" (#514) is the creation of a Riker-Troi-Ro triangle after the crew experiences collective amnesia. Despite complaints from the actors and the fans about the abandoned affairs, the writers were adamant about their decisions. Jeri Taylor, co-executive at the time, states:

> [The failed romances are] not anything we have any interest in developing because it leads you into constricting traps. We acknowledge that there was a relationship between Riker and Troi. They have a profound friendship. I don't think you should close any avenue off in a series that may go on for many more years. We draw on that relationship for subtext. I have no desire to make more of it than that, unless a story comes along that makes something of it [Altman, EG, Oct. 1992, 91].

Such a story emerges toward the end of sixth season. "Second Chances" introduces a "twin" brother for Riker, created eight years earlier by a transporter mishap. In a twist on sibling rivalry, Lt. Riker aggravates

Cmdr. Riker by rekindling his relationship with Troi.[18] In an interview with Mark Altman, Marina Sirtis remarked, "The most often asked convention question is what's happening to Troi and Riker. 'Second Chances' shows that Riker appears to have closed the door on that relationship. Troi would resume it immediately if Riker opened that door a little chink" (EG, Oct. 1993, 58). The writing staff made two bold decisions regarding the resolution of the episode. First, Troi is the one who squelches the romance with Riker's doppelganger. She rejects his marriage proposal and the offer to come with him to his next starship, bitterly reminding him that his "brother" made the same offer before leaving on the *Potemkin* eight years ago. Besides that, she is content with her life on the *Enterprise* and does not want to leave. Second, rather than killing Riker-2, which was the original plan, or Riker-1, which several writers advocated, both Rikers survive the episode (Altman "The Making of 'The Best'" 58).[19] Though *Next Generation*'s final season contains remnants of the love affair, such as Lwaxana Troi's caustic rejoinder to Riker in "Dark Page" (#707)—"If it weren't for you, she'd be married by now"—and a future Riker's angst over her death in "All Good Things..." the affair is all but dead. Co-producer Ronald D. Moore admits: "No one was really interested in revamping the Riker-Troi arc. There is a whole element of the fan base that is just obsessed with that. Our feeling [was] they were just boring together. No offense to the actors, but we just weren't interested in that relationship" (telephone interview).

Ultimately, the actors prevailed with the wedding of William T. Riker and Deanna Troi depicted in *Star Trek: Nemesis*, the tenth feature film. However, a relationship the writers *were* interested in developing came to fruition during the series' seventh year.

The Unlikely Couple: Worf and Troi

Beginning in the early years of *Star Trek: The Next Generation*, Michael Dorn, who plays Worf, and Marina Sirtis played subtextual tension between their characters. At a convention in February 1990, Dorn disclosed, "Worf dislikes Troi's empathic abilities and considers them an invasion of privacy." Sirtis, meanwhile, told convention audiences, "Troi is still a bit upset that Worf wanted to kill her baby in 'The Child' (#201)" (Trekon, Mar. 1993).[20] Being aware of this, the writers slowly conspired to bring the characters together. If the relationship involved real people, it would be a classic case of opposites attracting. Ron Moore expounds, "We were kind of aware that they were playing the antagonism subtext between the two of them. I think it was Michael Piller, at one point, who said, 'We should get those two together'" (telephone interview). Within the context of the series, Worf's son Alexander is the catalyst that unites them. Staff writer Brannon Braga posited, "It was a fun idea to give Worf a son this [fifth] season. I think Troi got a lot of attention this year as well, thanks to Worf's problems" (Altman, EG, Oct. 1992, 84). Braga refers to the fact that coping with fatherhood led Worf to consult Troi for advice more frequently.

Moore noted the effect of those counseling sessions:

> There was something intriguing about Worf and Troi in the scenes that they played together. When she was advising him, or he was ranting about something, even though they were playing antagonism, there seemed to be an interesting undercurrent between the two. And [we felt] that would be an interesting match-up [telephone interview].

The first significant step in the relationship appears in "Ethics" (#516) when Worf is paralyzed in an accident. Risking experimental surgery, he asks Deanna to raise Alexander in case he dies.[21] Later that season, they find themselves in a common situation when Lwaxana visits, deciding to take the impressionable Alexander under her wing in "Cost of Living" (#520). The episode ends with mother and daughter and father and son soaking in a mud bath. In the original script for "A Fistful of Datas" (#608), Alexander plans the holodeck adventure as a way to bring his father and the counselor together. Altman surmises that subplot was dropped in an "attempt to get away from the soap opera elements of Season Five" (EG, Oct. 1993, 43).

In the show's final year, the writers decided to develop the romance. Ron Moore explains: "We just started toying with it—throwing in little elements here and there, little dream sequences and that kind of stuff to see where it would go. We just kind of dug it: the writers really kind of fell in love with them falling in love. And we wanted to keep playing it and playing it as time went on" (telephone interview).

The first episode affected is "Parallels" (#711), in which Worf drifts between alternate realities, including several in which he and Troi are married. Episode scribe Brannon Braga annotates:

> Viewers who watched closely will see that we've been building their relationship for the past couple of years.[22] There was a temptation to do something [with Wesley], but I wanted to throw more attention on the Troi/Worf story and have Troi realize that there were realities where Worf never loved her, which is something we all think about. "What if's?" in our relationships [Altman "Seventh Season Episode Guide" 35].

The affair officially begins in the "real" time-frame in the episode's coda. Worf invites Troi to share his birthday dinner and orders champagne, as the *Enterprise* sails on. In "Eye of the Beholder" (#718), Deanna has an extended dream sequence in which she becomes romantically involved with him. In the *Star Trek: The Next Generation Episode Guide*, David R. Landis observes: "With this episode and 'Parallels' (#711), both Worf and Troi have seen what it would be like to be in a relationship together, *without* the other one knowing of the experience. If they both liked it, perhaps they *will* get together in reality (not in a dream or a different quantum universe)" (computer software, 1994).

The series finale "All Good Things..." (#725/726) begins and ends with the couple sharing a passionate moment—in what Landis calls "reality")—before the time-shifting Picard enters (*TNG Episode Guide*, computer software, 1994). When Worf expresses concern for hurting Riker's feelings, Troi reassures him to deal with their feelings—a sign she is over her former "imzadi."

Summary

Several conclusions can be drawn from the breadth and depth of dyadic relationships portrayed on *Star Trek: The Next Generation*. First of all, despite the rising divorce rate in contemporary American society, the family unit itself manages to survive and thrive in Roddenberry's 24th century. This concept was important enough to him that he equipped the *Enterprise-D* with accommodations so families could accompany crewmembers on their voyage. Next, mentor-protégé relationships are frequently portrayed. As captain, Picard serves as a role model for both male and female subordinates. His willingness to shepherd them indicates his maturity and strength as a leader. In the coda of "Skin of Evil" (#123), the holographic image of the fallen Lt. Yar poignantly describes, "[I]f there were someone in this universe I could choose to be like—someone who I would want to be proud of me—it's you."

Friendships, such as Data and La Forge's, are also a key element of the show. Although their relationship was never developed as fully as the Kirk-Spock dyad on classic *Trek*, the pairing of a "biologically-challenged" android with a physically-challenged human allowed the writers to explore how friends help each other grow and change. Finally, *Star Trek: The Next Generation*'s approach to romance is more mature (and less sexist) than classic *Star Trek*'s. Women are portrayed as equals rather than as *femmes-*

objets, who exist simply for men's pleasure (Blair "Sex and *Star Trek*" 292). The variety of interpersonal relationships highlight Roddenberry's belief that people must work together to build the future. Actor Whoopi Goldberg, who portrays the enigmatic Guinan in 29 episodes, explains her affection for that purview in the documentary *Gene Roddenberry: Star Trek and Beyond*. She describes, "For me Gene's vision was the idea of 'We.' Not 'I' but 'We.' And to me that's amazing, that's great because 'We' doesn't care about color, doesn't care about gender. You know, it's just 'We.' I like that." That concept of "We" is clearly an inherent component of *Trek*'s appeal.

"We"-ness can be explained in other contexts—specifically in the group and organizational contexts. Though the dyad is the basic unit of human communication, the addition of one or more persons creates a small group. Larger groups, in turn, become organizations. Primary concerns of a group or organization include leadership and the decision-making process, which are inextricably intertwined. The next contextual theories will show how *Star Trek: The Next Generation* characters performed as members of a group and organization.

Four

The Group and Organizational Contexts

Gene Roddenberry's vision of the future is one of the most unique aspects of *Star Trek*. In her essay "Filmmaker's Visions of Tomorrow" (1986), Mindy Machinac places movies about the future into three categories: "utopian projections," "dystopian scenarios," and "continuation films" (25). Utopian projections include "films [that] anticipate major improvements in human life or expect that we will incorporate technology smoothly into society without wiping ourselves out in the process" (25). Films in this class include the *Star Trek* films, Stanley Kubrick's *2001: A Space Odyssey*, and Lucasfilm's *Star Wars* franchise. Dystopian scenarios are those "in which humans are trapped in a horrible future." Examples include the *Planet of the Apes* series, *Logan's Run*, and James Cameron's *Terminator* movies. Finally, continuation films "show what might be if we continue on our current tracks. Often, these are dystopian, though they emphasize the extrapolation from the present." Stanley Kubrick's *A Clockwork Orange*, John Carpenter's *Escape from New York*, and Ridley Scott's *Blade Runner* are examples of continuation films. Despite the varying tones of the three categories, the films all tend to share a common theme—"the struggle to be human."

Pat Aufderheide notes this struggle is "something you can't do alone but only with other people under considerable stress.... [S]cience fiction offers a progress-addicted people hurtling into the future a chance to see themselves in the present" (35). In "The Neutral Zone" (#126) Capt. Picard remarks that in the 24th century, mankind has "eliminated hunger, want, the need for possessions" and has thereby "grown out of [its] infancy." Critics of *Star Trek: The Next Generation*, including some of its former writers, complain that such an idealized future makes creating dramatic conflict nearly impossible. In a March 1990 *Starlog* interview, first- and second-season writing producer Maurice Hurley groused:

> Gene sees this pollyanish view of the future where everything is going to be fine. If we keep going in this world the way we're going, there *is no* future, and the idea that humanity is going to go from its infancy, which is what he currently considers it to be in, to its adolescence in the next 400 years, I don't believe. But he does and that's why *Star Trek* is a success. It gives the audience a sense of hope. I don't believe it, but you have to suppress all that and put it aside. You suspend your own feelings and your own beliefs, and you get with his vision ... or you get *rewritten* [Gross 29].

Seven months later, Michael Piller, Hurley's successor as head of the writing staff, refuted his predecessor's claims:

> Gene's view of the future serves an important purpose in a very difficult time of our lives and history. When our daily lives are filled with smog, gangs and drugs, it's important to see that there is hope, that there are ways to solve our problems, that there's a future we can look forward to. I'm sure there's a fine, wonderful TV series to be made out of *Blade Runner*, but *I* wouldn't want to live there. I think it's terribly important on television that you provide an environment that people want to stay in. There are those who violently disagree with me, but I'd love to live in the 24th century that Gene Roddenberry has created [Gross 39–40].

Working within Roddenberry's vision, Piller led the staff to focus on the human equation. He said, "I'm not interested in how many Borg ships or Romulan ships are out there. I'm interested in what it ultimately means, what happens, what our characters learn about themselves, about life and so on" (Gross "Character Touches" 38). This researcher's examination of the group and organizational contexts hinges on understanding how Roddenberry's vision impacts the *Enterprise*'s command crew and Starfleet, respectively.

The Enterprise *Command Crew as a Group*

The Ensemble

Although classic *Star Trek* contained seven main characters—Kirk, Spock, McCoy, Scotty, Uhura, Sulu, and Chekhov—different critics classify the characters' relationships in different ways. This researcher observes the Kirk-Spock-McCoy command troika in semi-Freudian terms with Spock as superego, McCoy as id, and Kirk the mediating ego. Jane Elizabeth Ellington and Joseph W. Critelli, in "Analysis of a Modern

Myth: The *Star Trek* Series" (1983), take a different approach by applying the Meyers-Briggs personality inventory to Kirk, Spock, McCoy, and Scotty:

> If Jung's type system is applied to *Star Trek*, it becomes apparent that this television series represents a striking example of the universality of Jungian symbols across various cultures and artistic modes. A great deal of the extraordinary fascination with this series can be attributed to its provision of a unique symbol for the union of opposites: the four senior officers of the starship *Enterprise* form a perfect quaternity of opposing personality types. Taken together, the four, Kirk, Spock, McCoy, and Scott, form a highly articulated symbol of wholeness [243].

Noted "Trekspert" Mark Altman does not place too much stock in such analyses of the classic characters: "[The relationships] arose from dramatic, not psychological needs" (personal interview). No one can deny, however, that of the seven original characters, Kirk, Spock, and McCoy received the most screen time and particular emphasis was placed on the Kirk-Spock relationship.

This emphasis would change for *Star Trek: The Next Generation*. Larry Nemecek recounted that Roddenberry and his team sought to distance the new show from its forebear by avoiding the "dominating duality" of such a relationship. He explains, "This time [the writers] chose to divide the attributes of that dynamic pair [Kirk and Spock] among the new characters so that they could assemble an ensemble cast in the style of 1980s TV dramas like *Hill Street Blues*, *St. Elsewhere*, and *L.A. Law*" (13). Though television producer Steven Bochco, creator of *Hill Street* and *L.A. Law*, was renowned for honing the ensemble drama to an art form, Thomas Schatz traced the origins of that genre to the premiere of *Lou Grant* in September of 1977. In "*St. Elsewhere* and the Evolution of the Ensemble Series" (1985), he posited: "*Lou Grant* was less a clone of its predecessor [*The Mary Tyler Moore Show*, a situation comedy] than an experiment in generic recombination, with its unique blending of comedy and drama, of realism and stylization, of episodic and serial story lines, of social relevance and soap-opera melodramatics" (86).

Roddenberry and his creative team, in conceiving *Star Trek: The Next Generation*, fused the classic '60s *Trek* format with '80s dramatic sensibilities. Altman concurred, "*Star Trek: The Next Generation* is not about Picard, Riker, and Data. It is an ensemble show reflecting Bochco-esque casts, but retaining the structure of the original *Star Trek* rather than becoming serialized" (personal interview). The most essential differences regarding small groups in the series are encapsulated within the attributes of the different captains.

Picard vs. Kirk—The Real Differences

Family Matters

Despite the fact it took a few seasons for *Star Trek: The Next Generation* to emerge from the shadow of its predecessor, comparisons between the two series were inevitable. David Carren, fourth-season story editor with his partner Larry Carroll, offers this assessment:

> The old show worked because it basically was a family. It was more like Kirk was a big brother than a father figure and everyone else was kind of his siblings and Spock was the wise uncle. There were all kinds of interesting dynamics in their relationships. [Picard's crew] didn't really jell per se in this show until deep into the second season or even third, where it really comes together. I think Ten Forward [the *Enterprise* lounge] was an important part of that. It provided a family milieu and all those elements fell into place and you saw there's Picard and he's the father and here's the rest of the members of his family [Altman, EG, Oct. 1991, 43–44].

The two captains, then, serve different purposes with their surrogate families. As inheritor to Bochco-esque patriarchs, Picard's role is further delineated by Thomas Schatz, who annotates those functions:

> The authority figure and ideological touchstone in each of the ensemble dramas—*Trib* editor Lou Grant, Hill Street's precinct captain Frank Furillo, St. Eligius' Dr. Westphall—served as role models and patriarchs for their respective clans. Each figure favored conciliation over confrontation, negotiation over pontification, communication over authoritative administration. Yet there was never any doubt about where the buck stopped in each institutional hierarchy [92].

This "domestication of the workplace," as Schatz refers to it, makes Picard's *Enterprise* substantially different than Kirk's.

A superb example of the *Enterprise* crew as a family occurs in the seventh-season episode "Lower Decks" (#715). Dale Kutzera praises, "[This episode] offers a view of our regular cast from the perspective of outsiders, in this case the lower ranking officers who toil in anonymity, hoping for a big promotion" (76). Freelance writers Ronald Wilkerson and Jean Louise Matthias crafted the story from which this teleplay was written and were inspired by their affection for the British television series *Upstairs, Downstairs*. Commented Wilkerson:

> The main characters have staffs they work with. On a given day, they are probably interacting more with junior officers than the command crew. "Lower Decks" showed them in relationships with subordinates rather than peers and unknowns. When you have conventions, it's nice to break format and show those conventions that are usually taken for granted [personal interview].

The revelations that emerge from this shift of perspective are quite interesting, as Timothy Lynch analyzes them in the TNG *Episode Guide*.

From *our* point-of-view, [Riker's] the "fun-loving" commander in many ways, and he's also far less important to the grand scheme of things than Picard. Not, however, to the ensigns who serve on the bridge: there, Riker is the one who'll kick your [butt] if you screw up, the one who is so focused that he "probably sleeps in his uniform," and the one who you have to pay attention to if you want to know what's going on. Picard is [usually] too remote to make an impression. Similarly, we usually see Geordi as more of a subordinate. He's the one carrying out Picard's orders, the one who has to make things *work*. Not here. Here, we see him as "the boss," at least in Taurik's case [*TNG Episode Guide*, computer software, 1994].

One of the most innovative sequences in the episode is the juxtaposition of scenes in which the senior officers and junior officers play games with their respective peers. Like Thomas Schatz observes of the *Lou Grant* characters, Picard's crew "coalesced into an integrated constellation of characters from disparate backgrounds, working together, whose commitment to their work and to one another had become the governing force in their lives" (88).

LEADERSHIP STYLES

Perhaps the most tangible difference between Picard and Kirk is their styles of leadership. Altman contrasted, "Whereas Kirk's admonition to fellow officers might be a strict, 'Those are my orders, gentlemen,' Picard is most often seen nodding, 'Agreed'" (Altman, EG, Oct. 1991, 67). In a personal interview, he clarified:

> Picard uses consensus building rather than Kirk's autocracy. Picard solicited opinions and comments from his subordinates; Kirk didn't. The way the Gulf War was fought is analogous to Picard's leadership style. Kirk was a Kennedy-esque leader, with youth and charisma, and the early 1960s were a new frontier. Kirk might seek advice, but it was clear that he made the final decision.

Altman referred to the fact that when a decision has to be made, Capt. Picard often meets with his senior staff. These conferences often include phases of orientation, conflict, emergence, and reinforcement, the precepts of B. Aubrey Fisher's "interact system model of decision emergence" (140). Rick Marin, in his 1991 *TV Guide* article "Comparing the Captains: Kirk vs. Picard," interviewed prominent Trekkers to determine which captain is better. One respondent offered a precise evaluation:

> Mary Henderson, curator of a *Star Trek* exhibit opening in February at the Air and Space Museum in Washington, D.C., remembers watching the original series as a teenager and thinking Kirk was "really great." Twenty-five years later, however, he seems too "brash." She prefers the more "paternal" Picard. "Kirk is a man of the '60s. Picard is a man of the '90s" [5].

As Henderson implied, labeling either captain as better than the other is patently unfair; each leader is a product of his respective show's era. Picard's reliance on conferences and decision making is not a weakness but a sign that he acknowledges Fisher's belief that "groups do not *make* decisions. Decisions *emerge* from group interaction" (139).

A salient portrayal of the interact system exists in the *Star Trek: The Next Generation* episode "The Best of Both Worlds, Part II" (#401). In the wake of Picard's abduction and transformation, the newly promoted Capt. Riker must determine how to defeat his mentor and assembles his senior staff to solicit possible options. The following breaks down the steps of Fisher's model through the *Star Trek* characters' actions.

> *Orientation*
> Riker tells his officers, "Based on our latest communication, we can assume that the Borg survived the fleet's attack."
>
> *Conflict*
> - Lt. Cmdr. Shelby makes a proposal.
> - Lt. Cmdr. La Forge refutes Shelby's plan.
> - Lt. Cmdr. Data introduces his and Dr. Crusher's idea.
> - Dr. Crusher explains their proposal.
> - Lt. Cmdr. Shelby asks for clarification.
> - Dr. Crusher elucidates.
> - Capt. Riker asks how long the plan would take to implement.
> - Dr. Crusher reveals implementation time is problematic.
> - Counselor Troi sardonically concurs with Crusher's assessment.
>
> *Emergence*
> - Lt. Worf makes a proposal.
> - Lt. Cmdr. La Forge reinforces Worf's proposal.
>
> *Reinforcement*
> Since a major theme of the episode is Riker's crisis of confidence, writer Michael Piller allows an outside observer (Guinan) to bolster Riker's resolve. He ultimately merges Worf's proposal with a plan Shelby had proposed earlier (and Riker had soundly rejected), adding a third innovation of his own design. Successful in recovering Picard and defeating the Borg, Riker is praised for "brilliant but unorthodox strategy" ("The Best of Both Worlds, Part II").

Interpersonal Conflict

Star Trek: The Next Generation's most vocal critics have long denounced the lack of conflict between crew members. They felt one of the original series' most endearing qualities was the ongoing dispute between Mr. Spock and Dr. McCoy. Tracy Tormé, a first- and second-season staff writer remarked, "The weakness of the show at the beginning was that it was too passive. Everyone liked each other too much" (Engel 246). First-season producer Herb Wright, who returned to the show during its fifth season, concurs:

There's less conflict than ever, unless you are under the influence of cosmic rays, space drugs or alien possession, which we did a lot of. The basis of drama is conflict and the more conflict you have, the more drama you have. The one thing I liked about the original series—which I had not been a fan of when I came onboard *Star Trek* for the first time—was that they were always at each others' throats. It was not the joined-in-lockstep kind of crew that Gene [Roddenberry] envisioned for *The Next Generation* [Altman, EG, Oct. 1992, 67].

The season two "chemistry experiment" involving the change of doctors was apparently an attempt to emulate the Spock-McCoy relationship. The new doctor, Kate Pulaski, "was created somewhat in the image of Bones McCoy, as crusty and transporter-wary" (Nemecek 64). In addition, the second-season *Writers/Directors Guide* states Pulaski is "the only crewmember who treats [Data] like a machine" (17). Viewers, however, rejected the Data-Pulaski relationship. Though it and the Spock-McCoy dyad are ostensibly based on logic vs. common sense, Data—unlike Spock—is an innocent. Pulaski's coarse treatment of him, thus, seemed capricious to fans, "who fired up the show's first real protest letter-writing campaign" (Nemecek 64).

Michael Piller, who joined the show during season three and became an executive producer two years later, admitted the problems of portraying conflict to Mark Altman:

> It is much more difficult to find conflict here because you must get inside the characters and really know what they care about. But if they are real people then they will have natural conflicts because they will have different interests that bring them together. It doesn't mean black or white. It's shades of grey and that's what real writing is all about [EG, Oct. 1991, 42].

Firmly believing that "two people who like each other still can have conflict" (Gross, Oct. 90, 40–1), Piller encouraged *Star Trek: The Next Generation* writers to search for conflict in characters' contrasting motives. An example he cited is "The Best of Both Worlds" (#326/#401): "Shelby is not an evil character. She's bright and has an agenda. It puts her directly in conflict with [Riker] who has his own agenda. And they both feel very honorable and right about what they're trying to do" (Altman, EG, Oct. 1991, 41–42).

Jeri Taylor discussed another example of such conflict from "The Drumhead" (#421):

> If there's someone who is bad, there really has to be a reason for it. So we struggled with the character of Norah Satie, who was the McCarthy-esque kind of character, and realized that it's possible for people—for the best of motives and the best intentions—to take actions which ultimately turn in on themselves and become not the best but quite possibly the worst. And so we fashioned a character who out of a

passionate belief that the ideals of the Federation were paramount and must be protected at all costs. But it became distilled to the point where she became myopic and so rigid about her interpretation of those and so fearful for any challenge to those that she began to see enemies all around [personal interview].

The fact that even Worf gets swept up into Satie's "crusade" demonstrates the conceit that "people get caught up in things—they're tempted, they're lured, they think they're doing the right thing, and they lose the big picture when they get inside" (Taylor). *Star Trek: The Next Generation*'s precept of finding conflict in shades of grey, rather than black and white, carries over from the group context into the organizational.

Starfleet as an Organization

As with the preceding comparisons of Captains Picard and Kirk, to fully understand Starfleet and the United Federation of Planets, one must contextualize it within the time frames of the original series and *Star Trek: The Next Generation*.

Starfleet: Then and Now

THEN: COLD WAR IN SPACE

In "Captain Kirk: Cold Warrior" (1988), Rick Worland analyzes the original series in context with its mediation of Cold War themes (109). He determines that the series' emphasis altered in its second and third years due to the writers' creation of the United Federation of Planets: "The invention of the Federation, with its progressive implication that different alien races could cooperate peacefully, coincided with a virtual declaration of Cold War in outer space" (110). He elucidates further:

> After the creation of the Federation, Starfleet Command was understood to be the military arm of its government rather than the space force of the united Earth government of the twenty-third century. Thereafter, the *Enterprise*'s dual role as exploration vessel and warship came more and more to emphasize the latter function as Kirk and company were repeatedly locked in Cold War struggle with, yes, an evil empire, the Klingons [110].

Likening the Romulans to surrogates for the Red Chinese, and the Klingons to the Soviets, Worland notes, "[I]n no story did [the Romulans] clash with the Federation over Third World planets, colonies, resources, or the like, whereas the Klingons did so in virtually every appearance" (112). Rather than being analogous with the United Nations, then, the Federation "was more akin to the Cold War conception of 'the Free World,' with Starfleet as its NATO" (110).

Cultural Imperialism—Despite the pretense of cultural tolerance promised in Starfleet's Prime Directive of noninterference, classic *Star Trek* nevertheless advocated cultural imperialism. In "Sexuality and Sex-Role Stereotyping in *Star Trek*" (1985), Anne Cranny-Francis criticizes the series for that tenet:

> Kirk is a familiar figure from both the mainstream and popular culture of Western society. It is inevitably Kirk who argues (successfully) for active intervention in the internal organization of some small planet where he perceives that evil, in the shape of an alien force (usually those arch-fiends the Klingons), has either taken control or is in the process of doing so. He must intervene to protect [them] and so transfer to the Federation their forced allegiance to the Klingons (usually). Of course, it might then be argued that the "primitives" are simply trading one form of dominance, physical or military, for another, political or ideological. Within *Star Trek*, however, Kirk's ideology is presented not as ideology but truth. The Federation is the purveyor of truth and wisdom, and those who accept its domination are thereby participators in that truth [274–275].

Undoubtedly, Cranny-Francis would agree with Worland that "[i]ncreasingly in the second and third seasons of the series, Captain Kirk and the *Enterprise* crew were diverted from their scientific explorations in order to protect the weak and peaceful planets of the galaxy from the creeping menace of 'Klingonism'" (110).

Ironically, Roddenberry himself reviled classic *Trek*'s preoccupation with Klingons as the villains. He revealed:

> Klingons were invented by an episodic writer when he ran into "last act problems." They were never considered very imaginative but those of our writers who tended toward bad guys/good guys "hack" scripting loved them dearly. In fact, all in the original writer/producer team considered them rather clumsily drawn "bad guys" whom we planned to replace the moment we got a little time in which to invent more imaginative villains. But with producing a TV series being what it is, we never found that extra time [Alexander 516–517].

The overuse of Klingons as stock villains hearkens back to hoary generic conventions such as those used in Westerns. Roddenberry was especially troubled that many of the *Trek* films likewise portrayed Klingon antagonists. Despite being cast in that light, the Klingons of *Star Trek III: The Search for Spock* clearly denigrated their perception of the Federation's goal—cultural imperialism. After reviewing information on the Genesis Project—ideally a terraforming tool, but a powerful weapon if used improperly. Commander Kruge scornfully notes, "New cities, homes in the country, your woman at your side, children playing at your feet, and overhead, fluttering in the breeze, the flag of the Federation. (sarcastically) Charming." Roddenberry himself would rectify the "'tried and true' Klingon villainy" of the film series by making them allies on *Star Trek: The Next Generation* and placing Worf on the bridge of the *Enterprise*.[1]

Now: Glasnost in Space

Frank McConnell's "'Live Long and Prosper': The *Trek* Goes On" (1991) iterates that *Star Trek: The Next Generation*'s inclusion of Klingons as allies of Starfleet, rather than enemies, predates *glasnost*: "[T]he Klingons became our pals four years before Gorbachev and Yeltsin nailed that plot-change down in the real world" (654). Rather than being the snarling villains of classic *Star Trek*, the Klingons became noble. Ronald D. Moore, the writer-producer who crafted the "Klingon Saga," explains:

> When you had one of your own characters aboard that was a Klingon, you began to find honorable things about [them]. My model for the Klingons, in "Sins of the Father" and then after that, was the samurai families of Japan and warlords with interior honor and strict codes of behavior. In a lot of ways they were much more interesting than the Federation because [it's] kind of a boring place where everybody does get along. But there was something very Shakespearean and grand about the Klingons [telephone interview].

Some detractors responded unfavorably to such revisionism within the *Trek* canon. Melinda Snodgrass, a former *Star Trek: The Next Generation* writer, wrote a December 1991 *Omni* article accusing the show of being mired in contemporary, conservative politics and lacking its predecessor's liberalism (Altman, EG, Oct. 1992, 62). Rick Berman riposted:

> The original series dealt with the temperament and values of the '60s and ours deals with the temperament and values of '80s and '90s. America is quite a different place. It's more cynical than the Kennedy Camelot years, and television has grown up a great deal. TV today has gone in a different direction. There was nothing like *Civil Wars* or *Murphy Brown* or *LA Law* on TV in the '60s. [O]ur show is a reflection of contemporary values just as was the original show [Altman, EG, Oct. 1992, 62, 67].

Attempting to identify causes for "The Enduring Appeal of *Star Trek*" (1987), Christopher Pike reasons that the original series gave 1960s audiences optimism for the future while the world was in turmoil (34). Frank McConnell, in "'Live Long and Prosper'" (1991), theorizes that *Star Trek: The Next Generation* attempts to provide relevancy for today's audience: "How do we preserve our differences and our individuality in a New World Order that wants to make all of us the same?" (654). He adds, "I trust *Star*

Trek's answers to that question more than I trust anything offered by *anybody* currently in power anywhere on the planet" (654).

Cultural Tolerance—Probably the biggest change in the portrayal of Starfleet from one generation to the next has been strict adherence to Starfleet General Order #1—The Prime Directive. It mandates that "Starfleet personnel and spacecraft are prohibited from interfering in the normal development of any society, and that any Starfleet vessel or crew is expendable to prevent violation of this rule" (Okuda, Okuda & Mirek 385). Unlike Kirk who gave lip service to the Directive, yet routinely violated it, Picard takes the mandate quite seriously and rarely transgresses it. In "Symbiosis" (#122), he reminds Dr. Crusher, "It is not our mission to impose Federation or earth values on any others in the galaxy." In "The Drumhead" (#421), Admiral Norah Satie censures the captain for violating the Prime Directive nine times.[2] Although she is ultimately revealed to be a fanatic, one must note that Starfleet nevertheless holds Picard accountable for those infractions, unlike Kirk who was never reprimanded for his non-compliance.

Some Trekkers feared that after Roddenberry's death, his successors (Rick Berman and Michael Piller) would ignore the precept of "Infinite Diversity in Infinite Combinations," a call for universal tolerance. In a *TV Guide* interview, Berman confronts those charges:

> TVG: You've been attacked not only for taking a militaristic turn with *Trek*, but also for perpetuating racist stereotypes with your portrayals of evil aliens.
> RB: We have not treated aliens with any more enmity than we did when Gene was alive and at the helm. The same way Romulans and Klingons were bad guys in the original series, we've got bad guys on the current series. You need that kind of conflict [Logan 12].

An example that Berman and Piller have not forsaken their mentor's philosophy appears in "Emissary," the pilot episode of *Star Trek: Deep Space Nine*. The lead character, Cmdr. Benjamin Sisko, informs the non-linear, "wormhole" aliens, "We are explorers. We explore our lives day by day, and we explore the galaxy, trying to expand the boundaries of our knowledge. And *that* is why I am here—not to conquer you with weapons or with ideas, but to coexist and learn." Stephanie Foote extrapolates further in "We Have Met the Alien and It Is Us" (1992), written shortly after Roddenberry's death. She asserts that by "shift[ing] his focus from the alien without to the alien within" Roddenberry emphasized "evolution over revolution" (23–24). In short, Foote sees *Star Trek: The Next Generation*'s tolerance for different cultures as proof of its creator's optimism for human development.

The *Enterprise* Crew as a Subset of Starfleet

Robert Bloch, in his essay "Imagination and Modern Social Criticism" (1957), acknowledges "science fiction became the vehicle for social criticism" as a response to "main-stream writers [who produced] wonderful new stories in praise of the status quo" after World War II (102, 101). He continues,

> No wonder so many adolescents are attracted to this form of fiction; here, in a transparent disguise, is the story of revolt against organized society. The hero—with whom the adolescent identifies—defies the rules and the taboos of the authorities.
>
> While main-stream fiction glorifies the status quo, science fiction seemingly singles it out as the villain. Science fiction thus reassures people that they are the master of their fate, and that every mushroom cloud has a silver lining [104–105].

While social criticism itself is not necessarily bad, Bloch contends that most sf writers imply "future societies [will] need better government[s]" but few writers "suggest that we need better citizens" (114). Roddenberry's *Star Trek* universe addresses those concerns by presenting heroes who, by and large, are self-actualized individuals. Bloch lists seven main ingredients that formed the then-current paradigm for most science fiction:

1. A totalitarian state;
2. The underground;
3. Psychological warfare;
4. Science in collusion with the status quo;
5. Economic incentive;
6. The dominance of Anglo-Saxon culture;
7. Cultural imperialism [107–109].

The *Star Trek: The Next Generation* characters, as representatives of Starfleet, work within the status quo to affirm the dignity of man- and alien-kind alike.

Karl Weick's information systems approach to organizations can be used to show how the *Enterprise* command crew works as an organization to accomplish its mission. Weick postulates that organizations, to act effectively, must reduce uncertainty or ambiguity in their environments (Griffin 245). He states in *The Social Psychology of Organizing* (1969): "Interlocked behaviors are the basic elements that constitute any organization. They consist of repetitive, reciprocal contingent behaviors that develop and are maintained by two or more actors. Each actor uses and is used by the other person for the accomplishment of activities that neither alone could accomplish" (91). These behaviors occur in a three-stage process of enactment, selection, and retention. The interlocking attributes of Picard's staff allow them to organize and achieve gestalt, under his auspices. Although the following list of characters and corresponding traits may seem reductive, it usefully illustrates Weick's theory:

Riker	Pragmatism
Crusher	Ethics
Troi	Emotion
Data	Logic
La Forge	Technology
Worf	Aggression
Guinan	Mysticism[3]

Picard, as captain and organizer, encompasses all of his subordinates' characteristics. An episode that illustrates this process is "I, Borg" (#523).

Enactment

Weick himself describes, "The enactment process creates the information that the system adapts to, and in doing so removes a small amount of equivocality" (91). In "I, Borg," an Away Team consisting of Riker, Dr. Crusher, and Worf discovers an injured Borg among wreckage of a crashed ship. Crusher [ETHICS] persuades Riker [PRAGMATISM] and the Captain to bring the alien on board the *Enterprise* to treat it, despite Worf's suggestion to simply kill it [AGGRESSION]. Troi [EMOTION] asks Picard if feelings from his abduction by the Borg have resurfaced. As Em Griffin might note, Picard and crew have created "their environment rather than merely discovering it" during this enactment process (249).

Selection

The next stage, selection, consists of "[sorting] through the variety present in the equivocal information, [to put it] into orderly form" (Weick 92). As Crusher [ETHICS] and La Forge [TECHNOLOGY] respectively heal and repair their "guest," Picard plans to introduce a computer virus into the Borg to destroy its whole race. His rationale is to assure victory since the Borg's attack on the Federation at the Battle of Wolf 359 ("The Best of Both Worlds, Part II" #401) constituted war. Despite Picard's ulterior motive, Guinan criticizes the alien's presence on board, yet she too is prejudiced by the fact that the Borg destroyed her homeworld. This selection process, then, becomes a means of refining the previous action, which can be likened to "retrospective sense making" (Griffin 249).

Retention

Though essentially a storage process, retention "also removes some equivocality by integrating newer items with items previously retained" (Weick 92). During this final phase, Weick encourages leaders to challenge previously held assumptions, thereby gaining the flexibility of not relying too much on the past. Despite misgivings, La Forge [TECHNOLOGY] and Data [LOGIC] present plans for the Borg virus to a duly impressed Picard. But he rejects the engineer's doubts about the plan and its correlation with genocide—and orders him to sever his attachment with the Borg who calls himself "Hugh." Guinan [MYSTICISM] challenges Picard to reconsider. The captain reluctantly acquiesces and in a chilling scene impersonates Locutus,[4] attempting to bring out Hugh's Borg-like nature. Instead, the ruse prompts Hugh's individuality to emerge, and the captain realizes his moral obligation to abandon the Borg virus plan.

David Landis praises "I, Borg" for its powerful message: "It made the crew, and the viewer, examine their own prejudices and hatreds for the Borg. 'Hugh' [comes to be seen] as a person, and not as a hive member of a murderous alien species" (*TNG Episode Guide*, computer software, 1994). Mark Altman, on the other hand, criticizes the episode for "emasculating the single greatest antagonist ever created for *Star Trek*" but admits "[i]t's an astoundingly well-written, exceptionally well-performed installment" (1992, EG, 94).

Summary

In her article "My Appointment with the *Enterprise*: An Appreciation" (1994), Ursula K. Le Guin posits that *Star Trek: The Next Generation* transcended its space-opera roots, and perhaps even its predecessor, because the writers eschewed the "simplistic concept of Us/Nice/Real People vs. Them/Ugly/Villains" (32). Science fiction, to its detriment, has often inherited that stereotype from other genres such as westerns. By contrast, Roddenberry and his successors constantly surprised audiences by "humanizing" the bad guys, forcing the *Star Trek: The Next Generation* characters to reconsider their own prejudices. The way the *Enterprise* crew and Starfleet, as a group and an organization, express his belief in cultural tolerance, thus, is a crucial factor of *Trek*'s appeal. Though space may be the "final frontier," earthbound humans must first traverse "the social 'frontiers' that exist between our world's many different cultures" ("Where No Fan Has Gone Before..." 279). Roddenberry's most salient lesson remains that just because something is weird or threatening does not necessarily mean it is evil. Arthur C. Clarke opines that many modern politicians need to learn that lesson (8). Hopefully, the millions of Trekkers already know it by heart.

Star Trek writers intentionally imbue the show with "substance" to stimulate their audience's thinking. The willingness of viewers to enter this collaborative process is evidenced by their devotion to the series. Fans during the past five decades have transformed this mass communication artifact into a cultural phenomenon. This relationship will be explored in the next two chapters.

Five

The Mass Communication Context, Part I

This chapter will examine the relationship between viewers and *Star Trek: The Next Genera*tion as a mass communication text. The Audience-Artifact Relationship will be examined from issues rooted in two previous communication contexts: intrapersonal and interpersonal. Intrapersonal issues between audience and artifact will be explored by analyzing the philosophical underpinnings that Gene Roddenberry and the writers incorporated in the series. This section includes a survey of epistemological, ontological, and axiological concerns, as well as associated issues. Interpersonal issues will be examined via parasocial interactions—non-reciprocal interpersonal relationships formed by viewers with television characters. Horton and Wohl pioneered this concept in their 1956 *Psychiatry* article "Mass Communication and Para-Social Interaction: Observations on Intimacy at a Distance." The following chapter will examine the series as a mass communication text by scrutinizing fan culture through the group/organizational contexts.

Intrapersonal Issues: Philosophy of The Next Generation

In his *Time* article "Trekking Onward," Richard Zoglin writes, "Despite its techno-talk, *Star Trek* and *The Next Generation* were, at bottom, shows about the nature and meaning of being human" (77). When conceiving the original series, Gene Roddenberry aimed to infuse such concerns into an accessible, "space-opera" format. On February 12, 1965, he wrote, "We have an opportunity, like 'Gulliver's Travels' of a century or more ago, to combine spectacular excitement for a mass group along with meaningful drama and something of substance and pride" (Alexander 221). Legendary sci-fi/fantasy/horror author Richard Matheson[1] admitted the inherent risk in Roddenberry's venture: "I don't start out with [metaphysical concerns] in mind—that's deadly for a writer to plan on doing that up front. Because you'll become very pedestrian and hammy and preachy" (telephone interview). No one will deny that several episodes of classic *Star Trek* are didactic because of heavy-handed scripting. "Let That Be Your Last Battlefield"—an episode with warring aliens who are, respectively, black and white, and white and black—is as subtle as a proverbial sledgehammer to a viewer's forehead. But other episodes like "Balance of Terror" explore racism more deftly.

Of the three modes of didacticism described by Didier Coste in *Narrative as Communication* (1989)—deliberative, authoritarian, and demonstrative—*Star Trek: The Next Generation* relies heavily on the deliberative mode, which includes allegory as an effective technique (301–303). Executive producer Jeri Taylor, who also co-created and executive produced *Star Trek: Voyager*, discussed the approach her writing staff used to communicate with audiences:

> I think that the original series certainly treated stories in a different way from the way we do. They tended to be a little bit more straight forwardly about the issues. You've got people who were painted half-black and half-white, which really kind of told you what it was all about. We make an effort to sneak up on the situation a little bit—make it more oblique, let the audience have to struggle a little bit to work with us during the course of the show, to feel the impact of the message, rather than it just being broadly shot out in your face so that there's no question about it [personal interview].

Throughout all its incarnations, *Star Trek* has focused on intrapersonal issues that reflect the three dominant branches of philosophy—epistemology, metaphysics, and axiology. In their book *Introduction to Philosophy*, Norman L. Geisler and Paul D. Feinberg subdivide each philosophical area into pertinent questions.[2] This researcher will use those issues to clarify the philosophy displayed in *Star Trek: The Next Generation*'s episodes and to illustrate the messages the writers and producers hoped to convey to the audience.

Epistemology

The question of how knowledge is accumulated is central to philosophy. Does knowledge exist in the mind independent of experience (*a pri-

ori) or must it be discovered (*a posteriori*)? René Descartes (1596–1650) championed the former theory and argued that "innate ideas" are implanted in humans at birth. "[B]elief in innate ideas," Anthony Kenny writes, "came to be regarded as the hallmark of Cartesian rationalism in contrast to the empiricism of other seventeenth-century philosophers such as the Englishman John Locke" (128). Disagreeing with Descartes, Locke (1632–1704) believed "that man's mind begins as a *tabula rasa* (a blank slate) and that ideas are learned from experience in this life, not from prior exposure" (Geisler & Feinberg 40).

How Can We Know?

Star Trek has always been set in an idealized future. Since experience is central to the scientific method, the series clearly falls within the realm of Lockean philosophy. An episode that highlights this fact is "Darmok" (#502). Picard and Dathon, a Tamarian captain, "are forced to combine their efforts to fight a predatory electromagnetic creature" (Nemecek 176). Picard is initially unable to communicate with his counterpart until realizing Tamarian speech is based on allusion and metaphor. Applying this newfound knowledge, he recounts the Sumerian legend of Gilgamesh to the mortally wounded Dathon, sealing their bond. Executive producer Michael Piller lauded:

> I think "Darmok" is the prototype of what *Star Trek* should be. It dealt with a very challenging premise. [Scriptwriter] Joe Menosky created a whole language for that episode, [which] worked on every level. It had philosophy, dealing with language and what it does for us, two great performances, a monster and a space battle—it had everything [Altman, EG, Oct. 1992, 38].

How Do We Perceive the External World?

In all its incarnations, *Star Trek* has always been based on science. Gene Roddenberry predicted that portable computers, cellular phones, and the concept of warp speed would become science fact by the 21st century.[3] Yet despite being rooted in scientific realism, *Star Trek: The Next Generation* often asserted the existence of a realm transcending physical limits of time and space. The crew's first encounter with this plane occurs in "Where No One Has Gone Before" (#106) when engineering experiments plunge the *Enterprise* "into a dimension where the physical and mental worlds converge" (Nemecek 36). This episode introduces the Traveler, a mysterious being "whose race can travel among dimensions and time" (36). He advises Picard to encourage Wesley Crusher, who has the potential to become an engineering prodigy. Not surprising, episodes where the Traveler returns also focus on Wesley. In "Remember Me" (#405), the young intellect inadvertently traps his mother in an alternate universe, and in "Journey's End" (#720), he fulfills his destiny. (See Chapter Three for details.)

"Trekspert" Mark A. Altman critiques the latter episode:

> As long as the show is dealing with the fascinating political jockeying between the Federation and the Cardassia, and a band of Indians, [it] is quite effective. Unfortunately, Wesley's story is given short shrift. The idea of him not wanting to follow in his father's footsteps is intriguing. However, the resolution of Wesley's mystical awakening into a V'ger-like metamorphosis is completely unsatisfactory and an unwelcome intrusion of New Age nonsense into a secularly grounded series ["Seventh Season Episode Guide" 41].

Aside from the disjointed story elements, its handling of metaphysics was likewise flawed. David R. Landis notes:

> With the revelation that the shaman Lakanta was actually the Traveler, I felt cheated. Lakanta was an interesting character, a spiritual leader of his people, a member of the community for many years. To suddenly reveal him to be only "posing" as a tribal shaman trivialized the character and his culture—as if his beliefs and abilities would only be credible if he were a *weird* alien with *strange* powers [*TNG Episode Guide*, computer software, 1994].

Despite the two previous Traveler episodes that established the existence of a higher plane, Landis and Altman note the character's realm may transcend conventional space-time, but it is not a higher, spiritual plane.

How Are Beliefs Justified?

As with the previous question, the notion of belief is likewise problematic in the *Star Trek* universe. "Gene Roddenberry specifically did not want to deal with religions within the Federation," explains Landis. In fact, the third-season episode "Who Watches the Watchers" condemns religion as an "outdated and primitive superstition" (Altman, EG, Sept. 1990, 41). After Roddenberry's death, his successors circumvented his anti-religious bias by exploring belief from the vantage point of alien cultures. *Deep Space Nine*, the second *Star Trek* spinoff, centers on the Federation's involvement with the planet Bajor, whose inhabitants are deeply spiritual. The seminal statement of Berman and Piller's attitude toward religion is contained in the *Deep Space Nine* episode "In the Hands of the Prophets." Commander Sisko admonishes his son, "For over fifty years, the one thing that allowed the Bajorans to survive the Cardassian occupation was their faith. The Prophets were their only source of hope and courage.... It may not be what you believe, but that doesn't make it wrong."

That attitude was reflected in the sixth-season *Star Trek: The Next Generation* episode "Rightful Heir" (#623). Altman synopsizes, "While undergoing a spiritual crisis, Worf visits a Klingon monastery on Boreth where the image of the legendary Klingon warrior, Kahless, appears to him, seeking to reclaim his position as leader of the Klingon empire" (EG, Oct. 1993, 83). Despite the discovery that Kahless' resurrection is a hoax perpetrated by clerics via cloning, Worf proposes that the impostor be installed as a figurehead emperor to avert another Klingon civil war. This resolution paralleled "the Shogunate in 17th century Japan; where the Emperor [Kahless] was the spiritual leader of the people, but the Shogun [Gowron] held the real power" (Landis, *TNG Episode Guide*, computer software, 1994). Indirectly alluding to Jesus' prophesied Second Coming, the episode implies whether or not Kahless ever returned, "what is important is that we follow his teachings" ("Rightful Heir"). Belief, therefore, is validated by its utilitarianism—a bold statement for a science-fiction series grounded in secular humanism.

Metaphysics

Metaphysics is "the study of being or reality" (Geisler & Feinberg 433). Ostensibly interchangeable with "ontology," this researcher prefers the former term because the latter is often considered to be its subset. Aristotle is credited with the term *Metaphysics* because of a collection of his lectures, which bears that name.[4] Frederick Copleston describes: "Art, then, aims at production of some kind, but this is not Wisdom in Aristotle's view for the highest Wisdom does not aim at producing anything or securing some effect—it is not utilitarian—but at apprehending the first principles of Reality, *i.e.* at knowledge for its own sake" (287). Because the apprehension of reality requires knowledge, metaphysics is intertwined with epistemology.

What Is the Ultimate?

One of the most essential questions of metaphysics is the existence of God. In the 1960s, Roddenberry clearly tolerated the concept of a Supreme Being even if he did not believe in one himself. In the classic *Star Trek* episode "Bread and Circuses," Kirk and crew encounter an Earth-like world where the Roman Empire never fell. Though the episode satirizes the television industry as a gladiatorial competition, it contains an astonishing statement by Uhura. She informs her superior officers that the persecuted "sun worshipers" revered "not the sun up in the sky [but] the Son of God." Christianity, thus, is implied to exist in the 23rd century. But Roddenberry's attitudes changed during the ensuing decade. In the late 1970s, Terrance Sweeney, a Jesuit priest, interviewed several prominent Americans regarding their conceptions of God. Roddenberry's response was classic universalism:

> I think we intelligent beings on this planet are all a piece of God, are becoming God. In some sort of cyclical non-time thing we have to become God, so we can end up creating ourselves, so that we can be in the first place.... God equals consciousness. My own feeling is that relation to God as a person is a petty, superstitious approach to the All, the Infinite.... [T]o me the whole joy and glory of Jesus is the fact that he is one of us. Divine, yes. But so are we [Alexander 568, 570, 574].

Roddenberry's antipathy toward traditional monotheism continued to grow. By the time *Star Trek: The Next Generation* started production, he believed that by the 24th century, mankind would have transcended a need for God. As aforementioned, the episode "Who Watches the Watchers" (#304) is a scathing indictment of religion. Denizens of the primitive planet Mintaka III mistakenly believe Captain Picard is a god, but he allows himself to be shot with an arrow, proving his mortality. In retrospect, Roddenberry's religious intolerance regrettably violated his own precept of IDIC—Infinite Diversity in Infinite Combinations. At the very least, his successors acknowledge that religion can have utilitarian purposes even if there is no personification of an ultimate authority.

DOES MAN SURVIVE DEATH?

Not surprisingly, lack of belief in a Supreme Being generally precludes a belief in the hereafter. The first significant instance of *Next Generation*'s approach to death appears in the episode "Skin of Evil" (#123). Disappointed with the lack of development in her character, Denise Crosby (Lt. Tasha Yar) asked to be released from her contract. The producers obliged and decided to kill off her character.[5] Although Crosby did return first as an alternate timeline version of Yar ("Yesterday's Enterprise" #315), then as that character's half-Romulan daughter Sela ("Redemption" #426/#501 and "Unification" #507/8), and finally in a flashback sequence in the series finale ("All Good Things..." #725), the death was permanent—a rarity in the *Star Trek* universe. In a holographic message she left for her crewmates, Yar tells them, "Death is that state in which one exists only in the memory of others ... which is why it is not an end. No goodbyes. Just good memories" ("Skin of Evil").

The definitive *Star Trek: The Next Generation* statement about the notion of an afterlife is revealed five episodes later in "Where Silence Has

Lease" (#202). The *Enterprise* encounters an entity who wants to examine humans' reactions to death. Rather than have his crew be experimented with, Picard activates the ship's self-destruct mode. The entity, impersonating Data, asks the captain about death. He responds:

> Well, Data, some see it as a changing into an indestructible form, forever unchanging. They believe that the purpose of the entire universe is to then maintain that form in an earthlike garden which will give delight and pleasure through all eternity. On the other hand there are those who hold to the idea of our blinking into nothingness, with all of our experiences, and hopes, and dreams, merely a delusion. Considering the marvelous complexity of the universe, its clockwork perfection, its balances of this against that, matter, energy, gravitation, time, dimension, I believe that our existence must be more than either of these choices—that what we are goes beyond Euclidean or other practical measuring systems and that our existence is part of a reality beyond what we understand now as reality.[6]

This type of double-talk is symptomatic of the series when dealing with metaphysical issues. Picard and company freely acknowledge the existence of higher planes of existence; they simply refuse to equate them with the "limited" perspectives of traditional religions.

Other episodes that rationalized "supernatural" occurrences include "Power Play" (#515) and "Sub Rosa" (#714), both of which dealt with aliens posing as ghosts. In "The Next Phase" (#524), Geordi La Forge and Ro Laren are exposed to a Romulan cloaking experiment that leaves them incorporeal and presumed dead by the rest of the *Enterprise* crew. Comments Michael Piller, "It's a wonderful high-concept story. Ro thinks they're dead. Geordi doesn't buy into it" (Altman, EG, Oct. 1992, 99). Though Ro's spiritual explanation for their situation is disproven, the only reason it exists at all is because she is Bajoran, not human. The episode with the most tantalizing implication of existence after death is "Tapestry" (#615). Timothy W. Lynch offers this synopsis of the opening sequence:

> After being shot at close range with an energy weapon, Picard's artificial heart has malfunctioned, and he is dying on the surgical table. His vital signs begin to fade even further...
> And Picard looks around himself into a gulf of impenetrable whiteness. He sees nothing for a few moments, and then sees an angelic figure approaching him, shrouded in light. He takes this "angel's" hand, and the angel becomes more recognizable:
> "Welcome to the afterlife, Jean-Luc," says Q. "You're *dead*."
> Picard scoffs at the notion that he is dead, and even more so at Q's claim of being God. "I refuse to believe that the afterlife is run by *you*—the universe is not so badly designed!" [*TNG Episode Guide*, computer software, 1994].

Several *Star Trek: The Next Generation* episodes, thus, flirt with the concept of an afterlife but never make a conclusive statement.

Is Man Free?

"Tapestry" is doubly intriguing because it uses the above exchange as the inciting incident for Picard to learn—from Q of all people—not to regret actions he took as an impetuous youth.[7] Q offers Picard the chance to avoid a bar fight, which led to a serious heart injury and eventually to his "death." In altering that one incident, the captain completely changes his destiny to the point that he eventually finds himself a lieutenant, junior grade on the *Enterprise*, which is now commanded by Capt. Thomas Halliway. "This Picard never had a brush with death to add focus to his life," explains Lynch, "and always drifted from one job to the next—never standing out, and always playing it safe" (*TNG Episode Guide*, computer software, 1994). Realizing the changes were a mistake, Picard successfully implores Q to let him undo them. David Landis notes, "This episode examined how people view their past, both good things and bad, and how these events *actually* can shape them into the person they are now" (*TNG Episode Guide*, computer software, 1994). Despite the religious allusions at its opening, the episode ends implying that the scenario Q arranged for Picard may have just been a dream. Regardless, the episode shows the choices people make define their destinies.

What Is the Relationship Between Mind and Body?

Upon examination of *Star Trek: The Next Generation*'s 178 episodes, one would have difficulty discerning the intent of series with respect to the relationship between mind and body. However, this researcher notes a pattern that implies the relationship between mind and body seems inconsequential to the writers. They seem to fall in the category of people who erroneously believe "it is not a real problem" (Geisler & Feinberg 191). In 14 episodes,[8] *Enterprise* crew members become victims of alien mind control. One could merely perceive these multiple occurrences merely as over-reliance on a hoary plot device. Yet, the message implied is that the minds of 24th-century humans—or androids in the case of Data—are easily conquered by a myriad of alien threats.

The only instance in which a character is able to resist mind control is in "The Best of Both Worlds" (#326/401). Although captured, having his body surgically altered, and forced by the Borg to do their bidding, Picard attempts to resist and ultimately provides the solution for the *Enterprise*'s victory. Even more significant is the fact that "Family," the subsequent episode, serves as an epilogue to Picard's ordeal. He tearfully laments to his brother Robert, "I should have been able to stop them. I tried. I tried so hard. But I wasn't strong enough. I wasn't good enough! I should have been able to stop them." David Landis lauded, "It was refreshing to see that the producers gave the character a chance to deal with his torment, rather than simply throwing him into a new adventure and pretending that everything was fine" (*TNG Episode Guide*, computer software, 1994). Not surprisingly, since the "Best of Both Worlds" story arc portrays a character expressing the heroic ideal despite being mind-controlled, it transcends the cliché-ridden emptiness of the other dozen "mind-control" episodes. In Picard's case, even though his body was altered and enslaved, his mind resists and helps defeat a worthy adversary. This seems to be a deviation, however, from the series' overused trope of alien "mind-jacking."

Is Reality One or Many?

Whether reality is one or many has been argued by monists and pluralists since ancient times. In the opening decades of the 21st century, new theories have radically altered earlier views. Michio Kaku discussed contemporary conceptions of reality in his book *Hyperspace*:

> [T]he *theory of hyperspace* states that dimensions exist beyond the commonly accepted four of space and time. There is a growing acknowledgment among physicists worldwide, including several Nobel laureates, that the universe may actually exist in higher-dimensional space. Scientifically, the hyperspace theory goes by the names Kaluza-Klein theory and supergravity. But in its most advanced formulation is called superstring theory.... The usual three dimensions of space and one of time are now extended by six more spatial dimensions [vii-viii].

Hyperspace theory allows for the existence of alternate dimensions as well as parallel universes. Classic *Star Trek* focused on such topics in the 1960s when they were mere science fiction. Now that they are rooted in scientific theory, *Star Trek: The Next Generation* has used them frequently as a motif. "Parallels" (#711) is one such example. Returning to the *Enterprise* from an athletic competition, Lt. Worf finds himself drifting between parallel realities, including some in which he is married to Counselor Troi. Despite Mark A. Altman's criticism that the episode is "mired on enough techno-babble to fill a physics tome" and that the "interesting idea doesn't achieve [its] full potential" ("Seventh Season Episode Guide" 35), this researcher views it as solid storytelling extrapolated from quantum science.

Axiology

Axiology is the study of values or ethics. Like its antecedent, *Star Trek: The Next Generation* has often produced episodes with a moral message. Roddenberry, however, envisioned that interstellar travel would necessitate a new purview of morality. Jeri Taylor reveals how that concept informs the 1990s-era *Star Trek* series:

> [Ethics is] something that Gene Roddenberry felt very strongly about. And in terms of philosophy and approach to the show, we still very much have Gene with us and are consciously not violating the things that he held most dear. And one of those was that human values, in and of themselves, are not superior to any other values, and we must always respect alien cultures on their own terms and not presume to lecture them, change them, or even interfere in their natural development [personal interview].

What Is the Right?

This policy of noninterference—previously discussed in Chapter Four—is the crux of Starfleet General Order #1, the Prime Directive. Strict adherence to that precept guarantees that Starfleet will never become an agent of cultural imperialism. As such, Roddenberry's concept of Infinite Diversity in Infinite Combinations is aptly applied to all Federation citizens but is a cornerstone of Vulcan philosophy. Roddenberry's fervent belief in multi-culturalism began before its emergence as a tenant of postmodernism and was paramount to his extrapolation of human development in the twenty-third and twenty-fourth centuries. For this reason, "any Starfleet vessel or crew member is expendable to prevent violation of [the] rule" (Okuda, Okuda & Mirek 385). Right, thus, is loosely defined as the "greatest good to the greatest number of persons (in the long run)" (Geisler & Feinberg 357), which is a utilitarian conceit. Another means of expressing that view is expressed in the film *Star Trek II: The Wrath of Khan*. After sacrificing his life to save the *Enterprise*, Spock tells Kirk, "The needs of the many outweigh the needs of the few, or the one."

Is the Right Universal?

Though Right in the *Trek* universe is utilitarian, its universality is of a deontological nature. Geisler and Feinberg explain, "according to the rule-utilitarian view, the *obligation* is universal but the act is not necessarily an intrinsic and universal value" (409). That perspective is somewhat Machiavellian in that "the ends justify the means." On the other hand, the deontological view classifies a universal duty as "an *intrinsic value* that is binding on all men everywhere and always" (409). Thus, only ethical norms based on an absolute Good, i.e., the Prime Directive, are ultimately universal. An example of this dichotomy is the focus of "Suddenly Human" (#404). Captain Picard must decide whether to return a human teenager, Jono, to the alien who raised him. The captain's initial inclination is to return Jono to his biological grandfather, a Starfleet admiral, at the risk of war with the Talarians. Picard reconsiders, after realizing he failed to consider the youth's best interests.

As Richard Matheson related earlier, however, a writer's intent to moralize comes with the risk of being didactic. An additional peril is that of being misinterpreted by the audience. Jeri Taylor reveals "Suddenly Human" as such an episode:

> The interesting sidelight, I think in terms of communication in that script, was that while we did see it as a metaphor for foster parenting or step-parenting—which we think can be as valuable as any other kind, and that was the positive message we were trying to put out—many people saw the episode as being about child abuse and called to castigate us severely for allowing a child to "go back into an abusive home."
>
> Since this was remote from our intentions, it really caught us off guard. We were not really trying to portray that culture as abusive so much as different in its values from ours. And those were the ones that Jono was used to and enjoyed. So we were a little caught off guard to get a very, very strong response from people who thought we were putting out the message that it's okay to put a child back in an abusive home [personal interview].

While Picard's choice makes sense in the story world of the series, audience members bristled at the thought of returning a minor to an unsafe environment.

Do Moral Duties Ever Conflict?

Closely associated with the universality question is what should one do when moral duties conflict? There are three basic choices: denial, pursue the lesser evil, or pursue the greater good (Geisler & Feinberg 427). *Star Trek* characters usually opt for the latter alternatives. Yet those decisions are often mediated through cultural concerns. To wit, in the episode "Reunion" (#407), Lt. Worf avenges his mate K'Ehleyr's murder by killing Duras, the perpetrator. Picard is furious when he learns and admonishes Worf, "If anyone cannot perform his or her duty because of the demands of their society, they should resign."

Although Picard claims to be open-minded concerning other cultures' beliefs, his denunciation of Worf's behavior betrays a preference for the Federation bias against murder versus the Klingon precept of vengeful justice. Ironically, viewers expressed strong reactions to the show, not because Worf kills Duras but because Duras kills K'Ehleyr. Michael Piller responded, "[We] wanted to get to a place where Worf was going to take Duras apart, and there's no good reason for him to do it unless she dies" (Nemecek 146). By seeking vengeance, Worf prioritizes his duty to his dead mate above his duty to Starfleet, which earns him a rebuke from Picard.

What Is the Relationship Between Rules and Results?

Overall, ethical approaches can be divided into two categories: deontological ethics, which is duty-centered, and teleological ethics, which is end-centered (Geisler & Feinberg 397). Immanuel Kant, and Plato before him, firmly advocated the deontological approach. Anthony Kenny synopsizes, "For Kant, it is the painfulness of welldoing that is the real mark of virtue. It is only when it costs us something to do what is right that we can be sure we are acting from the motive of duty" (191). Proponents of teleological ethics included Jeremy Bentham and John Stuart Mill. From their perspective, "obligation is in regard to those actions required for the attainment of a certain end (for example, the actualization and harmonious integration of one's potentialities as a human being)" (Copleston "Absolute Idealism" 232).

"[A] comprehensive ethic will include both [approaches]," opine Geisler and Feinberg (397). They continue, "The rules are not determined by the results, but one should have results in view when decisions are made. Indeed, one of the rules of a duty ethic is to try to maximize the good or bring about the greatest good." Numerous episodes of *Star Trek: The Next Generation* applied this synthesis of teleological and deontological ethics. The most personal approach, however, occurred in "The First Duty" (#519), arguably the finest episode to focus on Wesley Crusher. For the first time in film or on television, the setting is Starfleet Academy, where Picard is to give the commencement address. Wesley participates in a cover-up with his squadron mates rather than reveal the truth about a fatal flight maneuver. Learning of his protégé's indiscretion, Picard "reads him the riot act," and Wesley makes the painful decision to turn in his friends. This choice was a controversial issue among the writing staff. Ron Moore, one of the episode's writers, felt that action "would amount to character assassination" (Altman "The Making of 'The First Duty'" 52). Michael Piller reveals:

> We had a long argument about whether it was the right thing to do, about what kind of message we wanted to give to our audience. Ultimately, Ron reluctantly agreed to go forward with the ending that the truth is the most important thing, which is what I want my kids to believe. Ron's a young writer who hasn't had any kids, so he doesn't know that yet [Altman 52–53].

By giving him a human flaw, the writers allow Wesley to transcend the "perfect, whiz kid" stereotype, which had previously caused many fans to despise the character.

Summary

Though the philosophy of *Star Trek* is akin to secular humanism, Gene Roddenberry's world view is unique unto itself. Ina Rae Hark in "*Star Trek* and Television's Moral Universe" (1979) asserts that while Roddenberry's morality has roots in "traditional Judeo-Christian thought," he abandons concepts of absolute good and evil (26). Though he believes humans can derive a system of ethics based on their enlightened nature, morality does not become obsolete but merely malleable. This conceit is not simply situational ethics, however, because Roddenberry's purpose is to affirm the dignity of all life, whether human or alien. Part of *Star Trek*'s appeal is that he managed to fuse "meaningful drama and something of substance and pride" with exciting space opera (Alexander 221). Accepting the perils of didacticism, Roddenberry succeeded. Wisely, he and his *Star Trek: The Next Generation* successors understood that the direct, didactic approaches, which worked on classic *Trek*, would not appeal to contemporary audiences.

By having "both the luxury and the albatross of being able to come at stories in a completely flip-flopped way," as Jeri Taylor commented, *Star Trek: The Next Generation* writers were able to teach viewers, without affronting their sensibilities. Such collaboration is a crucial element of didacticism (Coste 301). In addition, the characters themselves set examples for younger viewers to follow. Elaine Koste, who attended a recent convention with her husband and five-year-old daughter admitted she uses the show "as a tool to educate" her daughter: "It's good for her to see the characters deal with other races and teach good values" (Zoglin 76).

Interpersonal Issues: Parasocial Interactions

Another way to examine *Star Trek: The Next Generation* as a mass communication text is to examine how viewers interact with the series, specifically the characters portrayed. A parasocial interaction is a "one-sided interpersonal relationship that television viewers establish with media characters" (Rubin & McHugh 280). In their seminal 1956 *Psychiatry* article, "Mass Communication and Para-Social Interaction: Observations on Intimacy at a Distance," Horton and Wohl defined this pseudo-relationship. They argue that a viewer can develop a bond of intimacy with a media personality through "shared experiences existing only through viewing of the personality or persona over time" (Rubin & McHugh 280).

As continued viewings occur, the audience member and the character develop an illusionary "face-to-face relationship" (Horton & Wohl 185). Since the character is reliable, the viewer becomes a loyal "friend."

Theoretical Construct

In spring 1992, Parham and Wainer conducted a statistical survey of fans at a *Star Trek* convention in Virginia Beach, Virginia. The researchers' goal was "to determine if there is a relationship between *Star Trek* and the principles of the men's liberation movement" (13). If such a relationship exists, the duo theorized it could be a possible factor for the program's phenomenal success. They hypothesized:

H1—*Star Trek* appeals to men more than women.
H2—Viewers do perceive Picard as a mentor/father figure.
H3—There are differences between men's and women's perceptions of *Star Trek* [13].

Methodology

The researchers developed a questionnaire that was distributed to 120 participants at a *Star Trek* convention. The questionnaire consisted of three sections: viewing motivations, perceptions of *Star Trek* characters, and demography. Respondents were given detailed instructions to complete the survey but were not told the precise reason why the survey was being conducted (14).

Viewing Motivations

To determine viewing motivations, respondents were asked to indicate their agreement with each of 18 statements of reasons for watching *Star Trek*; their answers could range across five options for response, which included strongly agree, agree, somewhat agree, disagree, and strongly disagree. The statements were synthesized from items used by Rubin (148–149) and were drawn from six clusters: companionship, arousal, relaxation, escape, entertainment, and social interaction. Multiple statements were drawn from each cluster to establish reliability.

Perceptions of *Star Trek* Characters

The next section of the survey focused on viewers' opinions concerning dyadic relationships on *Star Trek: The Next Generation*. Respondents were asked to indicate their agreement with each of 25 statements about *Trek* characters. Those statements were subdivided by the researchers into three types: nine "type-A" statements centered on Picard as a mentor/father figure; three "type-B" statements focused on various male-male dyads; while the remaining 13 "type-C" statements were assorted observations about the crew. This construction allowed the researchers to analyze the appropriate groups of statements after data were collected.

DEMOGRAPHY

Demography accounted for the final section of the research instrument. In addition to information about gender, age, and ethnicity, four additional questions measured respondents' exposure to *Star Trek* in four of its incarnations—the original series, the feature films, *The Next Generation* and *Deep Space Nine*. Among other purposes, demographic information allowed the researchers to compare men's and women's answers with regard to sections one and two of the questionnaire.

Results

Out of 120 questionnaires distributed at the *Star Trek* convention on March 20–21, 1992, 73 participants responded.[9] Thirty-four respondents were male, while 38 were female. A plurality of respondents (37.5 percent) were in the 26- to 35-year-old age bracket, while precisely one-third ranged in age from 36 to 49 years old. The top three reasons, respectively, why respondents watched *Star Trek* were entertainment, relaxation, and excitement.

HYPOTHESIS 1

The hypothesis "*Star Trek* appeals to men more than women" was proven false. Statistically speaking, there was no significant difference between the reasons why men and women watch *Trek*. In fact, in the categories of entertainment and relaxation, women's mean scores (4.55 and 3.96) were slightly higher than the men's (4.52 and 3.74). Only in the realm of excitement was the men's mean higher than the women's (4.22 vice 3.92).

HYPOTHESIS 2

Parham and Wainer's next theory, however, was proven true: "Viewers do perceive Picard as a mentor/father figure." Correlation analysis of the nine dyadic statements regarding Picard rendered a Cronbach coefficient alpha of 0.611 for raw variables and 0.594 for standardized variables. When one statement (question #35) was removed, the Cronbach coefficient alpha increased to 0.690 and 0.693, respectively.[10] A rotated factor analysis was then performed. Three mathematically-determined factors confirmed concepts the researchers expected to prove

>FACTOR3 = Reverse code Q35 + Q33 + Q43 (Picard as a mentor)
>FACTOR4 = Q19 +Q22 (male friendships)
>FACTOR6 = Q25 + Q42 (Picard as a father figure)

Hypothesis 3

The statement "There are differences between men's and women's perceptions of *Star Trek*" was also proven to be false. Men's and women's perceptions across two categories—Picard as a father figure (Q25 + Q42) and male friendships (Q19 + Q22)—were compared. In the first category, the men's mean score was 3.121 and the women's mean score was 3.014; in the second category, the men's mean was 3.803 and the women's mean was 4.111. In neither category was the gender difference statistically significant.

Summary

Though only one of the researchers' hypotheses was validated—viewers' perception of Picard as a mentor/father figure—the results were encouraging. The finding that women view *Star Trek* for the same reasons as men is a testament to its broad-based appeal. In addition, despite the stereotype of "Trekkers" as isolated misfits, loneliness was the lowest rated viewing motivation for either men (mean score 1.615) or women (mean score 1.578). Most importantly, respondents did recognize that dyadic relationships exist on *Star Trek: The Next Generation*. Their ability to make judgments about the show's characters—evidenced by responses to section two of the survey—implies a high level of parasocial interactions. The high-level of fan engagement with the text through interpersonal and intrapersonal interactions helps explain the longevity and appeal that few television series have been able to match. Chapter Six will delve into fan culture through the lens of the group/organizational contexts.

Six

The Mass Communication Context, Part II

Group/Organizational Issues: Fans and Texts

The Fans

Star Trek fans are infamous for their exuberance and dedication to the show. A defining moment for them came on a *Saturday Night Live* skit in 1986. Richard Zoglin imparts:

> William Shatner—the indomitable Captain James Tiberius Kirk from the original TV series—was playing himself making a guest appearance at a *Star Trek* convention. After fielding a few dumb questions from the nerdy, trivia-obsessed fans, he suddenly exploded: "I'd just like to say.... Get a life, will you, people?! I mean, for crying out loud, it was just a TV show!" [72].

Despite Shatner's immediate recantation in the sketch that he was impersonating "the evil Captain Kirk" from episode 37, "the put-down was like a phaser to the heart" (72). Daryl G. Frazetti, professor of anthropology and sociology at California State University Channel Islands, conducted an online survey of 5,041 fans and makes this conclusion: "*Star Trek* fans are not simply teenage boys who live in their mother's basements as the stereotype goes. They are a diverse and vibrant cultural entity and are educated, with as many, if not more, female fans as male fans, and come to fandom from a broad spectrum of age and demographic."

For many fans, *Star Trek* is not simply a television show but a way of life. Frazetti explains, "[It] acts as a secular myth for contemporary times by providing cultural symbols and meanings that serve as a model for the formation of a distinct culture." Furthermore, posited Henry Jenkins, "[those] fans characterize their entry into fandom in terms of a movement from social and cultural isolation toward more and more active participation in a community receptive to their cultural productions, a community where they may feel a sense of belonging" (88). Professor Frazetti's survey allowed fans to rate their degree of involvement.

- 13 percent identified themselves as professional fans (fans who are now professional and working in Trek) and considered to be highly involved.
- Overwhelmingly, 82 percent considered themselves to be average to below-average in terms of involvement.
- 18 percent went all out to go into elaborate detail about how extremely involved they were as fans. This group reported such activities as attending more than ten conventions a year, belonging to two or more groups/clubs, having careers influenced by *Star Trek*, taking on Trek-related personas and being involved in costuming, and being either raised on *Star Trek* values or currently teaching others the values of Trek, including raising their own children on Trek.

Jean Louise Matthias, a freelance scriptwriter who co-wrote three episodes of *Star Trek: The Next Generation*, describes her entry into fandom in a manner consistent with Frazetti's and Jenkins' assertions. "When I was in high school," she divulges, "getting involved in *Star Trek* was a 'revenge of the geeks.' Kids who were disenfranchised from other venues in life, such as athletics or cheerleading, could become part of an interesting family" (personal interview). Adds David Carren, a *Star Trek: The Next Generation* fourth-season story editor, "On the original series Roddenberry had that basic kernel of an idea, which is that the Enterprise is one big, happy family ... and that's why you've got all these Trekkies dressing up in their uniforms and dreaming of being on the Enterprise" (Altman, EG, Oct. 1991, 44). "Rejecting aesthetic distance," postulates Jenkins, "fans passionately embrace favored texts and attempt to integrate media representations within their own social experience" (86). Mark Altman surmises this integration often arises from a sense of ennui: "Being set in the future, *Trek* allows people to use their own imagination. It takes them out of their present, humdrum worlds and allows them to 'be' [live vicariously] as Starfleet officers. In a sense, the phenomenon allows adults the opportunity to reach 'their inner child'" (personal interview). Immersion in the *Star Trek* phenomenon, then, becomes "a way of appropriating media texts and rereading them in a fashion that serves different interests, a way of transforming mass culture into a popular culture" (Jenkins 87).

Clearly *Star Trek* does appeal to fans because of the sense of community it provides. Karin Blair, in "The Garden in the Machine: The Why of *Star Trek*" (1979), even asserts the saucer section of the *Enterprise* itself can be seen as a mandala, a Jungian symbol of wholeness (183). But it is misleading to stereotype all fans as belonging to "marginalized subcultural groups (women, the young, gays, etc.)" as Jenkins did (87). Zoglin reports:

> General Colin Powell is a watcher; so are Robin Williams, Mel Brooks and Stephen Hawking, the best-selling physicist (*A Brief History of Time*) who made a guest appearance in an episode of *The Next Generation*.[1]
>
> According to Paramount TV research, *Star Trek*'s regular weekly audience of more than 20 million includes more high-income, college-educated viewers (as well as more men) than the average TV show. Even at the better than 200 Trekkie conventions held each year, the clientele is more likely to be middle-aged couples with kids in tow than computer geeks sporting Vulcan ears [75–76].

Jonathan Frakes, who portrayed Cmdr. William T. Riker, agrees: "If you go in looking for geeks and nerds, then yeah, you'll find some. But this is a show that doesn't insult the audience. It is intelligent, literate and filled with messages and morals—and that's what most of the people who watch are interested in" (Zoglin 76).

"Where no fan has gone before"

Another factor that made *Star Trek: The Next Generation* unique is the relationship specific fans formed with a character or set of characters. Lieutenant Commander Data, for example, became a role model for viewers on the Autism Spectrum Disorder. Taylor Soper from geekwire.com explains, "Often struggling to understand human emotion, 'Data' was one of the few characters on TV that people with autism or Asperger syndrome could relate to because he was trying to understand feelings and humanity in the same way they did." Actor Brent Spiner was unaware of this fact until he received a set visit from Oliver Sacks. The noted scientist describes the meeting: "On one occasion when I was in Los Angeles, I went to the studio and met Brent Spiner, who was Data. I told him he was the icon of autistic people everywhere, and I think he looked rather puzzled. And he wasn't quite sure what to make of my comment, which was meant to be a high compliment ("Science Fiction…")."

Years later when the cast reunited for a Blu-ray special feature, Spiner recounts a similar fan encounter.

> I had a moment recently at a convention where a young woman came to the table I was signing at, and she said, "I don't know if you know this, but your character was sort of the poster boy for children with Asperger's Syndrome. And I was one of those children because I could watch the show and see somebody grappling with how to express themselves and how to understand humanity. And it was the only

character on television that was like me." And I had no idea, but it was overwhelming ["Reunification"].

Spiner reflects, "I just think how lucky I was because I didn't have anything to do with it. I just showed up and played the part. It wasn't like I was trying to do that; it was just a tangential thing that happened to be bigger even than entertainment" (Soper).

Some fans' love of *Star Trek* has actually led to gainful employment. In the mid–1990s, Paramount Parks (then a division of Viacom) operated five theme parks, including Paramount's Great America in San Jose. Fans David Maddox and Kevin Miller were hired to portray *Star Trek* characters and walk around the park, mingling with guests.

> MADDOX: At the height of it, there were 32 *Star Trek* characters total. There were Bajorans, there a couple of humans—those were the guys who couldn't pull off the other aliens so they got demoted to being human. There were Vulcans, there were Klingons—a *lot* of Klingons—and a bunch of Romulans.
> MILLER: It was a great time. It was at the peak of *Next Generation*, *DS9*, and *Voyager*, so there was awareness; people knew who we were. For my three years, I was exclusively a Ferengi.
> MADDOX: I was a Vulcan, a Romulan, and a Klingon over the five years I worked there [personal interview].

Maddox confirms, "My love of *Star Trek* led me to the job." Miller adds, "The passion for *Star Trek* helped me transcend into the role, which made the job of walking around and talking to people just like a dream come true" (personal interview). Both men eventually relocated to Los Angeles after college and still remain close friends 20-plus years after their time together being employed to dress and perform as *Star Trek* aliens.

Perhaps no group epitomizes the extreme devotion of *Star Trek* aficionados than Klingon Fan Culture, which Mark Medeiros of the *Priority One* podcast contends, "has emerged amongst the most dedicated and passionate of Star Trek fans. They have taken fandom to a whole new level." The Klingon Fan Clubs and Groups homepage provides links to websites for 15 fan clubs and three language groups that span 23 countries across six continents—North and South America, Asia, Europe, Africa, and Australia. The Klingon Assault Group's webpage explains that club's purpose.

> **What does KAG do?**
> KAG has Fun.
> Our members go to fan conventions and intimidate other species.
> • We help charities with food and blood drives.
> • We win costume contests at conventions.
> • We throw excellent parties.

- We host events and weekend get-aways.
- We share in the richness of Klingon culture and the Klingon Language.

A 2016 copyright-infringement case even focused on whether Klingon "exists as an independent language" (Yuhas). Seeking to stop production of an unauthorized fan film, Paramount Pictures cited the Klingon language as one of numerous complaints. The studio's attorney argued, "A language is only useful if it can be used to communicate with people, and there are no Klingons with whom to communicate" (Yuhas). But a group of linguists filed an *amicus curiae*; their attorney, Marc Randazza, made a compelling counterargument.

> Given that Paramount Pictures commissioned the creation of some of the language, it is understandable that Paramount might feel some sense of ownership over the creation. But feeling ownership and having ownership are not the same thing. The language has taken on a life of its own. Klingon is not just a language. It is a state of mind—and that state cannot be constrained by copyright law [Yuhas].

Software developer John Lemay's experience as a member of the Klingon Legion of Assault Warriors (KLAW) provides an insider's perspective. He shares highlights of his time with KLAW.

> We met up at someone's house every two weeks to plan for conventions, make costumes and props. A couple of folks studied Klingon language, but mostly [we bonded] over our love of *Star Trek*. There was also a local Starfleet club, and we often had shared meetings with them. It was like we became a big family; there was certainly healthy rivalry between our groups, but we were all fast friends. In our heyday, my little club numbered over 200 with branches scattered around the southeast U.S. [personal interview].

KLAW members' activities eventually branched out into areas. "We had members start a Klingon rock band. Another club member "homebrewed beer. So he and some home winemakers made our own club-labeled beer, wine, and mead for room parties" (Lemay). "To this day," Lemay reflects, "this club brought me some of the closest friendships I ever had."

A reason why fans can form such close-knit communities is because of the mythology they share through the show. During a reunion to commemorate *Star Trek: The Next Generation*'s 25th anniversary, cast members traded stories about fan encounters. Actor Michael Dorn, who played Worf, recounts one that caught him off guard.

> Mine was in Vegas. It was a Klingon breakfast so everybody was dressed as Klingons. This guy came up to me—full Klingon stuff ... looked great! And he says, "You know, you saved my life." What're you talking about? He says he was in drugs and alcohol; he lost his job; he lost his family ... everything. And he said that the way the character was written and the way he was portrayed and all that stuff.... It

was honor and strength and blah blah blah. And I said, "I appreciate this, but it was you that did it. *You* did it" ["Reunification"].

Gates McFadden adds to the conversation, "It's like mythology for our times, and I started to realize that I'm a part of it. And it's quite remarkable to comprehend how important this has been to many, many, many people all over the world" ("Reunification").

The actors' observations bolster Frazetti's belief that "*Star Trek* is indeed a powerful myth that has acted as the basis for the formation of the fandom culture." Science-fiction writer David Gerrold, who launched his career by writing "The Trouble with Tribbles" for the original series, goes even further by saying, "*Star Trek* became the theology for modern culture. Its appeal is that as a theology for the modern man or modern person it says we can do better—we will do better—and here's what it could look like" (personal interview). While Gerrold's claims may seem hyperbolic, they are not inconsistent with Professor Frazetti's assertion that myths are "value-laden discourse that focus on the examination or explanation of the human condition." The specific core beliefs shared across fandom that he cites are

- the utopian future;
- Concept of IDIC (Infinite Diversity in Infinite Combinations); and
  the humanistic study of humanity [Frazetti].

Gerrold posits, "*Star Trek* is one of the few, positive visions of the future. It says there will be a future; we will survive our most critical problems, and we'll become a better people for it" (personal interview). Frazetti agrees: "*Star Trek* is a futuristic portal, allowing fans to learn from the past, make changes in the present, and strive for a Trek future."

Yet as the professor's research shows, devotees like Lemay, Maddox, and Miller are outliers and account for less than 20 percent of fandom. Gene Roddenberry hand-selected producer Rick Berman to guide the *Star Trek* empire, which he did until the tenth feature film, *Nemesis*. He concedes in a 1991 interview that *Star Trek: The Next Generation*'s phenomenal success is because of its broad appeal: "[A] large portion of the viewing audience, most of whom I would have to characterize as *not* being *Star Trek* fans, [have] embraced the show. Ratings and some specific demographic groups that are very important to advertisers have continued to soar, so we're all very happy" (Spelling 39).

Regardless of whether viewers characterize themselves as "hardcore" fans or not, Paramount Pictures is aware that the *Star Trek* franchise is quite lucrative. The thirteen films have grossed in excess of $1.4 billion at the box office, and "*Trek*-related merchandise, ranging from T-shirts and backpacks to a $2,200 brass replica of the *Enterprise*, has exploded in the past five years, with total revenues topping $1 billion" (Zoglin 74). Box-office receipts and licensed merchandise revenue demonstrate that *Star Trek* fans engage the series economically, as well as socially.

Constructed Narratives

From a communication standpoint, however, the exploration of ardent fans' reconstruction of the *Star Trek* narrative is a noteworthy pursuit. John G. Cawelti's "The Concept of Artistic Matrices" (1978) examined how the relationship between audience, critic-interpreters, and creators mediates and defines popular culture. He developed four models—communal, mythical, professional, and reflexive—to illustrate how art emerges from patterns within the larger culture. As discussed in Chapter One, the *Star Trek* phenomenon aligns with the mythical matrix. Cawelti explains:

> The crucial feature of this matrix is the special authority which is granted by participants in the matrix to the creator-performers, the genres they employ and possibly, in some cases, the medium that is used. In addition, the mythical matrix is characterized by a symbolic system consisting of an integrated body of narrative [298].

He raises two salient points here. First, the audience grants creator-performers "special authority." This observation helps explain fans' adulation of *Star Trek* actors and the willingness to pay exorbitant prices to attend conventions.[2] Second, fans regard all of the *Star Trek* series as a metanarrative. As such, they expect installments to be consistent with each other. Though not singling out *Star Trek*, Didier Coste posits in *Narrative as Communication* (1989), "It is still widely believed that [the] accumulation of strata of fictionality causes the reader to lose sight of 'referentiality' (that is, real reference)" (125). Berman concedes both points in an interview with Michael Walsh: "The laws of *Star Trek* are totally fictional but are held by the fans with such reverence that they have to be followed as if they were Newton's. You have to treat them very carefully, because there are people who for 25 years have considered them sacred" (77).

A deviation from Cawelti's mythical matrix is the blurring of the distance between audience and creator-performers. He surmises, "Because the creator-performer is given a special authority, he is somewhat distanced from the audience and tends to become more so as the culture develops" (298). A unique aspect of the *Star Trek* phenomenon is that fans of both series have been able to become creator-performers themselves to a certain extent. Loyal viewers of the original series, such as Bjo and John Trimble, organized campaigns to keep it on the air its second and third years. Kathryn Casey remarks, "Without [the Trimbles], *Star Trek*, rather than becoming a billion-dollar industry, might have died only a blip on the small screen" (31). Aside from that accomplishment, Bjo Trimble is renowned for writing the first reference book for fans, *The Star Trek Concordance*. She describes its origins:

> About midway through the first season of *Star Trek*, I noticed that Dorothy Jones, a fellow fan, was making extensive notes on the show, with cross-references to items and things mentioned, lists of who played what part, and so on. It seemed too interesting merely to keep it in a file box, so I suggested that we share it with other fans [*Star Trek Concordance* 8].

One must commend Trimble's fairly selfless motive for writing the tome and consider the near-Herculean scope of her task since the series was out of production and she was an outsider.[3] She differentiates, though, her book from the *Starfleet Technical Manual*, the *Starfleet Medical Reference Manual*, and other such books. "My book was based *entirely* on the TV show; no fannish extrapolation on what makes Vulcans tick on the inside or dreadnought ships never seen on the show. All other books have a great deal of imaginative additions by the authors to 'make things fit' as they see it" ("Ideas About Ideas" 21).

TEXTUAL POACHING ON CLASSIC *STAR TREK*

Whereas Trimble adhered to canon in the *Concordance*, other writers did not. In *Star Trek Creator: The Authorized Biography of Gene Roddenberry*, David Alexander relates, "There was one subject that Gene definitely wanted included in his biography, a subject for which he had particular irritation: they were 'the damn books!' as he characterized them" (484). The first *Star Trek* books were written by James Blish and were novelizations of episodes. Then, in 1970, Bantam Books published Blish's *Spock Must Die*, the first original novel. Alan Dean Foster novelized the animated episodes and other authors contributed other original novels. In addition to the authorized novels, fans began writing stories. Henry Jenkins III's essay, "*Star Trek* Rerun, Reread, Rewritten: Fan Writing as Textual Poaching" (1988), is a seminal examination of the fans' poaching. Aside from fulfilling a need for more material, the fan-generated stories allowed writers to reconstruct the *Star Trek* mythos making it more suitable for their own interests.

Jenkins asserts that men and women approach *Star Trek* fandom from different perspectives:

> Fan writing is an almost exclusively feminine response to mass media texts. Men actively participate in a wide range of fan-related activities, notably interactive games and conference planning committees, roles consistent with patriarchal norms that typically relegate combat—even combat fantasies—and organizational authority to the masculine sphere [90].

As discussed in Chapter Two, feminist critics like Anne Cranny-Francis clearly view the original series as paternalistic. Jenkins notes that female fan writers reconcile that bias by reconstructing the *Star Trek* mythos in their own image, so to speak. He writes, "Women, confronting a traditionally masculine space opera, chose to read it instead as a type of women's fiction" (96). He elucidates: "This need to reclaim feminine interests from the margins of masculine texts produces endless speculation, speculation that draws the reader well beyond textual boundaries into the domain of the intertextual" (91). Only by reconstructing the text, then, can these "women within a patriarchal society [seek] alternative pleasures within dominant media representations [i.e., *Star Trek*]" (Jenkins 88). Such reconstructions include "Lieutenant Mary Sue" stories, which "take the form of romantic fantasies about the series characters and frequently involve inserting glorified versions of [the authors] into the world of Star Fleet [*sic*]" (96–97).

A more controversial example is the K/S genre. "Hidden away in a few [fan-published magazines] were stories that appealed to a narrow spectrum of fans; homoerotic fiction featuring a speculative relationship between Kirk and Spock," explains Alexander (485). "As long as it remained on the fringes, Gene didn't care, although he once wondered why [Kirk] would have a sexual relationship with [Spock] who only became sexually active once every seven years" (485). "Some K/S fans frankly acknowledge the gap between the series characterizations and their own representations," reveals Jenkins, "yet refuse to allow their fantasy life to be governed by the limitations of what was actually aired" (102). Though the K/S stories are clearly not supported in the primary text,[4] Jenkins posits, "what K/S does openly, all fans do covertly" (102). He continues:

> In constructing the feminine countertext that lurks in the margins of the primary text, these readers necessarily redefine the text in the process of rereading and rewriting it.... If these fans have rewritten *Star Trek* in their own terms, however, many of them are reluctant to break all ties to the primary text that sparked their creative activity and, hence, feel the necessity to legitimate their activity through appeals to textual fidelity [102].

The true irony of all this reconstruction is that "the text [the fans] so lovingly preserve is the *Star Trek* that they created through their own speculations, not the one that Roddenberry produced for network air play" (Jenkins 100–101). Roddenberry, though, tolerated the range of fan-produced stories.

Bantam Books, the original licensee of *Trek* fiction, even published two volumes of *Star Trek: The New Voyages*. In the foreword to volume one, Roddenberry writes:

> [T]here is no more profound way in which people could express what *Star Trek* has meant to them than by creating their own very personal *Star Trek* things.
> It is now a source of great joy for me to see their view of *Star Trek*, their new *Star Trek* stories, reaching professional publication here [x].

Roddenberry's laissez-faire attitude about *Star Trek* fiction, however, changed a few years after Pocket Books—a division of Simon & Schuster, which was then owned by Paramount Communications—acquired the *Star Trek* franchise. Alexander recounts:

> In the mid–1980's, Pocket published a novel with elements of K/S as part of their continuing series of *Star Trek* novels. Gene received a few letters from outraged fans. He investigated and became livid.
> [He] took a closer look at all the proposed stories from then on, as well as how *Star Trek* was used in other outlets, including comic books. Gene's irritation grew out of authors who wanted to push their own characters and not the *Star Trek* regulars; authors who wanted to feature themselves in the story (the "Mary Sue" stories); and authors who wanted to change *Star Trek* history or format, or deviate from Gene's philosophical underpinnings [485–486].

Roddenberry eventually hired *Star Trek* expert Richard Arnold to be his watchdog (487).[5] He recalls, "Instead of five or six books a year, there were thirteen or fourteen books a year, and they were selling more and more of them. [Gene] was right again—there was not a finite amount of *Star Trek* merchandise that you can put out" (487). The linkages between fan poaching and licensed fiction are especially interesting when one considers Jenkins' assertion, "[T]he fans respect the original texts, yet fear that their conceptions of the characters and concepts may be jeopardized by those who wish to exploit them for easy profits [i.e., Paramount]" (100). Zoglin enumerates, "More than 63 million *Star Trek* books are in print, and new titles are appearing at the rate of more than 30 a year" (74). Despite fans' apparent concern with "Trek-sploitation," their hunger for new material seems insatiable.

Licensed Hunting on *Star Trek: The Next Generation*

Textual poaching on *Star Trek: The Next Generation* never became the "problem" it did for the original series. One of the reasons is that the producers eventually allowed fans themselves to submit story ideas and scripts. In an October 1990 *Starlog* interview, Michael Piller, who had just completed his first year heading the writing staff, reveals the following:

> [O]ne of the reasons that this past year [season three] has been so successful is that we generated six or seven shows off of speculative material. We probably get 500 to 1,000 scripts per year, more than *any* other TV show on the air. It's like having a staff of writers out there, and maybe one out of 100 tickle my fancy. It really comes down to a season full of ideas from fans, from viewers, from people who like to take a shot at it. That's where *fresh* ideas come from. It's been a real collaboration between the fans and the staff this year[6] [Gross 39].

The second-generation *Star Trek* shows had been unique among television series in that they were "open to script submissions from *anyone*, not just experienced television writers" (Reeves-Stevens 278). In the April 1995 "TV Market List" in the Writers Guild's *Journal,* only one of the 101 series included on the TV Market List specifically lists a separate phone number for submissions by writers without agents—*Star Trek: Deep Space Nine* (50–51).

After *Star Trek: The Next Generation*'s sixth season, Mark A. Altman interviewed several writing staffers for his 1993 *Cinefantastique* article "The Board and the Art of the Pitch." His account frankly but humorously describes how the staff culls through pitches from aspiring screenwriters:

> The writers have heard thousands of pitches since *The Next Generation*'s inception. Some of them have been utterly brilliant and been turned into episodes. Some have been mediocre and turned into episodes. Many writers have come in several times before selling a pitch, others have scored on just one, selling multiple premises. Most have been downright awful [52].

Some *Cinefantastique* readers might have been discouraged by the low acceptance rate or by the staffers' ridicule of prospective writers who had no concept of story structure. Executive producer Michael Piller, though, reveals why the process was beneficial: "There aren't a lot of good [pitches] but, ultimately, you have to listen to these ideas to keep fresh minds coming into the mix" (55). The true irony is that fans' demand for more *Star Trek* results in more fans being able to participate in the creative process by submitting scripts. Judith and Garfield Reeves-Stevens in *The Making of Star Trek: Deep Space Nine* encourage aspiring writers to submit scripts for *Trek*:

There are 79 original series episodes, 6 original series movies, and, by the end of 1994, there will be 176 [sic] *Next Generation* episodes, one *Next Generation* movie, and at least 46 *Deep Space Nine* episodes. That's more than 300 STAR TREK stories. Yet, if *Deep Space Nine* and *Voyager* go on to match *The Next Generation*'s success, then between now and 2001, Paramount's expecting to come up with 300 more!

Someone's going to write them. Why shouldn't it be you? [278, 303].

Summary

Fans' fascination with *Star Trek* and their ability to submerge themselves within the phenomenon has allowed them "to transform mass culture into a popular culture" (Jenkins 87). Their creativity unleashed, devotees find different ways to express their enthusiasm, such as writing stories, designing costumes, or collecting memorabilia. Moreover, the uniqueness of *Star Trek* fandom is that it transcends age, gender, physical, racial, and socioeconomic boundaries. Erik Davis' notation that a *Star Trek* convention is one "of the few social zones that bring together blacks and whites, Asians and Hispanics, men and women, toddlers and grandmothers" affirms the sense of community that pervades show's fans (81). That so many people from such varied backgrounds can participate in one phenomenon is a tribute to Gene Roddenberry's vision. *Star Trek* provides a place where people from all walks of life can fit in and participate as much, or as little, as they desire. As fan Kevin Miller surmises, "*Star Trek* allow[s] every culture and individual to have a value of their own. I don't see that in other television shows. That's what resonated with me the most" (personal interview). In essence, the *Star Trek* universe is a secular "kingdom of heaven."

Seven

Next Frontiers for Communication Contexts

An exciting aspect of using contextual communication theories to analyze *Star Trek: The Next Generation* is that this approach can be applied to other television series. The similarities in premises, cast designs, and narrative patterns of the subsequent *Star Trek* shows—*Deep Space Nine*, *Voyager*, *Enterprise*, and *Discovery*—make them ideal to examine using this paradigm. Moreover, by scrutinizing a sample communication context for each of those series, one can examine core components that help define them as *Star Trek* beyond the mere title.

Intrapersonal Issues on Star Trek: Discovery— *Michael Burnham and the Four Loves*

Each of the *Star Trek* series include a character through which the writers explore humanity or the human experience. Mr. Spock served this function in the original series. Several of the 79 episodes focused on his attempts to reconcile his mixed heritage, usually by trying to assert his Vulcan half at the expense of his human side. The first feature film, *Star Trek: The Motion Picture*, depicts events crucial to the development of Spock's character. Spock is reintroduced to audiences as he undergoes Kolinahr, a Vulcan ritual in which all emotion is shed. He abandons the ceremony, however, to rejoin his former shipmates on the refit *U.S.S. Enterprise*. Although detractors found the film overly cerebral and lacking action, Steve Smyth offered this assessment on the website *Quora*.

> I consider TMP just as much a culmination of Spock's story arc as it is a new beginning for Kirk. Spock's mind meld with V'ger opens the door to his realization that he is neither Terran nor Vulcan. He is Spock.

Once he gets to that place, he is actually a richer character. Remember, according to Spock, "Logic, is the beginning of wisdom."

Spock comes to weep for V'Ger—a massive entity revealed to be the space probe *Voyager 6*, which has become imbued with sentience albeit one representing pure logic and lacking emotion. This encounter prompts Spock to realize the way he should respond to his dual heritage is to "reframe" the dialectical tension between the two sides. In *Communication Theories in Action*, Julia T. Wood describes this process as "a perceptual transformation ... such that the two contrasts are no longer opposites" (211). Despite widespread criticism of *Star Trek: The Motion Picture*, sincere Trekkers acknowledge without Spock's encounter with V'ger in the film, his character would not have found inner peace he needed for the sequel, *Star Trek II: The Wrath of Khan*.

The subsequent *Star Trek* television series each contain a character whose function in the cast is to represent the exploration of humanity, usually from without. They include Data (*The Next Generation*), Odo (*Deep Space Nine*), Seven of Nine (*Voyager*), and T'Pol (*Enterprise*). A fascinating aspect of *Discovery*, the fifth spinoff series, is that series lead Michael Burnham fulfills this function. As *Variety*'s Maureen Ryan noted in her review, "[Burnham] is an outsider in many ways, which gives 'Discovery's writers a lot of interesting psychological territory to explore. Her professional relationships in the present and her personal bonds from the past are mostly fraught and complicated." In the series premiere, audiences learn that Burnham was orphaned at a young age because of a Klingon attack on Doctari Alpha and was raised by Spock's parents—Sarek and Amanda Grayson ("The Vulcan Hello"). The series sixth episode provides crucial backstory for the character. Sarek raised Burnham to embrace Vulcan logic and eschew human emotion. He asserts, "I have created with her a being of exquisite logic to rival the best of our species" ("Lethe").

Marriage and family therapist Dr. Andrea Brandt notes on *Psychology Today*'s blog that a way childhood trauma affects adults "is through the creation of *a false self*." She continued, "When we bury our emotions, we lose touch with who we really are, because our feelings are an integral part of us. We live our lives terrified that if we let the mask drop, we'll no longer be cared for, loved, or accepted" (Brandt). Ironically, the posthumous advice Burnham receives from Georgiou in her recorded will and testament proves salient: "The best way to know yourself is to know others" ("The Butcher's Knife Cares Not for the Lamb's Cry"). This guidance serves as a template to explore Burnham's intrapersonal reconciliation of emotions during season one. In *The Four Loves* C.S. Lewis discusses the four Greek words for love: *storge*—parental affection; *phileo*—friendship; *eros*—romance; agape—charity (unconditional "God" love). Though this paradigm is not a communication theory *per se*, by examining Burnham's relationships through the lens of Lewis' "four loves," one can trace her intrapersonal growth as she learns to reconnect with her own humanity.

Storge: Burnham and Parental Figures

Since Sarek strictly adhered to the Vulcan precept of logic over emotion, Amanda provided parental love to Michael (and Spock) that her husband was incapable of expressing. In a flashback from episode six, Burnham recalls receiving the book *Alice's Adventures in Wonderland*. Amanda tells her foster daughter, "This gift comes with a mother's advice. You've proven that you're as accomplished as any Vulcan, which is gonna serve you well as long as you never forget that you're human, too. You need to nurture that side" ("Lethe"). The episode hinges on Burnham's attempt to locate Sarek's shuttle before he succumbs to injuries inflicted by a terrorist attack. The conundrum of Burnham's character as a human raised by Vulcans is that Sarek fostered her with a specific intent. She reveals to roommate Sylvia Tilly, "I was supposed to be his proof that humans and Vulcans could coexist as equals" to which the cadet responds, "How can you put that kind of pressure on a child?" ("Lethe").

Burnham lived with guilt for not measuring up to those standards. The flashbacks, however, reveal that she *did* pass, but "the Group plans to allow only one of Sarek's children in, because neither of them are fully Vulcan" (Howell). Burnham, unaware at the time of his deception, joined Starfleet and was assigned to serve on the *U.S.S. Shenzhou*. Captain Philippa Georgiou recognized the challenges of serving as a strong mentor and maternal figure for the junior officer. Actor Michelle Yeoh, who plays Georgiou, explains further.

> When Michael Burnham arrived, she was like a solid piece of ice. Captain Georgiou and Sarek don't want to break her spirit, as she's worked so hard to be who she is. But they want her to understand that there is more than that, that it is okay to have these good emotions because they will help you, and guide you to make the right decisions [STDC 17].

During Burnham's seven years on the *U.S.S. Shenzhou*, she and Captain Georgiou forged a strong bond; yet Burnham's dedication to Vulcan logic still lead her to betray and attempt mutiny against her commanding officer ("The Vulcan Hello"). Convicted, demoted, and disgraced, Burnham is recruited to join *Starship Discovery*'s crew by the enigmatic Captain Gabriel Lorca ("Context Is for Kings").

After Georgiou's death, Burnham no longer has an active mentor/role model to guide her. Burnham suspects Lorca has an ulterior motive for taking her under his span of care. He quasi-confirms this after she confronts him: "I did choose you, but not for the reasons you think.... You chose to do the right thing over what was sanctioned, even at great cost to yourself. And that is the kind of thinking that wins wars. The kind of thinking I need next to me. Universal law is for lackeys" ("Context Is for Kings"). Unconvinced by that flattery, Burnham receives a measure of truth from Commander Landry: "Lorca isn't interested in what you are; he's interested in what you can do ... for him" ("The Butcher's Knife Cares Not for the Lamb's Cry"). After *Discovery*'s jump to the Mirror Universe, Burnham eventually deduces Lorca's true motivation for recruiting her upon meeting Georgiou's doppelgänger, the Terran Empress: "He needed me to get onto this ship; you wouldn't have let him on otherwise.... He needed me to get to you.... None of this was an accident. My so-called captain's not from my universe. He's from yours" ("Vaulting Ambition"). Through various plot undulations, the Burnham-Georgiou bond holds fairly steady and is crucial to resolving the Federation's conflict with the Klingons.

Phileo: Burnham and Tilly

Burnham has difficulty making friends upon her arrival on *U.S.S. Discovery*. "Though she's energetic and steadfast, she's not quite as comfortable in the Federation or even among humans as some of her fellow crew members" (Ryan). The first friend Burnham makes onboard the starship is Cadet Sylvia Tilly, who is initially eager to get to know her new roommate. Knowledge that Burnham is the infamous mutineer, however, makes Tilly reticent for them to become "besties." In fact, Tilly lies about having assigned stations in Engineering because she fears their association could pose a threat to her career aspirations. Similarly, Burnham has zero desire to befriend Tilly, which recalls Lewis' statement "Without Eros none of us would have been begotten and without Affection none of us would have been reared; but we can live and breed without Friendship. The species, biologically considered, has no need of it" (88). In an article for startrek.com, Mary Fan notes of the relationship, "Burnham, frosty and not easily impressed, initially finds the enthusiastic and awkward Tilly to be a nuisance, while Tilly is intimidated by Burnham's reputation and tries to avoid her. But they eventually warm up to each other and become trusted companions."

The tipping point occurs when Captain Lorca extends Burnham's stay aboard *U.S.S. Discovery* so she can contribute to the war effort. Surprised that she has not left the ship, Tilly confides her own aspirations to become a starship captain and requests Burnham's counsel since she was mentored by Captain Georgiou ("Context Is for Kings"). The friendship deepens as the cadet covertly helps her roommate bond with the tardigrade and also encourages her to deal with emotions.

> BURNHAM: I barely have a job here. I've never been less busy
> TILLY: Then that gives you the time and space to actually process what you're going through, emotionally.
> BURNHAM: I don't like it.
> TILLY: Really? I love feeling feelings! ["Choose Your Pain"].

Cheryl Eddy, a contributor to the *io9* website, initially hated the Tilly character but grew to see her value in precipitating a friendship with Burnham:

> [A]mid *Discovery*'s many insane and often frustrating dramatic twists, this friendship in particular helps keep things more emotionally grounded. Tilly's sole purpose isn't to make Burnham—who can be a challenging character to root for—more of a likable person, but it's definitely one of the reasons she's written the way she is, and the show is better for it.

Lest anyone think the relationship is non-reciprocal, Burnham coaches Tilly on nutrition and fitness to place her on the fast-track for captain. Plus, Burnham gives a rousing pep talk when the cadet has to impersonate her Mirror Universe counterpart: "You have the strength of an entire crew that believes in you. Fortify yourself with our faith in you. That's what a real captain does" ("Despite Yourself"). As their friendship deepens, a new possibility for companionship soon presents itself.

Eros: Burnham and Tyler

Having been raised on Vulcan, Burnham had neither the inclination nor the opportunity for a childhood crush or any kind of romance. In an interview conducted before the show's premiere, Executive Producer Aaron Harberts notes, "The fun thing about Burnham is that we actually get to watch a character sort of go through childhood and adolescence and adulthood over the span of a series, and that's really exciting" (cbs.com). Lieutenant Ash Tyler's arrival aboard *Starship Discovery* causes somewhat of a stir among the crew and presents a new first for Burnham—the opportunity for intimacy. After learning of Sarek's deception in episode six, "Lethe," she becomes overwhelmed with emotions and Tyler, whom she barely knows, serves as a sounding board.

> BURNHAM: All my life, the conflict inside me has been between logic and emotion. And now it's my emotions that are fighting. I think about [Sarek] and I want to cry. But ... I have to smile. And I feel angry. But I want to love. And I'm hurt, but there's hope. What is this?
> TYLER: Ah, it's just ... being human ["Lethe"].

Harry Mudd's scheme in "Magic to Make the Sanest Man Go Mad" accelerates the Burnham-Tyler coupling. The con man traps *Discovery* in a 30-minute time loop in order to glean the starship's secrets. However, since Lieutenant Stamets is the key to operate the spore drive, he exists outside the timeline and is aware of Mudd's manipulations.

"Stamets instructs Burnham to tell him a secret so that in future repetitions he won't have to waste time explaining himself," shares Eric Renner Brown (*ew.com*). That secret is that she's "never been in love." An episode later, Burnham and Tyler's romance progresses on an away mission to Pahvo where they share conversation and a kiss ("Si Vis Pacem, Para Bellum"), and he confides that seeing L'Rell triggered a post-traumatic stress disorder attack because the Klingon abused him physically, psychologically, and sexually. He tells Burnham, "I found peace ... right here," then kisses her tenderly ("Into the Forest I Go"). At this point during season one, many viewers were receptive to the Burnham-Tyler relationship; Casey Cipriani, writer for the website *Bustle*, is not one of them. She offers her criticism in "Why Discovery Should Drop Burnham's Romantic Subplot," which was released subsequent to the season one fall finale.

> There's a lot to explore with regard to her emotions, since Burnham was raised by Vulcans and taught to suppress her feelings. But the first emotion the show seems intent on exploring the deepest is love. [Her] exploration of love feels in line with stereotypical portrayals of female characters.

Ironically, one of the caveats Cipriani mentioned in her essay came to fruition when the truth about Ash Tyler is revealed.

The unfamiliar space where *Discovery* has jumped in the mid-season cliffhanger is the Mirror Universe, a parallel universe introduced in the original *Star Trek* series episode "Mirror, Mirror." *Entertainment Weekly*'s Eric Renner Brown opines, "the decision to revisit the Terran Empire—which [Specialist] Michael Burnham describes in 'Despite Yourself' as 'an oppressive, racist, xenophobic culture that dominates all known space—marks a bolder, more effective attempt to achieve political resonance"

("*Star Trek: Discovery* Recap"). Yet a thinly-veiled swiped at Trump-era American politics is not what the writers had in mind but carefully executed, character-driven story arcs. After being emotionally walled off most of her life, protagonist Michael Burnham risks falling in love for the first time with Ash Tyler. She knows he has "issues" resulting from being held captive by the Klingons, but he seems to be honest and forthright. Weary of posing as her Terran Empire counterpart, Burnham vents to her now-lover Tyler who reciprocates by sharing his feelings with her.

> My first year at the academy, I was terrified of open space. I could fly anything, no sweat, but I dreaded putting on that suit. Until I remembered the tether. They're mandatory the first few times a cadet goes out in an EV, and they link you back to what you know, what you love help you stay strong, even as you head out into that terrifying abyss. And that's you. You're my tether. You bring me back. You did it before we were stranded, and you're still doing it now ["The Wolf Inside"].

Then the writers drop a proverbial "truth bomb" on this romance.

An encounter with the Mirror Universe's Voq triggers suppressed memories within Tyler: he wasn't tortured by Klingons but surgically altered to look human and implanted with the *real* Ash Tyler's memories. Jordan Hoffman opines, "He's the echo of a dead Starfleet lieutenant with the submerged consciousness of the renegade Klingon Voq. So, naturally [he and Burnham] are going to fall in love!" (startrek.com). This was the caveat Cipriani mentions in her critique of the romance, and Hoffman notes its essentiality to the story and character arcs.

> Their relationship works as a reflection of where they are in their own self-discovery. Early in the season, Burnham still blames herself for Captain Georgiou's death and for triggering the Klingon War. When she begins to grow feelings for Tyler it is part of her path toward forgiving herself. But just as she begins to feel comfortable, Tyler gets the rug pulled from under him. He realizes he's not who he thinks he is, and betrays everyone who believes in him [startrek.com].

Sarek provides a measure of perspective when he learns of Tyler's betrayal and tells his foster daughter, "There is irony here, of course. The man you fell in love with was a Klingon.... There is also grace. For what greater source of peace exists than our ability to love our enemy" ("The War Without, the War Within"). Although the Burnham-Tyler romance did not continue in *Star Trek: Discovery* season two, the characters nevertheless share an intimate bond.

Agape: Burnham and Starfleet

The final love C.S. Lewis writes about in *The Four Loves* is perhaps the most difficult to examine without using religious terminology. Chapter

VI where he discusses agape is entitled "Charity," which he defines as "Divine Gift-love" (177). Stephen G. Post provides a more practical, secular definition in "The Tradition of Agape" where he calls it "altruism." He continues, "Altruistic love is an intentional affirmation of the other, grounded in biologically given emotional capacities that are elevated by worldview and imitation into the sphere of consistency and abiding loyalty" (51). Post links altruistic love to justice and distinguishes that its core definition "is not sacrifice but rather an affective, affirming participation in the being of the other" (52). In Michael Burnham's interior world, agape can be seen in her dedication to Starfleet, instilled in her during seven years of service with Captain Georgiou. The first line spoken in English during the series premiere is "We come in peace," uttered sardonically by the Klingon T'Kuvma. The line is repeated by Burnham on an away mission, "We come in peace, that's why we're here. Isn't that the whole idea of Starfleet?" to which Georgiou jocularly responds, "Hey, I taught you that" ("The Vulcan Hello").

The fact that later in this episode Burnham will momentarily abandon Starfleet's ethos is heartbreaking considering she will mutiny against and betray her mentor Georgiou. At the sentencing hearing, Burnham offers no defense for her actions.

> From my youth on Vulcan, I was raised to believe that service was my purpose. And I carried that conviction to Starfleet. I dreamed of a day when I would command my own vessel, and further the noble objectives of this great institution. That dream is over. The only ship I know in ruins. *My crew* ... gone. My captain ... my friend. I wanted to protect them from *war*. From the enemy. And now we are at war ... and I am the enemy ["Battle at the Binary Stars"].

Yet, one could argue that her journey during *Discovery*'s first season is one of redemption and rededication to Starfleet. Her concern for the health of the tardigrade, the creature that initially enabled the starship's spore drive to navigate the mycelial network, reflects the United Federation of Planets Charter "to reaffirm faith in the fundamental rights of sentient beings, in the dignity and worth of all lifeforms" ("The Void").

In the episode "Si Vis Pacem, Para Bellum," once the amorphous inhabitants of Pahvo initiate a dialogue with Saru, the away team's situation moves from one governed by Starfleet General Order One (aka the Prime Directive) to First Contact protocols. Eric Renner Brown elucidates, "As Burnham explains, now that they've revealed themselves to these sentient beings, they can't borrow or alter any Pahvan property without receiving consent—including the transmitter they wish to harness" (ew.com). Perhaps the clearest sign of Burnham's allegiance to Starfleet's principles is her revulsion to the Terran Empire in the latter episodes of season one: "It's been two days. But they're already inside my head. Every moment is a test. Can you bury your heart? Can you hide your decency? Can you continue to pretend to be one of them? Even as, little by little, it kills the person you really are?" ("The Wolf Inside"). Jordan Hoffman theorizes, "If you wanted to sum up *Discovery*'s entire first season in one scene, it's the moment where Burnham convinces Cornwell not to destroy Qo'noS" (*One Trek Mind*).

> CORNWELL: We do not have the luxury of principle.
> BURNHAM: That is all we have, Admiral! A year ago, I stood alone I believed our survival was more important than our principles. I was wrong. Do we need a mutiny today to prove who we are? ["Will You Take My Hand?"].

To use screenwriting terminology, this is the Obligatory Scene of the season one story arc (McKee 308); Burnham's convincing argument to uphold Starfleet ideals even at the risk of failure shows the most important value *Discovery*'s writers intend to express in the script, also known as the controlling idea. In the episode's dénouement, she gives a rousing speech: "We have to be torchbearers ... casting the light so we may see our path to lasting peace. We will continue exploring, discovering new worlds, new civilizations. Yes—that is the United Federation of Planets.... Yes—that is Starfleet.... Yes—that is who we are.... And who we will always be" ("Will You Take My Hand?"). Burnham's foster father Sarek presents her with Starfleet insignia; her conviction has been overturned and her rank restored.

Interpersonal Issues on Star Trek: Voyager

Interpersonal relationships comprise an area where the various *Star Trek* series have excelled for 50-plus years. From Captain Kirk's close-knit bond with Mr. Spock on the 1960s series to Lt. Cmdr. Data and Lt. Geordi La Forge's camaraderie on *The Next Generation* to Benjamin Sisko's unique bond with the Dax symbiont in hosts Curzon, Jadzia, and Ezri on *Deep Space Nine*, the writer/producers of the various *Star Trek* series clearly emphasize that exploring the final frontier is best done with friends to share the experience. *Star Trek: Voyager*, the third spinoff series, highlighted three dyadic relationships during its seven-year run on the United Paramount Network: the Janeway-Seven mentor-protégé dyad, the Paris-Kim friendship dyad, and the Paris-Torres romance dyad.

The Kathryn Janeway–Seven of Nine Mentor-Protégé Dyad

Author Paul Ruditis, in the *Star Trek: Voyager Companion*, opens his exploration of season one by synopsizing the series: "[T]he story of *Star Trek: Voyager* is the story of a makeshift family lost on the other side of the galaxy, thousands of light years from home, of a woman in command, of a combined crew of Starfleet heroes and Maquis rebels" (1). Although *Star Trek* series and movies had portrayed women in various command positions, *Voyager* was the first to be headlined by a female lead. For viewers like astrophysicist Dr. Erin Macdonald, it was about time. In the dedication to her doctoral thesis, she acknowledged the starship's fictional commanding officer by writing, "Finally, to Captain Kathryn Janeway. I cannot describe the level of inspiration she provided me right when I was on the verge of giving up." Dr. Macdonald explained further:

> Kathryn Janeway gave me the representation I needed right when I thought I wasn't capable anymore. I was able to see her going through situations more difficult than I was dealing with, all while openly dealing with recognizable issues unique to being a woman. Because we are able to see ourselves in these characters, we are given the guidance and strength to pursue careers that might otherwise be difficult, or lonely. *Star Trek* gives us the companionship we may not otherwise have in a field lacking in diversity, and shows us that we are strong, we are capable, and most importantly, we are not alone [*Women at Warp*].

Star Trek series have literally inspired generations of fans for decades; these real-world, parasocial interactions (see Chapter Five for more details) often spring forth from relationships portrayed on the series.

In Dr. Macdonald's case, Captain Janeway's key mentoring relationship on *U.S.S. Voyager* was with Seven of Nine, a character introduced in the fourth-season premiere, "Scorpion, Part II." The IMDb editors explain, "Assimilated by the Borg at the age of six, Seven of Nine joined the crew of the Voyager after her link to the Collective was severed. Seven, as she came to be known, [became] a key member of the Voyager's engineering team" ("To Boldly Go: The Women of 'Star Trek'"). Actor Kate Mulgrew, who played Kathryn Janeway told conference attendees at Star Trek Las Vegas 2018 that her character was brought to life by Seven.

> [Janeway] is given a blessing in the form of a half-human, half-Borg, very beautiful girl, who we call Seven of Nine. So, I am taught vulnerability. I am taught my limitations. I am taught how small I am, in the face of this kind of possible love. Seven of Nine is what brought Janeway to life, as a deeply human woman, I believe. And I am deeply grateful for that [TrekMovie.com].

Ruditis reflects on Seven's repatriation to humanity as "an uphill battle for Janeway and her crew, but each lesson learned and wall broken down not only serves to enhance the character, but provide commentary on the universe within and without the realm of the show" (194).

The Tom Paris–Harry Kim Friendship Dyad

Oxford Dictionaries added the word "bromance" in early 2011, defining it as "a close but non-sexual relationship between two men" (Shea). Prior to the word being officially sanctioned by Oxford, *Star Trek* viewers were well acquainted with portrayals of such friendships, especially between Captain Kirk and Mr. Spock from the original series and the first six feature films. Tom Paris and Harry Kim's "bromance" on Voyager begins in the pilot episode "Caretaker"; the former comes to the latter's rescue after Quark nearly cons the naïve junior officer into buying overpriced Lobi crystals on space station *Deep Space 9*. Actor Robert Duncan McNeill who portrayed Paris explains that art imitated life: "Garrett [Wang] and I worked the first scene of the show together, and we immediately bonded. He was a young actor, and I was a few years older. I was taking Garrett under my wing in the same way that Tom was taking Harry under his wing. A lot of the off-screen relationship translates" (Anders). Some viewers may not have realized that a friendship between an older, experienced sailor and a newbie has a real-world antecedent in the Royal Navy, as well as the United States Navy. A "Sea Daddy" is a "salty sailor [who] takes a boot-camp under his wing" (*Urban Dictionary*).

Not unlike *The Next Generation*'s Data and La Forge who often spend leisure time in holodeck adventures like Sherlock Holmes mysteries ("Elementary, Dear Data," "Ship in a Bottle"), Paris introduces Kim to Sandrínes, his favorite watering hole outside Marseilles, France ("The Cloud") and to *The Adventures of Captain Proton* holonovel ("Night"). Paul Ruditis notes: "Easily becoming a favorite escape among the cast and the fans, the Captain Proton program brings a unique look to *Star Trek* by emulating a fictional science-fiction serial circa the 1930s. It can't help but raise the question of how *Star Trek: Voyager* will be seen by viewers in the distant future" (254).

Despite their tight bond, their friendship's power dynamics are generally inequitable. To wit, Paris plays the titular Captain Proton in the holonovel while relegating Kim to a supporting role as sidekick Buster Kincaid. Though ostensibly the "beta male," Kim notably pushes back in the episode "Hunters" when nearly most of the crew is excited about receiving messages from home except Paris, who has a toxic relationship with his father. Kim snaps, "I am not you!" and walks out after Paris advises the ensign to downplay expectations. Perhaps the defining moment in their relationship appears in "The Chute" when both are wrongly convicted of terrorist activities, imprisoned by the Akritirian government, and psychologically tortured via neural implants. After their return to *Voyager*, Paris encourages a downcast Kim who laments nearly killing his comrade: "You want to know what I remember? Someone saying, 'This man is my friend; nobody touches him.' I'll remember that for a long time." Garrett Wang who played Kim reflects, "As we come to Season 3 ... Kim definitely becomes more of a calming influence on Paris and, as a result, becomes his own person instead of being under Paris's wing. Kim becomes much more of his equal" (Ruditis 251). The writers eventually "back burner" this bromance so they can focus on a new, more satisfying relationship.

The Tom Paris–B'Elanna Torres Romance Dyad

When Gene Roddenberry created *Star Trek: The Next Generation*, a new concept he incorporated was that space exploration was so demanding that some starships were equipped so families could accompany Starfleet personnel on extended missions. Yet aside from the few seasons that Beverly and Wesley Crusher were both aboard the *Enterprise*-D and the time Worf had custody of his son Alexander, family life was not consistently portrayed among the primary cast. And for a variety of reasons, romance was not in the proverbial cards for series leads, either. (See Chapter Three for details.) Thus, the writers' decision to make Tom Paris and B'Elanna Torres a couple was bold, as was allowing the relationship to progress organically across five seasons. The actors were enthused about this choice as well, according to McNeill: "Roxann and I were both excited initially when the producers decided to explore a relationship on our show and have these characters together. They both are very strong-willed people so it made for a very interesting relationship. And a very colorful relationship, for those two" (Ruditis 316).

Viewers also responded positively. In fact, Gregory Thompson commended the "fan favorite" couple for helping save the show: "A rocky courtship and realistic marriage portrayed made them the most genuine couple to come out of the show" (*ScreenRant*).

One could argue the Paris-Torres romance includes tropes typical of a romantic comedy. Though the *Star Trek: Voyager Bible* denotes that Paris "has an affection for B'Elanna, seeing in her a soul at war and reminding him of himself," she does not reciprocate. In fact, there's evidence to support that she initially regards him as immature and unworthy of her affections. In first season's "The Cloud," Torres has an unfortunate encounter with a character in the Sandríne's holodeck program and calls out Paris.

> TORRES: Paris? Did you program this guy?
> PARIS: Yeah. Why?
> TORRES: He's a pig. And so are you.

In the international best seller *The Peter Pan Syndrome*, psychologist Dan Kiley wrote about men who won't grow up (and the women who love them); Paris' back story of rebellion against authority and his bromance with Harry Kim suggests he may be "Peter Pan." Plus, Paris and Torres' personalities did not seem complementary. After all, "she was the hardworking engineer constantly concerned with the ship's operation, and he was the carefree pilot who enjoyed creating and starring in his own holonovels" (Thompson).

The turning point in their relationship occurs in season's three "Blood Fever," when Torres experiences *pon farr*-like symptoms after being attacked by Ensign Vorik. After her blood fever subsides, she and Paris have a frank discussion.

> PARIS: You're afraid that your big, scary Klingon side might have been showing. Well, I saw it up close and you know, it wasn't so terrible. In fact, I wouldn't mind seeing it again someday.
> TORRES: Careful what you wish for, Lieutenant.

Fourth season's "Day of Honor" includes playful banter…

> PARIS: Why is it we have to get beamed into space in environmental suits before I can initiate first contact procedures?
> TORRES: Why is it that if we're alone for more than thirty seconds, you start thinking about contact?
> PARIS: Oh, that is not fair.

But the episode ends with a startling confession:

> TORRES: I've been a coward about everything … everything that really matters.… I have to tell you the truth…
> PARIS: The truth about what?
> TORRES: Ah…. Ah…. I love you.

This declaration propels the relationship forward through the rest of the series.

The newly forged couple tries to keep their status secret, but Captain Janeway is nonplused by their clumsy, juvenile attempts to do so: "You are senior officers, and I expect you to maintain the standard for the rest of the crew, but this adolescent behavior makes me question my faith in you both. If you choose to pursue a relationship, that's your business. But you consider yourselves under orders to use better judgment about it ("Scientific Method").

The fifth season's "Extreme Risk" shows Torres grappling with depression after learning that her Maquis comrades have been massacred back in the Alpha Quadrant, and the final season's "Drive" shows her having doubts about the relationship while Paris becomes preoccupied with winning an inter-species space race. He ends up proposing, and they discuss name options for when they are married.

> TORRES: "B'Elanna Paris." That has a nice ring to it.
> PARIS: Thanks, but I already have a ring. Anyway, I kind of like the sound of "Tom Torres."
> TORRES: I hope you're kidding.
> PARIS: Hey.... It is the 24th century.

Despite the levity often depicted in their relationship, the revelation that Torres is pregnant in "Lineage" allows the writers to delve into several serious issues. These include her identity as a bi-racial (or more accurately, bi-species) humanoid, her relationship with her estranged father, and her contemplation of gene editing to remove Klingon DNA from the fetus *in utero*.

> PARIS: B'Elanna, I am never going to leave you.
> TORRES: You say that now but think about how hard it is to live with one Klingon. Pretty soon it'll be two.
> PARIS: Someday I hope it's three or four. I mean it, and I hope that every one of them is just like you. B'Elanna, I am not your father and you are not your mother, and our daughter is going to be perfect just the way she is.

Roxann Dawson who played Torres said this episode contained a "moment that I felt was so haunting to me" and divulged, "[I] wept when I read the episode.... It was a difficult and wonderful episode" (*50 Years of Star Trek*). Swapna Krishna calls it "a rare moment of devastation and vulnerability for her, and it makes clear that the best thing Tom Paris does in this series is be a good husband to B'Elanna" (*SyFy Wire*). *Star Trek: Voyager*'s finale "Endgame" marks two joyous moments in the characters' lives—their daughter Miral's birth and the starship's triumphant return to Earth.

Group/Organizational Issues on Star Trek: Deep Space Nine—Organizational Dissent and the Maquis

Deep Space Nine, the third *Star Trek* series, is sometimes affectionately known as the "anti–Trek show." Terry J. Erdmann describes the situation: "In 1993, the producers of *Star Trek* took a chance. They opted to break free of the established—an admittedly successful—format that had sustained the series for twenty-seven years. The new show would not take place on a giant starship [but] would be set in a frontier town located in space" (ix).

The summary of the initial draft Writers Bible's confirmed, "STAR TREK: DEEP SPACE NINE provides far more interpersonal conflict than we've seen before in the 24th century. If, as Gene Roddenberry always said, *Star Trek* is *Wagon Train* in space, think of *Deep Space Nine* as Fort Laramie on the edge of the frontier" (Reeves-Stevens 87). Aside from these format changes, the optimistic tone of classic *Star Trek* and *The Next Generation* would be supplanted with gritty realism.[1] Writer/producer Ronald D. Moore, who spent a decade in the *Star Trek* universe—five years on *The Next Generation*, plus co-writing the feature films *Generations* and *First Contact*, and five years on *Deep Space Nine*—would go on to reimagine *Battlestar Galactica* for the Sci-Fi Channel. Some aspects of the acclaimed series could be viewed as deconstructive criticism of his earlier work. This dialogue exchange between pilots Kara "Starbuck" Thrace and Lee "Apollo" Adama serves as an example:

> STARBUCK: You know the President says that we're saving humanity for a bright, shiny future on Earth. That you and I are never gonna see. We're not. Because we go out over and over again until someday, some metal motherfrakker is gonna catch us on a bad day and just blow us away.
> APOLLO: Bright, shiny futures are overrated anyway [*Battlestar Galactica* "Scar"[2]].

Noting the work history of several BSG writers, one cannot help but interpret this remark as a veiled reference to the optimism typically expressed in Gene Roddenberry's seminal space opera.

A macro-story arc that spanned three *Star Trek* series—*The Next Generation*, *Deep Space Nine*, and *Voyager*—focused on the Maquis, a group of Starfleet dissidents. "Journey's End," an episode from the first spinoff, lays the groundwork for the conflict [See Chapter 3 for a brief discussion], and establishes a Demilitarized Zone on Dorvan V, a planet that Federation colonists refuse to evacuate even though it's been returned to Cardassian control. *Voyager* co-creator Jeri Taylor explained, "So in order to avoid having some burdensome backstory and exposition in *Voyager*'s pilot, we decided we could plant the idea of the Maquis in the shows that were already on the air" (Erdmann 134). Tensions escalate in "The Maquis, Part I" when organized terrorists—who are revealed to be Starfleet renegades—intervene on the colonists' behalf. The notion itself of a group composed of Starfleet "renegades" might seem anathema to Roddenberry's idealized future, but there is historical precedent. Writer/producer Michael Piller reveals, "The Maquis was a name used for French freedom fighters during World War II" (134).

Dr. Jeffrey Kassing of Arizona State University, a leading researcher in the field of organizational dissent, notes that employees need to assess two key questions before engaging in dissent: "(1) Will dissent be perceived as adversarial or constructive? (2) And will it lead to retaliation?" (*International Encyclopedia of Communication*). In layman's terms, "count the cost." The *Deep Space Nine* writers specifically created the Maquis to establish them as dissidents/freedom fighters/renegades/terrorists, "people who are quite different, divulges Piller, "than the Starfleet human types we see all the time" (Erdmann 134). In *Anatomy of Rebellion*, Claude Emerson Welch describes a core precept of organizational dissent: "Organizations direct discontent into political objects; ideologies justify rebellious acts. Both must be coupled. Just as no rebellion can be said to be fully spontaneous—for it requires an organizational nucleus round which to crystallize—so too no rebellion can be said to be devoid of justification in its protagonists' eyes" (237). By creating Cal Hudson—an old friend of *Deep Space 9*'s commander Benjamin Sisko and science officer Dax—to serve as Starfleet's attaché to the colonies, the writers not only provide an "organizational nucleus" for the coming conflict but give two of the series leads personal stakes.

The tipping point, or "dissent trigger," is an event or circumstance "prompting the dissent" and causing the employee to "determine that speaking out about the issue is worth the risk of retaliation associated with dissent expression" (Kassing). In the case of the *Star Trek* shows, the Maquis do more than speak out to express dissent but take up arms against the Cardassians ... and if necessary, the Federation. The trigger seems to be cumulative rather than an isolated incident. The *Star Trek Encyclopedia* notes, "The Maquis grew in response to Cardassian hostilities toward these colonies and to the perception that they had been abandoned by the Federation government. Members had often been victims of violence directed toward them by the Cardassian military" (Okuda, Okuda & Mirek 287). Initially, Sisko is sympathetic to the colonists' plight.

> On Earth there is no poverty, no crime, no war. You look out the window at Starfleet Headquarters and you see paradise. Well, it's easy to be a saint in paradise. But the Maquis do not live in paradise. Out there, in the Demilitarized Zone, all problems have not been solved yet. There are no saints, just people; angry, scared, determined people who are going to do whatever it takes to survive, whether it meets with the Federation approval or not ["The Maquis, Part II"].

However, as the situation becomes more complicated, the station commander finds himself in a quandary.

Sisko must prevent war, rescue a kidnapped Cardassian leader (the loathsome Gul Dukat), and persuade Hudson to rejoin Starfleet. In a comment on *Jammer's Reviews'* critique of "The Maquis, Part I," William B provides a cogent analysis of Sisko's predicament.

> The two-parter is structured with Sisko, Hudson and Dukat as personal avatars for the overall philosophies and actions of Starfleet, the Maquis and Cardassia, with Sisko's loyalties torn between Hudson and Dukat.... [A]s the two-parter continues Sisko finds himself more and more (reluctantly) sympathetic to Dukat and his worldview and more and more disgusted and put off by Hudson's behaviour [Epsicokhan].

In addition to providing crucial back story for *Voyager*, the Maquis arc continues through *Deep Space Nine* for three more years with Sisko flummoxed by additional betrayals. In third season's "Defiant," Thomas Riker impersonates his "twin brother" Will and hijacks *U.S.S. Defiant*, the prototype warship assigned to the station, so he can fight with the Maquis. The following season in "For the Cause," Sisko learns his girlfriend, freighter captain Kasidy Yates, is smuggling for the Maquis. Their relationship survives, though, and after she serves her prison term, the couple eventually marries.

In the same episode, however, Michael Eddington, the Starfleet security officer assigned to *Deep Space 9*, defects to the Maquis. This is the betrayal that proverbially shakes Sisko to the core. Unlike Yates, Eddington swore an oath as a Starfleet officer to uphold the organization's principles. His bitter rebuke of them catches Sisko off guard.

> Open your eyes, Captain. Why is the Federation so obsessed with the Maquis? We've never harmed you. And yet we're constantly arrested and charged with terrorism.[3] Starships chase us through the Badlands and our supporters are harassed and ridiculed. Why? Because we've left the Federation, and that's the one thing you can't accept. Nobody leaves paradise. Everyone should want to be in the Federation. You know, in some ways you're even worse than the Borg. At least they tell you about their plans for assimilation. You're more insidious. You assimilate people and they don't even know it ["For the Cause"].

Executive producer Ira Behr discusses Eddington's transformation: "What if this guy who we originally conceived to be as true blue as possible suddenly realizes that there's something better out there?" (Erdmann 341). The character's disillusionment with Starfleet, thus, allowed him to abandon the organization and dedicate himself to the Maquis, who in his mind represented a higher purpose.

When Eddington returns in fifth season's "For the Uniform," his *Les Misérables* reference indicates Sisko's fixation: "All right, Javert. I'll give you what you want: Me!" *Star Trek: Deep Space Nine Companion* author Terry Erdmann embellishes, "Sisko's obsession with catching Eddington in this episode was something of a revelation, and it set the stage for the day when he would betray his principles for a greater good in 'In the Pale Moonlight'" (418). Sisko explains his antipathy to Dax.

> SISKO: He worked under me for a year and a half. I saw him almost every day. Read his reports. Had him to dinner. I even took him to a baseball game in the holosuite once. And I never saw it! It's my job to be a good judge of character, and what did I do? Not only did I not see it, I put him up for a promotion.
> DAX: He played his hand well.
> SISKO: He played me all right. And what is my excuse? Is he a Changeling? No. Is he a being with seven lifetimes of experience? No. Is he a wormhole alien? No. He's just a man, like me. And he beat me!

Eddington fully understands Sisko's enmity upon informing him of Cal Hudson's death: "You never forgave him. You can't forgive any of us. And not because we betrayed Starfleet or the Federation. But because we betrayed *you*" ("Blaze of Glory"). The Eddington/Maquis arc concludes with his death in that episode.

Audience/Artifact Relationship with Star Trek: Enterprise— *Reception Theory*

The fifth *Star Trek* series, *Enterprise*, earned the ignominious distinction of being the show that killed the franchise. As Darren Mooney notes, "Even *Star Trek: Voyager* was spared the indignity of killing an entire iteration of the franchise" (*the m0vie blog*). Part of the problem is that when the series debuted in 2001, the previous spinoffs had been on the air continuously for fourteen years. "Not only that," Mooney adds, "there had been twenty-one seasons of *Star Trek* produced in those fourteen years. It was possible that the franchise had reached (if not surpassed) the point of saturation, and that the whole thing might collapse in on itself." In their respective heydays, four versions of NBC's venerable *Law and Order* franchise aired concurrently, and CBS broadcast three *CSI: Crime Scene Investigation* series. Yet, as the Robert Frost poem states, "nothing gold can stay"; only *Special Victims Unit* remains of the *Law and Order* shows, and the *CSI*s have faded into broadcast memory.

Aware that *Star Trek* burnout was a distinct possibility, Rick Berman "begged [the studio] to let the franchise have a few years' rest," but Paramount wanted "to get another one up and going" (Altman & Gross 644). Graeme McMillan in his binge-watching guide to the series explains:

> A prequel to the original *Star Trek*, *Enterprise* let producers reset the franchise from the increasingly safe era of *The Next Generation* and *Voyager*, where technology could be relied upon to save the day and humanity had evolved past petty hatred and things that could provide easy drama. By showing the origins of Starfleet and the United Federation of Planets, the logic went, the series could delight long-time fans while also drawing in new viewers ... except that the reality proved to be almost entirely the opposite [*Wired*].

Chris Black (co-executive producer of *Enterprise* seasons one—three) adds, "We were trying to do something different. That was the whole point of setting it years before and rebooting the whole franchise" (Altman & Gross 684). One could argue that these factors helped doom *Enterprise* before its premiere.

Media theorist Stuart Hall pioneered Reception Theory, which examines how media texts are encoded and decoded. Producers encode a text with their "dominant or preferred" meaning (98); audiences can reject that meaning and replace it with their own "oppositional code" (103) or create a negotiated version that contains a mixture of those two approaches (102). Hall expounds.

> Decoding within the negotiated version contains a mixture of adaptive and oppositional elements: it acknowledges the legitimacy of the hegemonic definitions to make the grand significations (abstract), while, at a more restricted, situational (situated) level, it makes its own ground rules—it operates with exceptions to the rule [102].

Audiences' rejection of *Enterprise*, however, was not simply a matter of "television producers who find their message 'failing to get across'" (Hall 99) but one of oppositional rejection. Black reflects on the depth of audience antipathy season one.

> We would come into work on Monday and the voicemail box for the production office would be full. Overloaded. Completely full of people complaining and bitch-

ing. One guy shrieked into the voicemail, "Vulcans don't lie! Vulcans don't lie!" Just saying it over and over again [Altman & Gross 684].

Even co-creator Brannon Braga acknowledges the show's initial failings: "I felt like the first episode after the pilot was good, and then the third was good, and then there was some episode called 'Terra Nova' and it was dreadful. It was a stinker, and I thought, 'We're in trouble'" (Altman & Gross 679). McMillan summarizes, "The first two seasons of *Star Trek: Enterprise*—officially titled just *Enterprise*, the *Star Trek* didn't show up in the title until the third season—are uneven at best" (*Wired*). And the fans knew this and let the producers know, sometimes in harsh ways. Chris Black recounts a particular fan response. "We would get letters and vitriolic hate mail. Someone sent us a cardboard box where they had taken their kitchen wastepaper basket and dumped it into a box. Eggshells, coffee grounds. You know they sent us a box full of garbage. With a note that said, 'This is what you've done to *Star Trek*'" (Altman & Gross 684).

Steven Gordon describes in *Making Star Trek: Enterprise Even Better* that the series was "really the story of two different television shows. The first featured super-moral characters who could spend much of an episode talking about Malcom Reed's favorite food or writing letters to schoolchildren back home, still leaving time to solve an important ethical issue" (1). The second version of the show that Gordon references, however, did not appeal equally to all the fans.

Debuting on September 26, 2001, *Enterprise* was the first *Star Trek* series to air after the 9/11 terrorist attacks. Darren Mooney even theorizes, "The show was very much *Star Trek* for the Bush administration. There was a strong conservative and nationalist element to the plot, with Archer adamant about '*going it alone*' and fulfilling his father's dreams" (the m0vie blog). Although the pilot "Broken Bow" and the initial season one episodes were written in late spring/early summer of 2001, Mooney argues the specter of 9/11 looms large over the series:

> The thematic arc of the show's four-season run is one about coming to terms with the attacks and their impact on the popular consciousness. The first season is largely about denial, the production team trying to pretend that nothing has changed. The second season finds the show quietly stewing in the anger and confusion of the War on Terror.

"The Expanse," the season two finale, provided a "soft reboot" for the series. Graeme McMillan posits the episode "temporarily retooled the series as something more aggressive, with the *Enterprise* given bigger weapons and a new group of soldiers as they respond to a massive alien attack that killed millions by setting out to stop war at any cost possible" (*Wired*).

Although viewers perceived third season's year-long, story arc as the producers' response to 9/11, Braga disagrees: "We didn't do the Xindi arc as a 9/11 metaphor. We did it because an attack on Earth hadn't been done in awhile" (Altman & Gross 701). Yet according to Reception Theory, viewers have the right to reject the producers' preferred reading and either form an oppositional reading or a negotiated one. Thus, if Graeme McMillan, Darren Mooney, and other fan/critics decode the Xindi arc as a response to 9/11, Braga and the *Enterprise* writer/producers cannot privilege their dominant/preferred reading over the audience's. Mooney opines, "The third season was messy and raw. It was also ambitious and exciting." Furthermore, he conjectures that the Xindi storyline allowed producers to exorcise "all the worst tendencies that had taken root over the first two seasons of the show. All the xenophobia and hatred, all the paranoia and mistrust, all the anger and bloodlust." Yet even Mooney admits, "This was a premise that essentially challenged the franchise" (*the m0vie blog*). Season three has adherents like Steven Gordon who opines, "for the most part [it] was quite good (1), but most aficionados like Graeme McMillan recognize "in many important ways, it doesn't feel true to the ideals of Star Trek" (*Wired*).

David Gerrold, writer of the beloved, original series episode "The Trouble with Tribbles," objects to storylines like the Xindi arc based on their deviation from the classic formula.

> Subsequent iterations of *Star Trek* have gone much darker, much grittier, much less idealistic. And when you see the resignation, the bitterness, the critiques, the reactions of the fans, what they're reacting to is the loss of the optimism the essential optimism of the original series, and the fun of the original series has been leached out[4] [personal interview].

The two-part fourth—and final—season premiere wrapped up the controversial Xindi storyline. Then *Enterprise* focused on episodes that were prequels and/or sequels to original series and *Next Generation* episodes. New showrunner Manny Coto championed this approach. He reflects, "My idea was, let's find cool ideas that have some tie, some relevance with the original series; let's use this as a prequel. And let's have fun" (Altman & Gross 713). For many *Star Trek* fans, this is the version of *Enterprise* that the writers should have started with from the beginning and is the only season worth watching.

Summary

Examining each of the post–*Next Generation Star Trek* series through the lens of a sample communication context helps identify some of the core elements that make all the series uniquely *Star Trek*. Michael Burnham's intrapersonal growth on *Discovery* focuses on her reconnection to humanity after Sarek raised her to suppress emotions. Her journey of self-discovery fulfills *Star Trek: The Motion Picture*'s marketing tagline "The Human Adventure Is Just Beginning," one of creator Gene Roddenberry's core ethos. Another exemplar is highlighted by the interpersonal relationships portrayed on *Voyager*. The Maquis conflict depicted on *Deep Space Nine* serves as a cautionary tale for when organizational dissent goes awry and becomes a destructive force. Finally, scrutiny of *Enterprise*'s audience-artifact relationship shows the power—and potential financial consequences—of *Star Trek* fans who reject a series as unworthy of the franchise. As co-executive producer Chris Black notes, "There's nothing like the *Star Trek* people. They feel like they own the show. And if you make a choice they don't agree with or don't approve of, they get very upset" (Altman & Gross 684).

Conclusion

Twenty-seventeen marked the 30th anniversary of *Star Trek: The Next Generation*. No one knew what to expect when Paramount Pictures launched the first spinoff of its most successful franchise in 1987. On episode #202 of *Young Sheldon*, the titular character's mother epitomized audience feelings about *The Next Generation*: "When that first came on, you said a new *Star Trek* without Dr. Spock could never be good, but I've seen you watching it!" ("A Rival Prodigy and Sir Isaac Neutron"). Though that sitcom's writers have the benefit of hindsight, they accurately depict viewers' initial skepticism. Despite a shaky start creatively, *Star Trek: The Next Generation* ultimately garnered a total of 18 Emmy Awards (all in technical categories), two Hugo Awards, a Peabody Award, and an Emmy nomination for outstanding drama series in its final season. Most notable is the fact episodes averaged 20 million viewers a week in first-run syndication during its final year (Zoglin 75–76). The salient question remains: did *Star Trek: The Next Generation* merely extend the longevity of Paramount's crown jewel or did the series became a phenomenon in its own right, arguably eclipsing the popularity and influence of its progenitor?

Expanding the Universe

During the 78 years between James Tiberius Kirk's era and Jean-Luc Picard's—and the 18 years between the two series—Gene Roddenberry opened new storytelling possibilities on one hand and also limited them on the other. The Klingons became allies, albeit begrudging ones, of the Federation. Moreover, mankind had "eliminated hunger, want, the need for possessions [and had] grown out of its infancy," as Picard tells a 20th-century denizen awoken from suspended animation in the first season finale,

"The Neutral Zone." Dr. Alex Wainer, a professor of communication at Palm Beach Atlantic University, remarks: "It's pretty obvious Roddenberry was trying to conceive an extended universe that, though the same one as the original series, was actively not beholden whenever possible. Tone, characterization, and new races, planets, etc., seem to me deliberately different to escape close comparison with Kirk and company."

Josh Rubinstein, who worked in post-production on the Blu-ray restoration of *Star Trek: The Next Generation* season box sets, agreed, adding, "TNG expanded the story canvas of the *Star Trek* Universe by introducing story elements, such as Q and the Borg."[1] Wainer sees Q as a twist on an original series' adversary, "Q was Trelayne, grown up but still obnoxious. While [John] De Lancie was great in the part, I always hate it when a super being dominates our heroes—he was just the Squire of Gothos unleashed to generate similar plots." As for the Borg, they became the ultimate villains because their "Resistance is futile" philosophy was antithetical to Roddenberry's view of 24th-century mankind—epitomized by the self-actualized Jean-Luc Picard. In *American Science Fiction Film and Television*, Lincoln Geraghty explained, "The popularity of the Borg and their importance in flagging up issues relating to identity, our relationship to technology and the historical consequences of imperialism and colonialism meant that *TNG* continues to attract critical attention more than twenty years after it first aired" (80). Although another new *Star Trek: The Next Generation* race, the Ferengi, ended up not posing a true threat to Picard's *Enterprise*-D, the spinoff series *Deep Space Nine* used them to explore stories regarding the morality of capitalism run amok (Wainer).

Trek *Tech*

The original *Star Trek* dazzled audiences with technological devices like the communicator, phaser, and tricorder, as well as the transporter and warp drive. While these devices and others like them became mainstays of science fiction, variations of the first three have become commonplace in the 21st century. Cellular phones, once considered a luxury, are now a necessity. Laser pointers may not be able to stun or kill, but they can damage a person's eyes. And the variety of portable computing devices are nearly as capable as Mr. Spock's or Dr. McCoy's tricorders. IMDb reviewer Chris Brown wrote, "*The Next Generation* brought some very cool gadgets into our lives including tricorders, androids, and, of course, the most dreamed about invention the Holodeck!"

Another crucial innovation on the *Enterprise*-D was the prevalence of flat-panel computing devices, such as the bridge consoles and PADDs. Personal Digital Assistants (PDAs) and tablet computers have existed since the 1990s. But Apple's iPad, with its flat-panel touchscreen, looks like something straight out of a *Star Trek: The Next Generation* episode—the sixth season's "Relics,"[2] to be specific. Although no one can conclusively prove Jobs drew inspiration for the iPad from *TNG*'s PADD, the fact he played a clip from the 11th *Star Trek* film to demonstrate his device's capability at Apple's January 27, 2010, press event suggested there may be a causal link (Pascale). Mere days before its launch, a staff writer for the website *AppAdvice* posted the article "Steve Jobs Must be a *Star Trek* Fan—Captain Picard Has an iPad." He wrote:

> While channel surfing I saw a *Star Trek: The Next Generation* episode with James Doohan, aka Scotty. After watching a couple minutes the camera is in the captain's quarters and Captain Picard is holding a device that shares nearly the exact same form factor as an iPad. It looks like Picard rotated it to landscape maybe for a particular app that looks better in that perspective.

In addition to onscreen technological innovations, the ones behind-the-scenes were equally impressive. Paul Tonks lauded, "Like its predecessor in the 1960s, *TNG* pioneered visual effects on TV, making it an increasingly jaw-dropping show to look at." Rubinstein and others painstakingly approached their work while preparing the Blu-ray release of the series' seven seasons. The *Ain't It Cool News* informant known as Monty Cristo details their results on the restored pilot episode "Encounter at Farpoint":

> CBS/Paramount went back to the original 35mm camera negatives and re-scanned them. They re-composited the original effects shots, and everything looks absolutely astounding. Screen captures and video side-by-side comparisons can't do the difference justice. The creatures that appear toward the end of the episode are composed of the original shots re-composited at HD resolution. There is no CG enhancement, just re-scanning and re-compositing. What results is a magnificent testament to the original effects work done.

As with most science fiction, onscreen technology works best when it serves the story, such as in sixth season's "Ship in a Bottle" (#612). Writer René Echevarria used the *Enterprise-D*'s holodeck as a touchstone for a meditation on Platonic theories of ontology. When a simulation of Moriarty from a Sherlock Holmes adventure becomes self-aware, he uses his knowledge to trap Picard in a simulated holodeck, or "ship in a bottle." The captain eventually manages to outwit his adversary.

Although the immersive virtual reality depicted by the holodeck allowed for fictitious stories—such as Picard's Dixon Hill adventures, the aforementioned Sherlock Holmes mysteries ("Elementary, Dear Data" #203), mythical depictions of Robin Hood ("Qpid" #420), or the Old West ("A Fistful of Datas" #608)—too often the holodeck signified to represent the downside of *Star Trek: The Next Generation's* approach to technology. Paul Tonks explained this further:

> [W]hile technology was a useful tool in most crises, it now frequently seemed to be the cause of them too, as the show's writers continually warned about the dangers of over-reliance on technology (the Borg were the ultimate expression of this maxim). The word "technobabble" came to describe a weakness in many *TNG* scripts, which sacrificed the social and political allegories of the original and relied instead upon invented technological faults and their equally fictitious resolutions to provide drama within the *Enterprise*'s self-contained society.

Tonks conjectured that *Star Trek: The Next Generation's* "technobabble" appealed to a late 1980s audience, whose youth were the first generation to grow up with home computers and initiated the cliché of the "nerdy *Trek* fan."

The True Legacy

Perhaps the most impactful legacy of *Star Trek: The Next Generation* is its writers room, which became a training ground for some of the most prolific writers of contemporary television. This is largely because of the late Michael Piller's mentorship. His tenure as head writer began in third season when the show found its proverbial groove, creatively. Television veteran Jeri Taylor joined him the following season, serving as his "Number One." Writers Ronald D. Moore, Brannon Braga, René Echevarria, and Naren Shankar reminisced for a special feature on the season three Blu-ray. Echevarria compared Piller and Taylor to parents: "If Michael was our stern father, she was our nurturing mother. And somehow that combination worked in terms of getting the best out of us" ("*Star Trek: The Next Generation*, Inside the Writer's Room").

Under their mentorship, the "Class of TNG" helped foster careers of the following writers:

- 27 episodes—Ronald D. Moore (*Deep Space Nine, Battlestar Galactica, Outlander*)
- 20 episodes—Brannon Braga (*Voyager, Enterprise, 24*)
- 16 episodes—René Echevarria (*Deep Space Nine, Medium, Castle, Teen Wolf*)

9 episodes—Naren Shankar (*CSI: Crime Scene Investigation, Grimm, The Expanse*)

8 episodes—Hans Beimler (*Deep Space Nine, Profiler, The District*); Richard Manning (*TekWar, Farscape, When Calls the Heart*)

6 episodes—Tracy Tormé (*Sliders, Odyssey 5, Carnivàle*)

3 episodes—Hilary Bader (*The New Batman Adventures, Superman: The Animated Series, Batman Beyond*); Ira Steven Behr (*Deep Space Nine,* UPN's *The Twilight Zone, The 4400, Crash, Outlander*)

2 episodes—David Kemper (*seaQuest 2032, Farscape, Cult*); Philip LaZebnik (*Pocahontas, Mulan, The Prince of Egypt*)

In addition, writing staffs of the spinoff series *Deep Space Nine* and *Voyager* included future "superstar" television writers Bradley Thompson and David Weddle (*Battlestar Galactica, CSI: Crime Scene Investigation, Falling Skies, The Strain*) and Bryan Fuller (*Pushing Daisies, Hannibal, Star Trek: Discovery, American Gods*).

"The sky's the limit"

Star Trek: The Next Generation's success in first-run syndication paved the way for a multitude of other shows, including *Babylon 5, Hercules: The Legendary Journeys, Superboy,* and *Xena: Warrior Princess,* to name a few. None of those, however, achieved the critical or financial success of *Star Trek: The Next Generation,* which spawned four feature films. "Its success in maintaining a mainstream audience without the backing of a major network intimated that audiences wanted more series that offered weekly snapshots of distant worlds and intergalactic exploration," ascribed Lincoln Geraghty (79). Among the series' strongest assets was Sir Patrick Stewart's portrayal of Captain Picard. In the message the fallen Tasha Yar leaves for her comrades in "Skin of Evil" (#123) she tells him, "I wish I could say you've been like a father to me.... But I've never had one so I don't know what it feels like. But if there was someone in this universe I could choose to be like—someone who I would want to make proud of me—it's you. You who have the heart of an explorer and the soul of a poet." These sentiments reflect those of viewers for whom Stewart's character had become a mentor and role model. Plus, the actor's Shakespearean training and mellifluous, baritone voice helped inject the series with a gravitas its predecessor never achieved.

In the foreword to *Make It So: Leadership Lessons from Star Trek: The Next Generation*, Dr. Wess Roberts and Bill Ross wrote: "[E]pisodes from this series can also teach us valuable lessons about respect for life and acceptance of people without regard to race, gender, or culture ... one can also learn a great deal about the value of others' views and opinions, and that the unknown is not to be feared, but understood" (x).

More important, Picard's role as a father figure helped satisfy audience needs. In the introduction to the 2003 edition of the *Star Trek: The Next Generation Companion*, Larry Nemecek opined the series' appeal extended beyond its initial run. "If there was any doubt as to the cool factor of Picard and his crew, it can be seen in the post–9/11 yen for family, heroes, and old-fashioned values—even if they come via the 24th century. It's an old twist on the ongoing quest or the essence of *Star Trek*'s appeal, and one that is not likely to diminish anytime soon" (x).Those words turned out to be prophetic.

On August 4, 2018, Sir Patrick Stewart made a stunning announcement on stage at the *Star Trek* Las Vegas convention.

> During these past years, it has been humbling to hear many stories about how "The Next Generation" brought people comfort, saw them through difficult periods in their lives or how the example of Jean-Luc inspired so many to follow in his footsteps, pursuing science, exploration and leadership. I feel I'm ready to return to him for the same reason—to research and experience what comforting and reforming light he might shine on these often very dark times [Otterson].

Star Trek: Picard will stream on CBS All Access along with *Star Trek: Discovery* and other shows set in the *Star Trek* universe. Much like Arthurian folklore predicts the king's resurrection in England's greatest hour of need, *Star Trek: The Next Generation*'s Captain Picard will return to provide guidance for generations of fans yearning for an idealized future like the one Gene Roddenberry envisioned more a half-century ago. Truly, *Star Trek* is modern mythology at its best.

Appendix A
List of Star Trek: The Next Generation *Episodes*

Season One

Encounter at Farpoint (telefilm)
The Naked Now
Code of Honor
The Last Outpost
Where No One Has Gone Before
Lonely Among Us
Justice
The Battle
Hide and Q
Haven
The Big Goodbye
Datalore
Angel One
11001001
Too Short a Season
When the Bough Breaks
Home Soil
Coming of Age
Heart of Glory
The Arsenal of Freedom
Symbiosis
Skin of Evil
We'll Always Have Paris
Conspiracy
The Neutral Zone

Season Two

The Child
Where Silence Has Lease
Elementary, Dear Data
The Outrageous Okona
Loud as a Whisper
The Schizoid Man
Unnatural Selection
A Matter of Honor
The Measure of a Man
The Dauphin
Contagion
The Royale
Time Squared
The Icarus Factor
Pen Pals
Q Who
Samaritan Snare
Up the Long Ladder
Manhunt
The Emissary
Peak Performance
Shades of Gray

Appendix A

Season Three

Evolution	A Matter of Perspective
The Ensigns of Command	Yesterday's Enterprise
The Survivors	The Offspring
Who Watches the Watchers	Sins of the Father
The Bonding	Allegiance
Booby Trap	Captain's Holiday
The Enemy	Tin Man
The Price	Hollow Pursuits
The Vengeance Factor	The Most Toys
The Defector	Sarek
The Hunted	Ménage à Troi
The High Ground	Transfigurations
Déjà Q	The Best of Both Worlds

Season Four

The Best of Both Worlds II	Clues
Family	First Contact
Brothers	Galaxy's Child
Suddenly Human	Night Terrors
Remember Me	Identity Crisis
Legacy	The Nth Degree
Reunion	Qpid
Future Imperfect	The Drumhead
Final Mission	Half a Life
The Loss	The Host
Data's Day	The Mind's Eye
The Wounded	In Theory
Devil's Due	Redemption

Season Five

Redemption II	Conundrum
Darmok	Power Play
Ensign Ro	Ethics
Silicon Avatar	The Outcast
Disaster	Cause and Effect
The Game	The First Duty
Unification I	Cost of Living
Unification II	The Perfect Mate
A Matter of Time	Imaginary Friend
New Ground	I, Borg
Hero Worship	The Next Phase
Violations	The Inner Light
The Masterpiece Society	Times Arrow

List of Star Trek: The Next Generation *Episodes*

Season Six

Times Arrow II
Realm of Fear
Man of the People
Relics
Schisms
True Q
Rascals
A Fistful of Datas
The Quality of Life
Chain of Command I
Chain of Command II
Ship in a Bottle
Aquiel

Face of the Enemy
Tapestry
Birthright I
Birthright II
Starship Mine
Lessons
The Chase
Frame of Mind
Suspicions
Rightful Heir
Second Chances
Timescape
Descent

Season Seven

Descent II
Liaisons
Interface
Gambit I
Gambit II
Phantasms
Dark Page
Attached
Force of Nature
Inheritance
Parallels
The Pegasus
Homeward

Sub Rosa
Lower Decks
Thine Own Self
Masks
Eye of the Beholder
Genesis
Journey's End
Firstborn
Bloodlines
Emergence
Preemptive Strike
All Good Things... (telefilm)

The Movies

Star Trek Generations
Star Trek: First Contact
Star Trek: Insurrection
Star Trek: Nemesis

Appendix B
Research Instrument for Star Trek *Survey*

Section I

For sections I & II, please answer with a number from 1 to 5.
(1 = strongly disagree, 2 = disagree, 3 = somewhat agree,
4 = agree, 5 = strongly agree)

I watch *Star Trek* ...
1. So I won't have to be alone. (__)
2. Because it's thrilling. (__)
3. Because it relaxes me. (__)
4. So I can forget about school, work, or other things. (__)
5. Because it entertains me. (__)
6. Because it's something to do when friends come over. (__)
7. Because it makes me feel less lonely. (__)
8. Because it's exciting. (__)
9. Because it allows me to unwind. (__)
10. So I can get away from what I'm doing. (__)
11. Because it's enjoyable. (__)
12. So I can be with other members of the family or friends when they are watching. (__)
13. When there's no one else to talk to or be with. (__)
14. Because it peps me up. (__)
15. Because it's a pleasant rest. (__)
16. So I can get away from the rest of the family or others. (__)
17. Because it amuses me. (__)
18. Because I watch it with my friends. (__)

Section II
19. Wesley Crusher has learned much from Riker's influence. (__)
20. Picard's age and experience are what make him an effective commanding officer. (__)
21. Dr. Crusher has benefited from Picard's influence on Wesley. (__)

Research Instrument for Star Trek Survey

22. The friendship between LCdr. Data and LCdr. LaForge is interesting to observe. (__)
23. Without Picard's influence, Wesley would not have made it to Starfleet Academy. (__)
24. Dr. Pulaski was a more effective medical officer than Dr. Crusher. (__)
25. Picard has accepted having children on his ship. (__)
26. The relationship between Riker and Troi is a main reason I watch the show. (__)
27. Picard has helped Deanna Troi develop as a counselor. (__)
28. Data has become more "human" as the show has progressed. (__)
29. Troi's counseling has helped Picard develop as a leader. (__)
30. Ens. Ro and Lt. Yar are positive role models for young women. (__)
31. Troi, more than Picard, has helped Barclay adjust to shipboard life. (__)
32. I would like to see more episodes focusing on the friendship between Dr. Crusher and Counselor Troi. (__)
33. Under Capt. Picard's leadership, Cdr. Riker has become a highly competent first officer. (__)
34. Fatherhood has tempered Worf's aggressive tendencies. (__)
35. Riker has not grown as a leader under Picard's command. (__)
36. Guinan often serves as a surrogate mother to crew members. (__)
37. Wesley blames Picard for his father's death. (__)
38. Worf would have abandoned Starfleet if not for his friends on the *Enterprise*. (__)
39. Picard has been vital in helping Lt. Worf become a part of Starfleet. (__)
40. Wesley has become more likable as the series has progressed. (__)
41. Despite his age and experience, Data has child-like qualities. (__)
42. Picard is the father Riker really wanted. (__)
43. I would enjoy working for someone like Picard. (__)

Section III

Please circle the appropriate response.

44. I am male/female.
45. I am (1) 17 or under (2) 18–25 (3) 26–35 (4) 36–49 (5) 50 or over
46. I am (1) Caucasian (2) African American (3) Hispanic (4) Asian or (5) Other

Please answer with a number from 1 to 5.
(1 = none, 2 = a few, 3 = some, 4 = most, 5 = all)

I have seen ____ of ...

47. The original *Star Trek* episodes. (__)
48. The *Star Trek* films. (__)
49. The *Star Trek: The Next Generation* episodes. (__)
50. The *Star Trek: Deep Space Nine* episodes. (__)

Chapter Notes

Introduction

1. Ironically, an animated version of *Star Trek* would become a part of NBC's Saturday morning children's programming in 1973.
2. Paramount's enthusiasm withstanding, the space shuttle *Enterprise* (Orbiter OV-101) was built "as a test vehicle and used [solely] for landing tests in 1977. [It] was not intended for space flight" (Joels 1.9).

Chapter One

1. A term coined by R.N.B. Lockhart in "Jules Verne as Prophet," *New Statesman*, 11 Feb. 1928: 560.
2. G. K. Chesterton rightly criticized Wells for ignoring "man's proneness to evil" in formulating his utopia.
3. Such magazines included *Galaxy*, which has emphasized sociological concerns over technological details, and *The Magazine of Fantasy and Science Fiction*, which also focuses more on humanistic concerns. Both magazines set the tone for modern sci fi, which often incorporates satirical overtures to classic themes.
4. Ellison was renowned for his strong and often controversial opinions. But his assessment of *The Thing*—of which this excerpt has been considerably shortened—is thoroughly warranted.
5. Some of Roddenberry's influences included Robert A. Heinlein's "Future History" series, Arthur C. Clarke's *Profiles of the Future* (1962), and Isaac Asimov's entire body of work (Alexander 188).
6. In *Where No One Has Gone Before*, author J. M. Dillard alleges that CBS described their series as being "more 'adult'" than *Star Trek*. Anyone who has seen both shows would beg to differ.
7. In his *Star Trek* database for the Macintosh, David R. Landers gives this synopsis for "The Cage": "Captain Pike becomes part of a scientific experiment in which he must mate with Vina, the lone survivor of a crash landing on a planet."
8. Despite Asherman's assertion, CBS' *Lost in Space* also had a "lost" pilot. The network rejected producer Irwin Allen's first attempt "Nowhere to Hide" because it lacked sufficient conflict and greenlit a second pilot "The Reluctant Stowaway," which introduced the villainous Dr. Zachary Smith.
9. Years later, after Roddenberry's death, his successors would cast a woman as second-in-command on *Star Trek: Deep Space Nine* and finally a female captain on *Star Trek: Voyager*.
10. Ironically, Majel Barrett Roddenberry is the only actor who has appeared—or been heard—in all incarnations of *Star Trek* that existed before her death in 2008.
11. NBC executives thought Kelley had played so many villains that audiences would not accept him as a "good guy"; his role as a criminologist in Roddenberry's *Police Story* pilot changed their minds (Dillard 17–18).
12. Episodes with such a concern include "Balance of Terror," "Arena," "The

Devil in the Dark," "Metamorphosis," and the heavy-handed "Let That Be Your Last Battlefield."

13. Ellison had written the award-winning "City on the Edge of Forever," widely acknowledged as the original *Star Trek*'s finest episode.

14. The roster of "The Committee" was a veritable "Who's who in sci fi": Harlan Ellison, Theodore Sturgeon, Richard Matheson, A. E. Van Vogt, Robert Bloch, Lester del Ray, Phil Farmer, Frank Herbert, and Pohl Anderson.

15. Freiberger is sometimes referred to as the "man who killed *Star Trek*." Not surprisingly, many fans felt betrayed by Roddenberry's desertion. Sci-fi pioneer John Campbell wrote *Star Trek*'s creator in January 1969 asking why he abdicated his direct involvement with the show. Roddenberry replied by explaining his brinkmanship with NBC and a desire to move on from *Star Trek* to newer endeavors (Alexander 362–64).

16. His exclusion was caused by union rules concerning voice-over actors.

17. Spock was excluded for a variety of reasons, including that Leonard Nimoy was in a Broadway show at the time and was also involved in a dispute with Paramount concerning *Star Trek* merchandising.

18. Edward Gross reports that Wise was instrumental in assuring Nimoy's return ("*Star Trek II*" 57).

19. The books *Star Trek Movie Memories*, *Gene Roddenberry: The Man and the Myth Behind Star Trek*, and *Trek Creator* all include thorough discussions of these disputes.

20. Joel Engel in Roddenberry's unauthorized biography reiterates that Roddenberry's decision was based largely on the fact his ego was bruised when he was "emasculated from having the producer's role" of the film series (221).

21. Ironically, Ronald D. Moore admits in a special feature on the seventh season TNG box set that he advocated a similar approach to avoid "the oppressive weight of continuity" before J. J. Abrams received the assignment.

22. Lee J. Cronbach labeled this phenomenon as the "implicit personality theory" in his 1955 article "Processes Affecting Scores on 'Understanding of Others,' and 'Assumed Similarity.'"

23. Griffin cites the benign, "I'm not sure I understand what you're saying" as an example of a clarifying statement.

Chapter Two

1. Though Counselor Troi is also a half-breed—half-human and half-Betazoid—her dual heritage is never a primary focus in the series.

2. Altman refers to a mid-1970s science-fiction show that tried to satiate *Trek* fans but whose quality was wildly uneven. Of note is the fact that during *Space: 1999*'s second (and final) season, Fred Freiberger—the man blamed for killing classic *Trek*—was brought in to oversee the series.

3. In his defense, Ron Moore was assigned to develop the script from someone else's story, a common practice in television writing.

4. The only exception was Dr. Katherine Pulaski, TNG's second-season medical officer. Allegedly, the reason the Dr. Crusher character returned to the series the next year was because of adverse fan reaction to Pulaski's negative relationship with Data.

5. Snodgrass' script, her first for television, was nominated for a Writers Guild award.

6. "Manhunt" falls flat and the writer, Tracy Tormé, used a pseudonym to protest revisions he felt were unnecessary (Altman, EG, Sept. 1990, 38).

7. Worf later investigates rumors of his father, Mogh's survival in a Romulan P.O.W. camp in the episode "Birthright" (#616/17), but the rumors are incorrect.

8. Although alluded to in "Heart of Glory" (#120), Worf's foster parents make their first appearance in "Family" (#402) and Nikolai in "Homeward" (#713).

9. Worf's relationship with K'Ehleyr will be discussed in Chapter Five, "The Interpersonal Context." Her death was highly controversial among *Star Trek* fans, but the producers felt it was necessary to justify Worf's killing of Duras.

10. A humorous intratextual criticism of such writing appears in "The Emissary." After an argument with Worf, K'Ehleyr storms into her quarters and breaks a glass table. Troi enters and states the obvious, "You're upset." K'Ehleyr responds, "Your finely honed Betazoid sense tell you that?" to which Troi ripostes, "Well, that and the table."

11. Though David Gerrold and Gene Roddenberry had a bitter parting of ways during *Star Trek: The Next Generation*'s launch phase—which is described in both the authorized and unauthorized Roddenberry biographies—no one can deny Gerrold's valuable input during the series' inception.

12. That episode was recycled from an unused script from the ill-fated *Star Trek: Phase Two* series from the 1970s, because of the 1988 Writers Guild strike.

13. At a *Star Trek* convention, Sirtis joked to the audience that her husband asked, "Honey, when Troi loses her powers, why does she turn into Marina?" (20 Mar. 1993).

14. Nemecek notes that Worf and Riker's conflict over the "right to die" reflects Dr. Crusher's disagreement with Dr. Toby Russell (a guest character) over the use of experimental medical procedures (193).

15. A search of the TNG Episode Guide indicates that Picard is prominent in 105 episodes and Riker in 35. The last number seems insufficient when one considers that 43 episodes are about Data.

16. Jonathan Frakes took the commotion in stride: "[The writers] seemed to be more concerned about it than I was. I figured as long as there was still a bearded officer on the ship I would still have a job" (Altman 58).

17. This "experiment" is explained in Chapter Four.

18. Not coincidentally. Brannon Braga and Ron Moore's script for *Star Trek Generations* has Data, attempting to be spontaneous, push Crusher off a sailing ship into the ocean.

19. La Forge's parents do figure prominently in the seventh-season episode "Interface" (#703). However, despite Burton's sensitive portrayal of his character's difficulty in accepting his mother's apparent death, that circumstance could have been easily ascribed to any of the *Star Trek: The Next Generation* characters.

Chapter Three

1. Though a second-season episode "The Icarus Factor" (#214) centers on Cmdr. Riker's relationship with his estranged father, Kyle, that dyad never recurs in future episodes.

2. Another factor is that Dr. Crusher's character was replaced during the second season, only to return in the third year for the rest of the series' run.

3. Ronald D. Moore reveals that one of the reasons Worf's son Alexander was brought on board the *Enterprise* was to "tap into some storylines that we couldn't really get to otherwise [,] the tough warrior who has to deal with the young son, who doesn't necessarily want to follow in his father's footsteps" (telephone interview, 10 Apr. 1995).

4. Actor Wil Wheaton even complained to the producers that *he* was tired of Wesley saving the ship all the time (Drennan 28–32, 64).

5. After three years of the writers contriving to keep the character on board the starship.

6. His third guest appearance was insubstantial—a cameo in "Parallels" (#711) as the Wesley Crusher of a parallel universe.

7. A vision quest is a common initiation formerly practiced by certain tribes of Native Americans: "the Indian simply rides off into the wilderness alone, seeking his own challenges and ready to receive any divine validation of manhood that happens to be tossed his way" (Raphael 198).

8. Ron was in Naval Reserve Officer Training Corps at Cornell University, eventually realizing he had chosen a prospective military career because he thought his family expected that of him.

9. Especially since the Federation's treaty with the Cardassian Union provides crucial back story for both *Deep Space Nine* and *Voyager*.

10. La Forge did eventually receive cy-

bernetic eyes in the *Next Generation* feature films, starting with *First Contact*.

11. A reference to Geordi's own ineptitude with affairs of the heart.

12. Jeri Taylor explains, "While Gene was alive, he had apparently been in discussions with gay and lesbian groups about doing a story or including a character in the 24th century that was gay. His feeling and ours now is that it would be no big deal. You couldn't really tell a story about that, or even have a continuing character that was gay, because there would be no issue. There would be no controversy. There would be no conflict. But we did feel the issue was important enough to address, and on *Star Trek* we have both the luxury and the albatross of being able to come at stories in a completely flip-flopped way" (personal interview).

13. Soren was played by Melinda Culea, a female.

14. That episode is excluded from this analysis because Picard's life (and relationships) as "Kamin" occur in his mind as part of the Kataan probe.

15. The dissolution of the Picard-Daren relationship seems inconsistent considering *Star Trek* has previously portrayed a husband and wife in the same chain of command. However, considering that Michael Piller proposed Picard's marriage at the end of the third season—an idea rejected by Paramount executives—the resolution of "Lessons" seemed inevitable (Altman, EG, Oct. 1991, 43).

16. *Star Trek* novelist Peter David pokes fun at this trope in his novel *Q-Squared*. On its final page, Crusher repeats the phrase, and David supplies six permutations: "Jean-Luc, you're the best friend I ever had; Jean-Luc, I think it's time I moved on; Jean-Luc, it's about Wesley; Jean-Luc, I'm dying; Jean-Luc, I want to have sex with you; Jean-Luc, I love you" (434).

17. Despite Roddenberry's statement, Jonathan Frakes admits on a Blu-ray special feature, "Marina and I always played it like we were lovers. We always sat next to each other in the conference room, for instance, whenever we could" ("Relativity: The Family Saga of *Star Trek: The Next Generation* Part Two: Posterity").

18. Riker's negative reaction to his brother was foreshadowed in an earlier episode, "Up the Long Ladder" (#218). When requested to give a cell sample so the Mariposans could clone him, he responded, "One William Riker is unique, perhaps even special. But a hundred of him, a thousand of him, diminishes me in ways I can't even imagine."

19. Since then, Thomas Riker has appeared on *Star Trek: Deep Space Nine* in the third-season episode "Defiant."

20. On the *TNG* set, however, Dorn and Sirtis were close friends (Sirtis).

21. A call back to that scene occurs in one of the alternate realities of "Parallels" (#711). Worf asks Deanna to be Alexander's "so'chim" ("godmother"), which would make her his "stepsister." When she retorts that Lwaxana would then become his "stepmother," Worf reacts with a look of surprised horror: "I had not considered that possibility! [But] I am willing to take that risk." Never realizing Deanna is simply teasing him, his reaction is wonderful (Landis, *TNG Episode Guide*, computer software).

22. In one alternate reality, Worf learns the romance started soon after his near-lethal back injury in the episode "Ethics" (#516).

Chapter Four

1. Herb Wright purports that he, David Gerrold, and Rick Berman fought to put a Klingon on the bridge (Altman, EG, Oct. 1992, 84).

2. The episodes involved are "Justice" (#108), "Angel One" (#114), "Pen Pals" (#215), "Up The Long Ladder" (#218), "The Ensigns of Command" (#302), "Who Watches the Watchers" (#304), "The High Ground" (#3–12), "Legacy" (#406), and "First Contact" (#415) (Landers).

3. Guinan, Whoopi Goldberg's enigmatic bartender, appears in only 29 episodes and the film *Star Trek Generations*. She is included in this list, however, because she plays a vital role in the episode to be discussed.

4. Locutus is the name given to the cybernetically-altered Picard in "Best of

Both Worlds." David Landis opines, "Picard's use of his buried 'Locutus' persona was quite unexpected and shocking when first viewed. Even though we know it's not true, the question 'what if all the Borg isn't gone from Picard?' comes back in that moment. It was a chilling scene, perfectly played by Stewart and by Jonathan Del Arco as "Hugh" (*TNG Episode Guide*, computer software, 1994).

Chapter Five

1. Matheson also wrote "The Enemy Within" for classic *Star Trek*.
2. In order, and subdivided, those questions are as follows: *Epistemology* (1) How can we know? (2) How do we perceive the external world? (3) How are beliefs justified? *Metaphysics* (1) What is the Ultimate? (2) Does Man survive death? (3) Is Man free? (4) What is the relationship between mind and body? (5) Is reality one or many? *Axiology* (1) What is the Right? (2) Do moral duties ever conflict? (3) What is the relationship between rules and results?
3. In fact, *The Science of Star Trek* documentary substantiates the only significant *Star Trek* technology that is completely implausible is the transporter, which disassembles then reassembles physical matter across spatial distances.
4. Copleston notes, "The name *Metaphysics* simply refers to the position of the *Metaphysics* in the Aristotelian Corpus, i.e., as coming after the *Physics*." Ironically, the book is metaphysical because it "involves a higher degree of abstraction than does the *Physics*" (287).
5. Ironically, Crosby's departure was quite beneficial because it allowed the producers to realign the billets of the bridge crew, thus tightening the ensemble cast.
6. Patrick Stewart delivered this speech as part of a eulogy at Roddenberry's memorial service (Alexander 551–52).
7. The story parallels the themes of *It's a Wonderful Life*, which in turn was inspired by Dickens' *A Christmas Carol*. Mark A. Altman reports that writer Ronald D. Moore's first draft was actually entitled

"A Q Carol" ("The Making of 'Tapestry'" 56).
8. Those episodes are "Lonely Among Us" (#107), "The Battle" (#109), "The Schizoid Man" (#206), "The Best of Both Worlds" (#326/401), "The Mind's Eye" (#424), "The Game" (#506), "Conundrum" (#514), "Power Play" (#515), "Man of the People" (#603), "Descent" (#626/701), "Sub Rosa" (#714), and "Masks" (#717).
9. Although Parham and Wainer ideally hoped for 100 completed questionnaires, the 60.8 percent response rate they received was greater than 50 percent, which is considered acceptable for survey completion. Nevertheless, these results can only be applied to attendees of this particular convention, although they provide hints as to the show's broad-based appeal.
10. That question was "Riker has not grown as a leader under Picard's command." Had the researchers remembered, they would have informed their data analyst to reverse the answers for that question, which would have provided an even stronger correlation for that section.

Chapter Six

1. Hawking played poker with *Star Trek: The Next Generation*'s Data and holographic re-creations of Albert Einstein and Sir Isaac Newton in the episode "Descent, Part I)." The scientist quipped to Jonathan Frakes, "Between solving quantum physics problems, I like to sneak in the occasional TV appearance" ("Reunification").
2. For example, general admission tickets for Creation Entertainment's official *Star Trek* 2018 convention, which was held August 1–5 in Las Vegas, Nevada, cost $50 Wednesday, $55 per day Thursday and Friday, $75 Saturday, and $65 Sunday. An estimated 15,000 fans attended along with more than 100 celebrities.
3. By contrast, *The Star Trek Chronology*, *The Star Trek Encyclopedia*, and *Next Generation Technical Manual* were spearheaded by Rick Sternbach, Michael Okuda, and Denise Okuda, who were *Star Trek: The Next Generation* staff members.

4. Roddenberry includes a lengthy footnote in his novelization of *Star Trek: The Motion Picture* to dispel once and for all the K/S "*lovers* rumor" (22).

5. Alexander explains this step was necessary because of Roddenberry's increasing involvement in other projects, including the preproduction phase of *Star Trek: The Next Generation*, which started in fall 1986 (487).

6. Third-season episodes developed from spec scripts are "The Bonding," "Yesterday's Enterprise," "The Offspring," "Sins of the Father," "Tin Man," "Hollow Pursuits," and "Sarek."

Chapter Seven

1. Although similarities between the premises of J. Michael Straczynski's *Babylon 5* and *Star Trek: Deep Space Nine* cannot be easily dismissed, the two series diverged drastically as their respective story arcs unfolded. Despite suspicions that Paramount appropriated Straczynski's ideas and overlaid them into the *Star Trek* universe, there are science-fiction fans who can appreciate and acknowledge both series for their strengths and weaknesses.

2. Episode scribes David Weddle and Bradley Thompson are also *Star Trek* veterans, having served with *Deep Space Nine*'s writing staff for four years.

3. Future *Battlestar Galactica* showrunner Ronald D. Moore would return to the concept of turning protagonists into terrorists with his acclaimed "New Caprica" story arc. As the American Film Institute noted when the series was cited as a 2005 program of the year, "[W]hen at war, when does a society become that which it opposes?"

4. Gerrold attributes the darker *Star Trek* films and sequel series to *Star Wars*. He describes, "Those first few [*Star Wars*] films created such a financial asteroid hitting the Hollywood planet that everybody has been imitating *Star Wars* ever since. 'What can we blow up?' 'Who can we fight?' 'How big a villain?' And we've seen that in subsequent *Star Trek* pictures" (personal interview).

Conclusion

1. The super being Q, introduced in the series premiere "Encounter at Farpoint," recurred in several episodes of *Star Trek: The Next Generation* and later appeared on *Deep Space Nine* and *Voyager*.

2. "Relics" introduced James Doohan's beloved character Montgomery ("Scotty") Scott to Captain Picard and the *Enterprise*-D crew.

Bibliography

Aldiss, Brian W., with David Wingrove. *Trillion Year Spree: The History of Science Fiction.* New York: Atheneum, 1986. Print.
Alexander, David. *Star Trek Creator: The Authorized Biography of Gene Roddenberry.* New York: Roc, 1994. Print.
"All Good Things..." Writ. Ronald D. Moore, Brannon Braga. Dir. Winrich Kolbe. Exec. Prod. Rick Berman, Michael Piller, Jeri Taylor. *Star Trek: The Next Generation.* Paramount Television. 23 May 1994. Television.
"Allegiance." Writ. Richard Manning, Hans Beimler. Dir. Winrich Kolbe. Exec. Prod. Gene Roddenberry, Rick Berman. *Star Trek: The Next Generation.* Paramount Television. 24 Mar. 1990. Television.
Altman, Mark A. "The Acting Ensemble." *Cinefantastique* Oct. 1993: 44–5. Print.
_____. "The Board and the Art of the Pitch." *Cinefantastique* Oct. 1993: 52–5. Print.
_____. "Episode Guide." *Cinefantastique* Sept. 1990: 26–30, 32–8, 40–6, 48–51. Print.
_____. "Episode Guide." *Cinefantastique* Oct. 1991: 19, 21–2, 24, 26–30, 32, 34–6, 38, 40, 42–3, 45–6, 48, 50–1. Print.
_____. "Episode Guide." *Cinefantastique* Oct. 1992: 35, 37–8, 43, 45–6, 51, 53–4, 59, 61–2, 67, 69–70, 75–6, 78–9, 85–6, 91, 93–4, 99, 101–2. Print.
_____. "Episode Guide." *Cinefantastique* Oct. 1993: 19, 21, 29–30, 35, 37–8, 43, 45–6, 51, 53–4, 59, 61–2, 67, 69–70, 75, 77–78, 83, 85–87. Print.
_____. "The Importance of Being Data." *Cinefantastique* Sept. 1990: 36–7, 59. Print.
_____. "Jonathan Frakes: Actor/Director." *Cinefantastique* Oct. 1991: 47. Print.
_____. "The Making of 'Tapestry.'" *Cinefantastique* Oct. 1993: 56–7. Print.
_____. "The Making of 'The Best of Both Worlds.'" *Cinefantastique* Oct. 1991: 48–50, 61. Print.
_____. "The Making of 'Birthright.'" *Cinefantastique* Oct. 1993: 71–4. Print.
_____. "The Making of 'The First Duty.'" *Cinefantastique* Oct. 1992: 52–3. Print.
_____. "Marina Sirtis, Betazoid Beauty." *Cinefantastique* Oct. 1993: 64–6. Print.
_____. Personal Interview. 2 Dec. 1994.
_____. "Seventh Season Episode Guide." *Sci-Fi Universe* Aug./Sept. 1994: 30–1, 33–6, 38–9, 41–2, 44–5. Print.
_____. "These Were the Voyages..." *Sci-Fi Universe* Sept. 1994: 28–45. Print.
_____. "Will Riker, to Be or Not to Be?" *Cinefantastique* Oct. 1993: 58. Print.
Altman, Mark A., and Edward Gross. *The Fifty-Year Mission: The Next 25 Years.* New York: Thomas Dunne Books, 2016. Print.
Anders, Charlie Jane. "From Star Trek Actor to Chuck Producer: The Evolution of Robert Duncan McNeill." *io9.* Gizmodo, 22 Apr. 2010. Web. 31 Dec. 2018.
Anderson, Craig W. *Science Fiction Films of the Seventies.* Jefferson, NC: McFarland, 1985. Print.

"Angel One." Writ. Patrick Berry. Dir. Michael Rhodes. Exec. Prod. Gene Roddenberry. *Star Trek: The Next Generation*. Paramount Television. 23 Jan. 1988. Television.
"The Arsenal of Freedom." Writ. Richard Manning, Hans Beimler. Dir. Les Landau. Exec. Prod. Gene Roddenberry. *Star Trek: The Next Generation*. Paramount Television. 9 Apr. 1988. Television.
Asherman, Allan. *The Star Trek Companion*. 20th anniv. ed. New York: Pocket Books, 1986. Print.
"Attached." Writ. Nicholas Sagan. Dir. Jonathan Frakes. Exec. Prod. Rick Berman, Michael Piller, Jeri Taylor. *Star Trek: The Next Generation*. Paramount Television. 6 Nov. 1993. Television.
Aufderheide, Pat. "Earth: Love It or Leave It." *The Progressive* Oct. 1986: 35–9. Print.
"Balance of Terror." Writ. Paul Schneider. Dir. Vincent McEveety. Exec. Prod. Gene Roddenberry. *Star Trek*. NBC. WNBC, New York. 15 Dec. 1966. Television.
Banks, Jane, and Jonathan David Tankel. "Science as Fiction: Technology in Prime Time Television." *Critical Studies in Mass Communication* 7 (1990): 24–36. Print.
"Battle at the Binary Stars." Writ. Gretchen J. Berg, Aaron Harberts, Bryan Fuller. Dir. Adam Kane. *Star Trek: Discovery*. CBS All Access. 24 Sept. 2017. Television.
Behr, Ira Steven, et al. Panel Discussion. Writers Guild of America, West, Los Angeles. 30 Nov. 1994.
"The Best of Both Worlds." Writ. Michael Piller. Dir. Cliff Bole. Exec. Prod. Gene Roddenberry, Rick Berman. *Star Trek: The Next Generation*. Paramount Television. 16 June 1990. Television.
"The Best of Both Worlds, Part II." Writ. Michael Piller. Dir. Cliff Bole. Exec. Prod. Gene Roddenberry, Rick Berman. *Star Trek: The Next Generation*. Paramount Television. 22 Sept. 1990. Television.
"The Big Goodbye." Writ. Tracy Tormé. Dir. Joseph L. Scanlan. Exec. Prod. Gene Roddenberry. *Star Trek: The Next Generation*. Paramount Television. 9 Jan. 1988. Television.
Blair, Karin. "The Garden in the Machine: The Why of *Star Trek*." *Television: The Critical View*, 3d ed. Ed. Horace Newcomb. New York: Oxford University Press, 1982. 181–97. Print.
_____. "Sex and *Star Trek*." *Science-Fiction Studies* 10 (1983): 292–7. Print.
"Blaze of Glory." Writ. Robert Hewitt Wolfe, Ira Steven Behr. Dir. Kim Friedman. Exec. Prod. Rick Berman, Ira Steven Behr. *Star Trek: Deep Space Nine*. Paramount Television. 12 May 1997. Television.
Bloch, Robert. "Imagination and Modern Social Criticism." *The Science Fiction Novel: Imagination and Social Criticism*. Chicago: Advent Publishers, 1959. 97–121. Print.
"Blood Fever." Writ. Lisa Klink. Dir. Andrew Robinson. Exec. Prod. Rick Berman, Jeri Taylor. *Star Trek: Voyager*. UPN. New York, WWOR. 5 Feb. 1997. Television.
Bloom, Melanie M. "Sex Differences in Ethical Systems: A Useful Framework for Interpreting Communication Research." *Communication Quarterly* 38 (1990): 244–54. Print.
"The Bonding." Writ. Ronald D. Moore. Dir. Winrich Kolbe. Exec. Prod. Gene Roddenberry, Rick Berman. *Star Trek: The Next Generation*. Paramount Television. 21 Oct. 1989. Television.
Bonds, Martha J. "Harve Bennett: Beauty and Death in the World of *Star Trek*." *Starlog* Mar. 1983: 46–49. Print.
Bradbury, Ray. "The Ardent Blasphemers" (Introduction). *20,000 Leagues Under the Sea*. By Jules Verne. Toronto: Bantam Books, 1962. 1–12. Print.
Brandt, Andrea. "4 Ways That Childhood Trauma Impacts Adults." *Psychology Today*. Psychology Today, 1 June 2017. Web. 26 Dec. 2018.
"Bread and Circuses." Writ. Gene Roddenberry, Gene L. Coon. Dir. Ralph Senensky. Exec Prod. Gene Roddenberry. *Star Trek*. NBC. WNBC, New York. 15 Mar. 1968. Television.

"Broken Bow." Writ. Rick Berman, Brannon Braga. Dir. James L. Conway. Exec Prod. Rick Berman, Brannon Braga. UPN. New York, WWOR. 26 Sept. 2001. Television.
Brooks, Cleanth, John Thibaut Purser, and Robert Penn Warren. "General Introduction." *An Approach to Literature*, 5th ed. New York: Appleton-Century-Crofts, 1964. 1–8. Print.
Brown, Chris. Rev. of *Star Trek: The Next Generation*. IMDb.com. Internet Movie Database, 9 Sepy. 2000. Web. 13 Apr. 2012.
Brown, Eric Renner. "*Star Trek: Discovery* Recap: 'Despite Yourself.'" ew.com. Entertainment Weekly, 8 Jan. 2018. Web. 26 Dec. 2018.
____. "*Star Trek: Discovery* Recap: 'Magic to Make the Sanest Man Go Mad.'" ew.com. Entertainment Weekly, 29 Oct. 2017. Web. 26 Dec. 2018.
____. "*Star Trek: Discovery* Recap: 'Si Vis Pacem, Para Bellum.'" eww.com. Entertainment Weekly, 5 Nov. 2017. Web. 26 Dec. 2018.
"The Butcher's Knife Cares Not for the Lamb's Cry." Writ. Jesse Alexander, Aron Eli Coleite. Dir. Olatunde Osunsanmi. *Star Trek: Discovery*. CBS All Access. 8 Oct. 2017. Television.
Canary, Robert H. "Science Fiction as Fictive History." *Many Futures, Many Worlds*. Ed. Thomas D. Clareson. Kent, OH: Kent State University Press, 1977. 164–81. Print.
"Captain's Holiday." Writ. Ira Steven Behr. Dir. Chip Chalmers. Exec. Prod. Gene Roddenberry, Rick Berman. *Star Trek: The Next Generation*. Paramount Television. 31 Mar. 1990. Television.
"Caretaker." Writ. Rick Berman, Michael Piller, Jeri Taylor. Dir. Winrich Kolbe. Exec. Prod. Rick Berman, Michael Piller, Jeri Taylor. UPN. New York, WWOR. 16 Jan. 1995. Television.
Casey, Kathryn. "The Woman (and the Man) Who Saved *Star Trek*." *TV Guide—Star Trek: Four Generations* Spring 1995: 30–2. Print.
Cassidy, Marsha F. "*Dallas* Refigured." *Television Studies: Textual Analysis*. Ed. Gary Burns and Robert J. Thompson. New York: Praeger, 1989. 41–56. Print.
Cawelti, John G. "The Concept of Artistic Matrices." *Communication Research* 5 (1978): 283–304. Print.
CBS Television Studios. "Bryan Fuller Set as Co-Creator and Showrunner of the New 'Star Trek' Television Series Alongside Executive Producer Alex Kurtzman." CBS Television Studios, 2016. Print.
Chavers, Alexander. "Why Deep Space Nine Is the Best Star Trek Series (in 5 Reasons)." Medium.com. Medium, 25 June 2017 Web. 12 Jan. 2019.
"The Child." Writ. Jaron Summers, Jon Povill, Maurice Hurley. Dir. Rob Bowman. Exec. Prod. Gene Roddenberry. *Star Trek: The Next Generation*. Paramount Television. 19 Nov. 1988. Television.
"Choose Your Pain." Writ. Kemp Powers, Gretchen J. Berg, Aaron Harberts. Dir. Lee Rose. *Star Trek: Discovery*. CBS All Access. 15 Oct. 2017. Television.
Christenson, Gary D. Rev. of *Star Trek: The Next Generation*. *TV Guide* 23 July 1988: 39. Print.
"The Chute." Writ. Kenneth Biller, Clayvon C. Harris. Dir. Les Landau. Exec. Prod. Rick Berman, Jeri Taylor. *Star Trek: Voyager*. UPN. New York, WWOR. Television.
Cipriani, Casey. "Why 'Star Trek: Discovery' Should Drop Burnham's Romantic Subplot." bustle.com. Bustle, 15 Nov. 2017. Web. 28 Dec. 2018.
Clareson, Thomas D. "Lost Lands, Lost Races: A Pagan Princess of Their Very Own." *Many Futures, Many Worlds*. Ed. Thomas D. Clareson. Kent, OH: Kent State University Press, 1977. 117–39. Print.
Clarke, Arthur C. "Reflections on the Final Frontier." *TV Guide—Star Trek: Four Generations* Spring 1995: 6–8, 11. Print.
"The Cloud." Writ. Tom Szollosi, Michael Piller, Brannon Braga. Dir. David Livingston. Exec. Prod. Rick Berman, Michael Piller, Jeri Taylor. *Star Trek: Voyager*. UPN. New York, WWOR. 13 Feb. 1995. Television.

"Coming of Age." Writ. Sandy Fries. Dir. Mike Vejar. Exec. Prod. Gene Roddenberry. *Star Trek: The Next Generation.* Paramount Television. 12 Mar. 1988. Television.
"Context Is for Kings." Writ. Gretchen J. Berg, Aaron Harberts, Craig Sweeny, Bryan Fuller. Dir. Akiva Goldsman. *Star Trek: Discovery.* CBS All Access. 1 Oct. 2017. Television.
"Conundrum." Writ. Barry M. Schkolnick, Joe Menosky. Dir. Les Landau. Exec. Prod. Gene Roddenberry, Rick Berman, Michael Piller. *Star Trek: The Next Generation.* Paramount Television. 15 Feb. 1992. Television.
Copleston, Frederick, S. J. "Absolute Idealism." *A History of Philosophy* VIII (1967). New York: Image Books, 1985. 219–236. Print.
____. "The Metaphysics of Aristotle." *A History of Philosophy* I (1946). New York: Image Books, 1985. 287–319. Print.
"Cost of Living." Writ. Peter Allan Fields. Dir. Winrich Kolbe. Exec Prod. Gene Roddenberry, Rick Berman, Michael Piller. *Star Trek: The Next Generation.* Paramount Television. 18 Apr. 1992. Television.
Coste, Didier. *Narrative as Communication.* Minneapolis: University of Minnesota Press, 1989. Print.
Cranny-Francis, Anne. "Sexuality and Sex-Role Stereotyping in *Star Trek.*" *Science-Fiction Studies* 12 (1985): 274–84. Print.
Cristo, Monty. Rev. of *Star Trek: The Next Generation—The Next Level. aintitcool*.com. Ain't It Cool News, 30 Jan. 2012 Web. 9 Apr. 2012.
Crumley, Bruce, Julie K. L. Dam, and Emily Mitchell. "Voyage to the Dark Center of the Future." Rev. of *Paris in the 20th Century.* By Jules Verne. *Time* 3 Oct. 1994: 59. Print.
"Dark Page." Writ. Hilary J. Bader. Dir. Les Landau. Exec. Prod. Rick Berman, Michael Piller, Jeri Taylor. *Star Trek: The Next Generation.* Paramount Television. 30 Oct. 1993. Television.
"Darmok." Writ. Joe Menosky. Dir. Winrich Kolbe. Exec. Prod. Gene Roddenberry, Rick Berman, Michael Piller. *Star Trek: The Next Generation.* Paramount Television. 28 Sepy. 1991. Television.
David, Peter. *Q-Squared.* New York: Pocket Books, 1994. Print.
Davis, Erik. "True Believers." *TV Guide—Star Trek: Four Generations* Spring 1995: 78–82. Print.
"Day of Honor." Writ. Jeri Taylor. Dir. Jesús Salvador Treviño. Exec. Prod. Rick Berman, Jeri Taylor. *Star Trek: Voyager.* UPN. New York, WWOR. 17 Sept. 1997. Television.
"The Defector." Writ. Ronald D. Moore. Dir. Robert Scheerer. Exec. Prod. Gene Roddenberry and Rick Berman. *Star Trek: The Next Generation.* Paramount Television. 30 Dec. 1989. Television.
"Defiant." Writ. Ronald D. Moore. Dir. Cliff Bole. Exec. Prod. Rick Berman and Michael Piller. *Star Trek: Deep Space Nine.* Paramount Television. 21 Nov. 1994. Television.
Delany, Samuel R. "Critical Methods: Speculative Fiction." *Many Futures, Many Worlds.* Ed. Thomas D. Clareson. Kent, OH: Kent State University Press, 1977. 278–91. Print.
"Descent (Part I)." Writ. Ronald D. Moore. Dir. Alexander Singer. Exec. Prod. Rick Berman, Michael Piller. *Star Trek: The Next Generation.* Paramount Television. 19 June 1993. Television.
"Despite Yourself." Writ. Sean Cochran. Dir. Jonathan Frakes. *Star Trek: Discovery.* CBS All Access. 7 Jan. 2018. Television.
Dillard, J. M. *Star Trek: "Where No One Has Gone Before."* New York: Pocket Books, 1994. Print.
Dorn, Michael. Address. Beach Trek III, Virginia Beach. 10 Feb. 1990.
Drennan, Kathryn M. "Wil Wheaton: Acting Ensign." *Starlog* Apr. 1988: 28–32, 64. Print.
"Drive." Writ. Michael Taylor. Dir. Winrich Kolbe. Exec. Prod. Rick Berman, Brannon Braga. *Star Trek: Voyager.* UPN. New York, WWOR. 18 Oct. 2000. Television.

"The Drumhead." Writ. Jeri Taylor. Dir. Jonathan Frakes. Exec. Prod. Gene Roddenberry, Rick Berman. *Star Trek: The Next Generation.* Paramount Television. 27 Apr. 1991. Television.
Ebert, Roger. *Roger Ebert's Movie Home Companion.* Kansas City: Andrews and McMeel, 1992. Print.
Elderkin, Beth. "*Deep Space Nine* Is *Star Trek*'s Best World, Because It's the Real World" *io9.* Gizmodo, 7 Sept. 2016. Web. 12 Jan. 2019.
"Elementary, Dear Data." Writ. Brian Alan Lane. Dir. Rob Bowman. Exec. Prod. Gene Roddenberry. *Star Trek: The Next Generation.* Paramount Television. 3 Dec. 1988. Television.
Ellington, Jane Elizabeth, and Joseph W. Critelli. "Analysis of a Modern Myth: The *Star Trek* Series." *Extrapolation* 24 (1983): 241–50. Print.
Ellison, Harlan. "Ellison Reviews *Trek*." *Starlog* Apr. 1980: 60–3. Print.
_____. "Lurching Down Memory Lane with It, Them, the Thing, Godzilla, HAL 9000 ... That Whole Crowd: An Overview of the Science Fiction Cinema." *Omni's Screen Flights/Screen Fantasies.* Ed. Danny Peary. New York: Doubleday/Dolphin, 1984. 1–14. Print.
Ellul, Jacques. *The Technological Society.* New York: Random House, 1964. Print.
"Emissary." Writ. Michael Piller. Dir. David Carson. Exec. Prod. Rick Berman, Michael Piller. *Star Trek: Deep Space Nine.* 2 Jan. 1993. Television.
"Encounter at Farpoint." Writ. D.C. Fontana, Gene Roddenberry. Dir. Corey Allen. Exec. Prod. Gene Roddenberry. *Star Trek: The Next Generation.* Paramount Television. 26 Sept. 1987. Television.
"Endgame." Writ. Kenneth Biller, Robert Doherty, Rick Berman, Brannon Braga. Dir. Allan Kroeker. *Star Trek: Voyager.* UPN. New York, WWOR. 23 May 2001. Television.
Engel, Joel. *Gene Roddenberry: The Man and the Myth Behind Star Trek.* New York: Hyperion, 1994. Print.
"The Ensigns of Command." Writ. Melinda M. Snodgrass. Dir. Cliff Bole. Exec. Prod. Gene Roddenberry, Rick Berman. *Star Trek: The Next Generation.* Paramount Television. 30 Sept. 1989. Television.
Epsicokhan, Jamahl. *Jammer's Reviews.com.* Jammer's Reviews. Web. 31 Dec. 2018.
Erdmann, Terry, with Paula M. Block. *Star Trek: Deep Space Nine Companion.* New York: Pocket Books, 2000. Print.
"Ethics." Writ. Ronald D. Moore. Dir. Chip Chalmers. Exec. Prod. Gene Roddenberry, Rick Berman, Michael Piller. *Star Trek: The Next Generation.* Paramount Television. 29 Feb. 1992. Television.
"The Expanse." Writ. Rick Berman, Brannon Braga. Dir. Allan Kroeker. Exec Prod. Rick Berman, Brannon Braga. UPN. New York, WWOR. 21 May 2003. Television.
"Extreme Risk." Writ. Kenneth Biller. Dir. Cliff Bole. Exec. Prod. Rick Berman, Brannon Braga. *Star Trek: Voyager.* UPN. New York, WWOR. 28 Oct. 1998. Television.
"Eye of the Beholder." Writ. René Echevarria, Brannon Braga. Dir. Cliff Bole. Exec. Prod. Rick Berman, Michael Piller, Jeri Taylor. *Star Trek: The Next Generation.* Paramount Television. 26 Feb. 1994. Television.
"Family." Writ. Ronald D. Moore. Dir. Les Landau. Exec. Prod. Gene Roddenberry, Rick Berman. *Star Trek: The Next Generation.* Paramount Television. 29 Sept. 1990. Television.
Fan, Mary. "Trek's Fabulous Female Friendships." startrek.com. CBS Entertainment, 24 Oct. 2018. Web. 27 Dec. 2018.
Farrand, Phil. *The Nitpicker's Guide for Next Generation Trekkers.* New York: Dell, 1993. Print.
50 Years of Star Trek. Writ. Joe Braswell. Dir. Ian Roumain. Exec. Prod. Mark A. Altman, Joe Braswell, Brian Volk-Weiss. History Channel. 14 Aug. 2016. Television.
"Final Mission." Writ. Kasey Arnold-Ince, Jeri Taylor. Dir. Corey Allen. Exec. Prod. Gene

Roddenberry, Rick Berman. *Star Trek: The Next Generation*. Paramount Television. 17 Nov. 1990. Television.
"The First Duty." Writ. Ronald D. Moore, Naren Shankar. Dir. Paul Lynch. Exec. Prod. Gene Roddenberry, Rick Berman, Michael Piller. *Star Trek: The Next Generation*. Paramount Television. 28 Mar. 1992. Television.
"First Officer Michael Burnham Is a Woman of Two Worlds on Star Trek: Discovery." cbs.com. CBS, 19 Sept. 2017. Web. 11 Dec. 2018.
"Firstborn." Writ. René Echevarria. Dir. Jonathan West. Exec. Prod. Rick Berman, Michael Piller, Jeri Taylor. *Star Trek: The Next Generation*. Paramount Television. 23 Apr. 1994. Television.
Fisher, B. Aubrey. *Small Group Decision Making: Communication and the Group Process*. New York: McGraw-Hill, 1974. Print.
"A Fistful of Datas." Writ. Robert Hewitt Wolfe, Brannon Braga. Dir. Patrick Stewart. Exec. Prod. Rick Berman, Michael Piller. *Star Trek: The Next Generation*. Paramount Television. 7 Nov. 1992. Television.
Foote, Stephanie. "We Have Met the Alien and It Is Us." *The Humanist* Mar./Apr. 1992: 21–24, 33. Print.
"For the Cause." Writ. Ronald D. Moore, Mark Gehred-O'Connell. Dir. James L. Conway. Exec Prod. Rick Berman, Ira Steven Behr. *Star Trek: Deep Space Nine*. Paramount Television. 6 May 1996. Television.
"For the Uniform." Writ. Peter Allan Fields. Dir. Victor Lobl. Exec Prod. Rick Berman, Ira Steven Behr. *Star Trek: Deep Space Nine*. Paramount Television. 3 Feb. 1997. Television.
"Force of Nature." Writ. Naren Shankar. Dir. Robert Lederman. Exec. Prod. Rick Berman, Michael Piller, and Jeri Taylor. *Star Trek: The Next Generation*. Paramount Television. 13 Nov. 1993. Television.
Foss, Sonja K. *Rhetorical Criticism: Exploration & Practice*. Prospect Heights, IL: Waveland Press, 1989. Print.
Frazetti, Daryl G. "Star Trek and the Culture of Fandom." startrek.com. CBS Entertainment, 26 Apr. 2011. Web. 21 Sept. 2018.
Fredericks, S. C. "Revivals of Ancient Mythologies in Current Science Fiction and Fantasy." *Many Futures, Many Worlds*. Ed. Thomas D. Clareson. Kent, OH: Kent State University Press, 1977. 50–65. Print.
Geisler, Norman L., and Paul D. Feinberg. *Introduction to Philosophy*. Grand Rapids: Baker Book House, 1980. Print.
Gene Roddenberry: Star Trek and Beyond. Writ. Ruben Norte. Prod. Ruben Norte. Exec. Prod. Robb Weller, Gary H. Grossman. Los Angeles: The A&E Television Networks, 1994. Television.
Geraghty, Lincoln. *American Science Fiction Film and Television*. New York: Berg, 2009. Print.
Gerrold, David. "Generations: The Next Phase." *Starlog* May 1987: 14–15. Print.
_____. Personal Interview. 7 Jan. 2019.
_____. "Spockalypse Now." *Starlog* Apr. 1980: 24, 70. Print.
_____. "The *Star Trek* Experience." *Starlog* Nov. 1982: 40–43. Print.
_____. "*Star Trek* Report: February 21, 1987." *Starlog* June 1987: 20–21. Print.
_____. *The World of Star Trek*. 50th anniv. ed. San Diego: Comicmix, 2016. Print.
Gianetti, Louis. *Understanding Movies*. 5th ed. Englewood Cliffs, NJ: Prentice Hall, 1990. Print.
Gilligan, Carol. *In a Different Voice: Psychological Theory and Women's Development*. Cambridge: Harvard University Press, 1982. Print.
Goldberg, Lesley. "'Star Trek: Discovery' Renewed for Season 2 on CBS All Access." hollywoodreporter.com. The Hollywood Reporter, 23 Oct. 2017. Web. 23 Oct. 2017.
Gordon, Steven. *Making Star Trek: Enterprise Even Better (Analysis, Second Edition)*. Petulant Pomeranian Press, 2017. Print.

Greenberg, Harvey R. "In Search of Spock: A Psychoanalytic Inquiry." *Journal of Popular Film and Television* 12 (1984): 53–65. Print.
Grenz, Stanley J., and Roger E. Olson. *20th-Century Theology.* Downers Grove, IL: InterVarsity Press, 1992. Print.
Griffin, Em. *A First Look at Communication Theory.* New York: McGraw-Hill, 1991. Print.
Gross, Edward. "Character Touches." *Starlog* Oct. 1990: 38–45, 87. Print.
_____. "Matters of Honor." *Starlog* Mar. 1990: 29–33, 64. Print.
_____. "*Star Trek II: The Lost Generation.*" *Starlog* Nov. 1988: 45–8, 57. Print.
"Half a Life." Writ. Peter Allan Fields. Dir. Les Landau. Exec. Prod. Gene Roddenberry, Michael Piller. *Star Trek: The Next Generation.* Paramount Television. 4 May 1991. Television.
Hall, Stuart. "Encoding, Decoding." *The Cultural Studies Reader.* Ed. Simon During. New York: Routledge, 1993. 90–103. Print.
Harding, Christopher, ed. *Wingspan: Inside the Men's Movement.* New York: St. Martin's Press, 1992. Print.
Hark, Ina Rae. "*Star Trek* and Television's Moral Universe." *Extrapolation* 20 (1979): 20–37. Print.
"Haven." Writ. Tracy Tormé. Dir. Richard Compton. Exec. Prod. Gene Roddenberry. *Star Trek: The Next Generation.* Paramount Television. 28 Nov. 1987. Television.
"Heart of Glory." Writ. Maurice Hurley. Dir. Rob Bowman. Exec. Prod. Gene Roddenberry. *Star Trek: The Next Generation.* Paramount Television. 19 Mar. 1988. Television.
Heinlein, Robert A. "Science Fiction: Its Nature, Faults and Virtues." *The Science Fiction Novel: Imagination and Social Criticism.* Chicago: Advent, 1959. 14–48. Print.
"Hero Worship." Writ. Joe Menosky. Dir. Patrick Stewart. Exec. Prod. Gene Roddenberry, Rick Berman, Michael Piller. *Star Trek: The Next Generation.* Paramount Television. 25 Jan. 1992. Television.
"The High Ground." Writ. Melinda M. Snodgrass. Dir. Gabrielle Beaumont. Exec. Prod. Gene Roddenberry, Rick Berman. *Star Trek: The Next Generation.* Paramount Television. 27 Jan. 1990. Television.
Hoffman, Jordan. "ONE TREK MIND: Discovery's Top 7 Relationships." startrek.com. CBS Entertainment, 16 Feb. Web. 27 Dec. 2018.
"Hollow Pursuits." Writ. Sally Caves. Dir. Cliff Bole. Exec. Prod. Gene Roddenberry, Rick Berman. *Star Trek: The Next Generation.* Paramount Television. 28 Apr. 1990. Television.
Holloway, Daniel, and Joe Otterson. "'Star Trek: Deep Space Nine' at 25: Through the Wormhole With the Cast and Creators." *variety.com.* Variety, 3 Jan. 2018. Web. 3 Jan. 2018.
Horton, Donald, and R. Richard Wohl. "Mass Communication and Para-Social Interaction: Observation on Intimacy at a Distance." *Inter-Media*, 3d ed. Ed. Gary Gumpert and Robert Cathcart. New York: Oxford University Press, 1986. Print.
"The Host." Writ. Michael Horvat. Dir. Marvin V. Rush. Exec. Prod. Gene Roddenberry, Rick Berman. *Star Trek: The Next Generation.* Paramount Television. 11 May 1991. Television.
Howell, Elizabeth. "*Star Trek: Discovery* Shows Logic at Its Prettiest and Ugliest in Episode 6." space.com. Future plc, 23 Oct. 2017. Web. 12 Dec. 2018. Web.
"The Hunted." Writ. Robin Bernheim. Dir. Cliff Bole. Exec. Prod. Gene Roddenberry, Rick Berman. *Star Trek: The Next Generation.* Paramount Television. 6 Jan. 1990. Television.
"Hunters." Writ. Jeri Taylor. Dir. David Livingston. Exec. Prod. Rick Berman, Jeri Taylor. *Star Trek: Voyager.* UPN. New York, WWOR. 11 Feb. 1998. Television.
"I, Borg." Writ. René Echevarria. Dir. Robert Lederman. Exec. Prod. Gene Roddenberry, Rick Berman, Michael Piller. *Star Trek: The Next Generation.* Paramount Television. 23 May 1992. Television.
"The Icarus Factor." Writ. David Assael, Robert L. McCullough. Dir. Robert Iscove. Exec.

Prod. Gene Roddenberry. *Star Trek: The Next Generation.* Paramount Television. 22 Apr. 1989. Television.
Illich, Ivan. *Tools for Conviviality.* New York: Harper & Row, 1973. Print.
IMDb Editors. "To Boldly Go: The Women of 'Star Trek.'" IMDb.com. Internet Movie Database, 24 Oct. 2017. Web. 31 Dec. 2018.
"In the Hands of the Prophets." Writ. Robert Hewitt Wolfe. Dir. David Livingston. Exec Prod. *Star Trek: Deep Space Nine.* Paramount Television. 20 June 1993. Television.
"In Theory." Writ. Ronald D. Moore, Joe Menosky. Dir. Patrick Stewart. Exec. Prod. Gene Roddenberry, Rick Berman. *Star Trek: The Next Generation.* Paramount Television. 1 June 1991. Television.
"The Inner Light." Writ. Morgan Gendel, Peter Allan Fields. Dir. Peter Lauritson. Exec. Prod. Gene Roddenberry, Rick Berman, Michael Piller. *Star Trek: The Next Generation.* Paramount Television. 6 June 1992. Television.
"Interface." Writ. Joe Menosky. Dir. Robert Wiemer. Exec. Prod. Rick Berman, Michael Piller, Jeri Taylor. *Star Trek: The Next Generation.* Paramount Television. 2 Oct. 1993. Television.
"Into the Forest I Go." Writ. Bo Yeon Kim, Erika Lippoldt. Dir. Chris Byrne. *Star Trek: Discovery.* CBS All Access. 12 Nov. 2017. Television.
Isrig, Matt. "*Star Trek: The Next Generation*'s Place in Gene's Universe." *Star Trek: The Official Fan Club Magazine* June/July 1994: 45. Print.
Jenkins, Henry, III. "*Star Trek* Rerun, Reread, Rewritten: Fan Writing as Textual Poaching." *Critical Studies in Mass Communication* 5 (1988): 85–107. Print.
Joels, Kerry Mark, Gregory P. Kennedy, and David Larkin. *The Space Shuttle Operator's Manual.* New York: Ballantine Books, 1982. Print.
Johnson, Diane. Introduction. *Frankenstein.* By Mary Shelley. 1818. New York: Bantam Books, 1981. vii-xix. Print.
"Journey's End." Writ. Ronald D. Moore. Dir. Corey Allen. Exec. Prod. Rick Berman, Michael Piller, Jeri Taylor. *Star Trek: The Next Generation.* Paramount Television. 26 Mar. 1994. Television.
Kagle, Steven. "Science Fiction as Simulation Game." *Many Futures, Many Worlds.* Ed. Thomas D. Clareson. Kent, OH: Kent State University Press, 1977. 224–36. Print.
Kaku, Michio. *Hyperspace.* New York: Oxford University Press, 1994. Print.
Kassing, Jefffrey W. "Dissent." *International Encyclopedia of Communication.* Ed. Craig R. Scott. Hoboken: John Wiley & Sons, 2017. Print.
Kenny, Anthony. "Descartes to Kant." *The Oxford History of Western Philosophy.* Ed. Anthony Kenny. New York: Oxford University Press, 1994. 107–92. Print.
Khemorex Klinzhai (Klingon Fan Clubs and Groups). Home page. *khemorex-klinzhai.de.* Web. 28 Sept. 2018.
Kiley, Dan. *The Peter Pan Syndrome: Men Who Have Never Grown Up.* New York: Avon Books, 1983. Print.
King, J. Norman. "Theology, SF, and Man's Future Orientation." *Many Futures, Many Worlds.* Ed. Thomas D. Clareson. Kent, OH: Kent State University Press, 1977. 237–59. Print.
Klingon Assault Group FAQs. Home page. *khemorex-klinzhai.de.* Web. 28 Sept. 2018.
Krishna, Swapna. "A Star Trek: Voyager Episode Guide for B'elanna Torres." SyFyWire.com. SyFy, 10 Nov. 2017. Web. 31 Dec. 2018.
Kutzera, Dale. "Episode Guide." *Cinefantastique* Oct. 1992: 47–50, 54, 56, 59–60, 62, 66, 68, 72, 76, 79–80, 82, 87, 89–90, 92–93. Print.
Landis, David R. *Star Trek: The Next Generation Episode Guide.* Ver. 2.1. Computer software. Oak Mountain Software, 1994.
Le Guin, Ursula K. "My Appointment with the *Enterprise*: An Appreciation." *TV Guide* 14 May 1994: 31–2. Print.
Lee, John. *At My Father's Wedding: Reclaiming Our True Masculinity.* New York: Bantam Books, 1991. Print.

"Legacy." Writ. Joe Menosky. Dir. Robert Scheerer. Exec. Prod. Gene Roddenberry, Rick Berman. *Star Trek: The Next Generation*. Paramount Television. 27 Oct. 1990. Television.

Lemay, John. Personal Interview. 10 Oct. 2018.

"Lessons." Writ. Ronald Wilkerson, Jean Louise Matthias. Dir. Robert Wiemer. Exec. Prod. Rick Berman, Michael Piller. *Star Trek: The Next Generation*. Paramount Television. 3 Apr. 1993. Television.

"Let That Be Your Last Battlefield." Writ. Oliver Crawford, Lee Cronin. Prod. Gene Roddenberry. Dir. Jud Taylor. *Star Trek*. NBC. WNBC, New York. 19 Jan. 1969. Television.

"Lethe." *Star Trek: Discovery*. Writ. Joe Menosky, Ted Sullivan. Dir. Douglas Aarniokoski. *Star Trek: Discovery*. CBS All Access. 22 Oct. 2017. Television.

Lewis, C. S. *The Four Loves*. San Diego: Harcourt Brace Jovanovich, 1960. Print.

_____. "On Science Fiction." *Of Other Worlds: Essays & Stories*. Ed. Walter Hooper. New York: Harcourt Brace Jovanovich, 1966. 59–73. Print.

Liao, Shannon. "We Can Do Better Than the Bechdel Test." *The Verge.com*. The Verge, 22 Dec. 2017. Web. 11 Jan. 2019.

Lichtenberg, Jacqueline, Sondra Marshak, and Joan Winston. *Star Trek Lives*. New York: Bantam Books, 1975. Print.

"Lineage." Writ. James Kahn. Dir. Peter Lauritson. Exec. Prod. Rick Berman, Brannon Braga. *Star Trek: Voyager*. UPN. New York, WWOR. 24 Jan. 2001. Television.

Littlejohn, Stephen W. *Theories of Human Communication*. 4th ed. Belmont, CA: Wadsworth, 1992. Print.

Logan, Michael. "Trek Troika." *TV Guide—Star Trek: Four Generations* Spring 1995: 12–7. Print.

"The Loss." Writ. Hilary J. Bader, Alan J. Adler, Vanessa Greene. Dir. Chip Chalmers. Exec. Prod. Gene Roddenberry, Rick Berman. *Star Trek: The Next Generation*. Paramount Television. 29 Dec 1990. Television.

"Lower Decks." Writ. Rene Echevarria, Ronald Wilkerson, Jean Louise Matthias. Dir. Gabrielle Beaumont. Exec. Prod. Rick Berman, Michael Piller, Jeri Taylor. *Star Trek: The Next Generation*. Paramount Television. 5 Feb. 1994. Television.

Lynch, Lawrence. *Jules Verne*. New York: Twayne, 1992. Print.

Macdonald, Erin. "Finding Female STEM Mentors in Star Trek." womenatwarp.com. Women at Warp: A Roddenberry Star Trek Podcast, 11 Oct. 2017. Web. 31 Dec. 2018.

Machanic, Mindy. "Filmmaker's Visions of Tomorrow." *The Futurist* Nov./Dec. 1986: 24–7. Print.

Maddox, David, and Kevin Miller. Personal Interview. 9 Jan. 2019.

"Magic to Make the Sanest Man Go Mad." Writ. Aron Eli Coleite, Jesse Alexander. Dir. David M. Barrett. *Star Trek: Discovery*. CBS All Access. 29 Oct. 2017. Television.

"Man of the People." Writ. Frank Abatemarco. Dir. Winrich Kolbe. Exec. Prod. Rick Berman, Michael Piller. *Star Trek: The Next Generation*. Paramount Television. 3 Oct. 1992. Television.

Mancini, Marc. "The Future Isn't What It Used to Be." *Film Comment* May-June 1985: 11–15. Print.

"Manhunt." Writ. Terry Devereaux. Dir. Rob Bowman. Exec. Prod. Gene Roddenberry. *Star Trek: The Next Generation*. Paramount Television. 17 June 1989. Television.

"The Maquis, Part I." Writ. James Crocker, Rick Berman, Michael Piller, Jeri Taylor. Dir. David Livingston. Exec. Prod. Rick Berman, Michael Piller. *Star Trek: Deep Space Nine*. Paramount Television. 24 Apr. 1994. Television.

"The Maquis, Part II." Writ. Ira Steven Behr, Rick Berman, Michael Piller, Jeri Taylor. Dir. Corey Allen. Exec. Prod. Rick Berman, Michael Piller. *Star Trek: Deep Space Nine*. Paramount Television. 1 May 1994. Television.

Marin, Rick. "Comparing the Captains: Kirk vs. Picard." *TV Guide* 31 Aug. 1991: 4–6. Print.

Matheson, Richard. Telephone Interview. 9 Mar. 1995.
McConnell, Frank. "'Live Long and Prosper': The 'Trek' Goes On." *Commonweal* 118 (1991): 652, 654. Print.
McKee, Robert. *Story: Substance, Structure, Style and the Principles of Screenwriting.* New York: ReganBooks, 1997. Print.
McMillan, Graeme. "Wired Binge-Watching Guide: Star Trek: Enterprise." Wired.com. Wired, 29 July 2015. Web. 6 Jan. 2019.
Mead, George H. Mead. *Mind, Self, & Society: From the Standpoint of a Social Behaviorist.* Ed. Charles W. Morris. Chicago: University of Chicago Press, 1934. Print.
"The Measure of a Man." Writ. Melinda M. Snodgrass. Dir. Robert Scheerer. Exec. Prod. Gene Roddenberry. *Star Trek: The Next Generation.* Paramount Television. 11 Feb. 1989. Television.
Medeiros, Mike. "The Spirit of Trek—The Klingon Phenomenon." priorityonepodcast.com. Priority One: A Roddenberry Star Trek Podcast. Web. 28 Sept. 2018.
"Ménage à Troi." Writ. Fred Bronson, Susan Sackett. Dir. Robert Legato. Exec. Prod. Gene Roddenberry, Rick Berman. *Star Trek: The Next Generation.* Paramount Television. 26 May 1990. Television.
Mendelson, Scott. "Paramount Has Canceled 'Star Trek 4,' and Disney's 'Star Wars' Is to Blame." Forbes.com. Forbes, 10 Jan. 2019. Web. 10 Jan. 2019.
"Mirror, Mirror." Writ. Jerome Bixby. Dir. Marc Daniels. Exec. Prod. Gene Roddenberry. *Star Trek.* NBC. WNBC, New York. 6 Oct. 1967. Television.
Mooney, Darren. "*Star Trek: Enterprise* Reviews." them0vieblog. The Movie Bl0g, 9 Sept. 2016. Web. 6 Jan. 2019.
Moore, Ronald D. Telephone Interview. 10 Apr. 1995.
"The Most Toys." Writ. Shari Goodhartz. Dir. Timothy Bond. Exec. Prod. Gene Roddenberry, Rick Berman. *Star Trek: The Next Generation.* Paramount Television. 5 May 1990. Television.
Naisbitt, John. *Megatrends: Ten New Directions Transforming Our Lives.* New York: Warner Books, 1982. Print.
"The Naked Now." Writ. J. Michael Bingham. Dir. Paul Lynch. Exec. Prod. Gene Roddenberry. *Star Trek: The Next Generation.* Paramount Television. 3 Oct. 1987. Television.
Nemecek, Larry. *Star Trek: The Next Generation Companion.* Rev. ed. New York: Pocket Books, 2003. Print.
"The Neutral Zone." Writ. Maurice Hurley. Dir. James L. Conway. Exec. Prod. Gene Roddenberry. *Star Trek: The Next Generation.* Paramount Television. 14 May 1988. Television.
"The Next Phase." Writ. Ronald D. Moore. Dir David Carson. Exec. Prod. Gene Roddenberry, Rick Berman, Michael Piller. *Star Trek: The Next Generation.* Paramount Television. 30 May 1992. Television.
"Night." Writ. Brannon Braga, Joe Menosky. Dir. David Livingston. Exec. Prod. Rick Berman, Brannon Braga. *Star Trek: Voyager.* UPN. New York, WWOR. 14 Oct. 1998. Television.
"The Offspring." Writ. René Echevarria. Dir. Jonathan Frakes. Exec. Prod. Gene Roddenberry, Rick Berman. *Star Trek: The Next Generation.* Paramount Television. 10 Mar. 1990. Television.
Okuda, Michael, Denise Okuda, and Debbie Mirek. *The Star Trek Encyclopedia: A Reference Guide for the Future.* Rev. ed. New York: Pocket Books, 1997. Print.
O'Quinn, Kerry. "Miracle Worker?" *Starlog* Nov. 1987: 6. Print.
Osherson, Samuel. *Finding Our Fathers: The Unfinished Business of Manhood.* New York: The Free Press, 1992. Print.
Otterson, Joe. "Patrick Stewart to Return as Capt. Picard in New 'Star Trek' Series for CBS All Access." Variety.com. Variety, 4 Aug. 2018 Web. 4 Aug. 2018.
"The Outcast." Writ. Jeri Taylor. Dir. Robert Scheerer. Exec. Prod. Gene Roddenberry,

Rick Berman, Michael Piller. *Star Trek: The Next Generation*. Paramount Television. 14 Mar. 1992. Television.
"The Outrageous Okona." Writ. Burton Armus, Les Menchen, Lance Dickson, David Landsberg. Dir. Robert Becker. Exec. Prod. Gene Roddenberry. *Star Trek: The Next Generation*. Paramount Television. 10 Dec. 1988. Television.
Paglia, Camille. "Dear Mr. Data, You Made Me Love You." *TV Guide—Star Trek: Four Generations* Spring 1995: 46–7. Print.
"Parallels." Writ. Brannon Braga. Dir. Robert Wiemer. Exec. Prod. Rick Berman, Michael Piller, Jeri Taylor. *Star Trek: The Next Generation*. Paramount Television. 27 Nov. 1993. Television.
Parham, Thom, and Alex Wainer. "Marketed Mentorship: The Cultural Phenomenon of *Star Trek*." Film and American Culture, Virginia Humanities Conference, Williamsburg. 2 Apr. 1993.
Pascale, Anthony. "Steve Jobs Uses Star Trek to Introduce iPad." TrekMovie.com. Trek Movie, 27 Jan. 2010. Web. 14 Apr. 2012.
Pike, Christopher. "The Enduring Appeal of *Star Trek*." *Moving Up* Dec. 1987: 32–4. Print.
"Plato's Stepchildren." Writ. Meyer Dolinsky. Dir. David Alexander. Exec. Prod. Fred Freiberger. *Star Trek*. NBC. WNBC, New York. 22 Nov. 1968. Television.
Post, Stephen G., et al. *Altruism and Altruistic Love: Science, Philosophy, and Religion in Dialogue*. New York: Oxford University Press, 2002. Print.
"Power Play." Writ. Rene Balcer, Herbert J. Wright, Brannon Braga. Dir. David Livingston. Exec. Prod. Gene Roddenberry, Rick Berman, Michael Piller. *Star Trek: The Next Generation*. Paramount Television. 22 Feb. 1992. Television.
"The Price." Writ. Hannah Louise Shearer. Dir. Robert Scheerer. Exec. Prod. Gene Roddenberry, Rick Berman. *Star Trek: The Next Generation*. Paramount Television. 11 Nov. 1989. Television.
Proto-Swim-Jetman. UrbanDictionary.com. UrbanDictionary, 11 Feb. Web. 31 Dec. 2018.
"Qpid." Writ. Ira Steven Behr. Dir. Cliff Bole. Exec. Prod. Gene Roddenberry, Rick Berman. *Star Trek: The Next Generation*. Paramount Television. 20 Apr. 1991. Television.
"Redemption." Writ. Ronald D. Moore. Dir. Cliff Bole. Exec. Prod. Gene Roddenberry, Rick Berman. *Star Trek: The Next Generation*. Paramount Television. 15 June 1991. Television.
"Redemption II." Writ. Ronald D. Moore. Dir. David Carson. Exec. Prod. Gene Roddenberry, Rick Berman, Michael Piller. *Star Trek: The Next Generation*. Paramount Television. 21 Sept. 1991. Television.
Reeves-Stevens, Judith, and Garfield. *The Making of Star Trek: Deep Space Nine*. New York: Pocket Books, 1994. Print.
"Relativity: The Family Saga of *Star Trek: The Next Generation* Part Two: Posterity." *Star Trek: The Next Generation*, Season Four. Dir. Roger Lay, Jr. Writ./Prod. Roger Lay, Jr., Robert Meyer Burnett. CBS Home Entertainment, 2013. Blu-ray.
"Relics." Writ. Ronald D. Moore. Dir. Alexander Singer. Exec. Prod. Rick Berman, Michael Piller. *Star Trek: The Next Generation*. Paramount Television. 10 Oct. 1992. Television.
"Remember Me." Writ. Lee Sheldon. Dir. Cliff Bole. Exec. Prod. Gene Roddenberry and Rick Berman. *Star Trek: The Next Generation*. Paramount Television. 20 Oct. 1990. Television.
"Reunification: 25 Years After *Star Trek: The Next Generation*." *Star Trek: The Next Generation* Season Two. Dir. Roger Lay, Jr. Writ. Roger Lay, Jr., Robert Meyer Burnett. Prod. Roger Lay, Jr., Robert Meyer Burnett. CBS Home Entertainment, 2012. Blu-ray.
"Rightful Heir." Writ. Ronald D. Moore, James E. Brooks. Dir. Winrich Kolbe. Exec Prod. Rick Berman, Michael Piller. *Star Trek: The Next Generation*. Paramount Television. 15 May 1993. Television.

"A Rival Prodigy and Sir Isaac Neutron." Writ. Damir Konjicija, Dario Konjicija, Tara Hernandez, Chuck Lorre, Steven Molaro, David Bickel. Dir. Mark Cendrowski. Young Sheldon. CBS. WCBS, New York. 27 Sept. 2018. Television.

Roberts, Wess, and Bill Ross. *Make It So: Leadership Lessons from Star Trek: The Next Generation*. New York: Pocket Books, 1996. Print.

Roddenberry, Gene. *Star Trek: The Motion Picture*. New York: Pocket Books, 1979. Print.

_____. Foreword. *Star Trek: The New Voyages*. Ed. Sondra Marshak and Myrna Culbreath. New York: Bantam Books, 1976. Print.

_____. *Star Trek: The Next Generation Writers/Directors Guide*. 2d ed. Los Angeles: Paramount Pictures, 1988. Print.

_____. *Star Trek: The Next Generation Writers/Directors Guide*. Los Angeles: Paramount Pictures, 1987. Print.

Roth, Dany. "Star Trek TNG: Guinan's 5 Most Quintessential Moments." SyFywire.com. SyFy, 27 Sept. 2017 Web. 11 Jan. 2019.

Roush, Matt. "An Enterprise with Big Shoes to Fill." *USA Today* 4 Jan. 1993: D1–2. Print.

Rubin, Rebecca B., and Michael P. McHugh. "Development of Parasocial Relationships." *Journal of Broadcasting & Electronic Media* 31 (1987): 279–92. Print.

Rubinstein, Josh. Personal Interview. 17 Mar. 2012.

Ruditis, Paul. *Star Trek: Voyager Companion*. New York: Pocket Books, 2003. Print.

Ryan, Maureen. "TV Review: 'Star Trek: Discovery' on CBS and CBS All Access." Variety.com. Variety, 24 Sept. 2017 Web. 29 Dec. 2018.

"Samaritan Snare." Writ. Robert L. McCullough. Dir. Les Landau. Exec. Prod. Gene Roddenberry. *Star Trek: The Next Generation*. Paramount Television. 13 May 1989. Television.

"Scar." Writ. David Weddle, Bradley Thompson. Dir. Michael Nankin. Exec. Prod. Ronald D. Moore, David Eick. *Battlestar Galactica*. Sci-Fi Channel. 3 Feb. 2006. Television.

Schatz, Thomas. "*St. Elsewhere* and the Evolution of the Ensemble Series." *Television: The Critical View*. Ed. Horace Newcomb. 4th ed. New York: Oxford University Press, 1987. 85–100. Print.

Schmidt, Stanley. "The Science in Science Fiction." *Many Futures, Many Worlds*. Ed. Thomas D. Clareson. Kent, OH: Kent State University Press, 1977. 27–49. Print.

"Science Fiction, Star Trek and Meeting Mr. Spock." WebofStories.com. Web of Stories. Web. 30 Aug. 2018.

The Science of Star Trek. Prod. Barry Stoner. Exec. Prod. Bill Kurtis. Kurtis Productions Ltd., WTTW/Chicago. A&E Television Networks. 18 Jan. 1995. Television.

"Scientific Method." Writ. Lisa Klink, Sherry Klein, Harry "Doc" Kloor. Dir. David Livingston. Exec. Prod. Rick Berman, Jeri Taylor. Star Trek: Voyager. UPN. New York, WWOR. 29 Oct. 1997. Television.

"Scorpion, Part II." Writ. Brannon Braga, Joe Menosky. Dir. Winrich Kolbe. Exec. Prod. Rick Berman, Jeri Taylor. *Star Trek: Voyager*. UPN. WWOR, New York. 3 Sept. 1997. Television.

"Second Chances." Writ. René Echevarria. Dir. LeVar Burton. Exec. Prod. Rick Berman, Michael Piller. *Star Trek: The Next Generation*. Paramount Television. 22 May 1993. Television.

Selly, April. "'I Have Been, and Ever Shall Be, Your Friend': *Star Trek, The Deerslayer* and the American Romance." *The Journal of Popular Culture* 20 (1986): 89–104. Print.

Shatner, William, with Chris Kreski. *Star Trek Memories*. New York: HarperCollins, 1993. Print.

_____. *Star Trek Movie Memories*. New York: HarperCollins, 1994. Print.

Shea, Ammon. "Wake Up and Smell ODO's Latest Additions!" blog.oxforddictionaries.com. Oxford Dictionaries, 24 Feb. 2011. Web. 31 Dec. 2018.

"Ship in a Bottle." Writ. René Echevarria. Dir. Alexander Singer. Exec. Prod. Rick, and Michael Piller. *Star Trek: The Next Generation*. Paramount Television. 23 Jan. 1993. Television.

"Si Vis Pacem, Para Bellum." Writ. Kirsten Beyer. Dir. John Scott. *Star Trek: Discovery.* CBS All Access. 5 Nov. 2017. Television.
"Silicon Avatar." Writ. Jeri Taylor. Dir. Cliff Bole. Exec. Prod. Gene Roddenberry, Rick Berman, Michael Piller. *Star Trek: The Next Generation.* Paramount Television. 12 Oct. 1991. Television.
Simpson, Janice C. "*Star Trek*: The Next Frontier." *Time* 28 Dec. 1992: 63. Print.
"Sins of the Father." Writ. Ronald D. Moore, W. Reed Moran. Dir. Les Landau. Exec. Prod. Gene Roddenberry, Rick Berman. *Star Trek: The Next Generation.* Paramount Television. 17 Mar. 1990. Television.
Sirtis, Marina. Address. Trekon, Virginia Beach. 20 Mar. 1993.
"Skin of Evil." Writ. Joseph Stefano, Hannah Louise Shearer. Dir. Joseph L. Scanlan. Exec. Prod. Gene Roddenberry. *Star Trek: The Next Generation.* Paramount Television. 23 Apr. 1988. Television.
"The Sky's the Limit: The Eclipse of *Star Trek: The Next Generation* Part One: Umbra." *Star Trek: The Next Generation* Season Seven. Dir. Roger Lay, Jr. Writ./Prod. Roger Lay, Jr., Robert Meyer Burnett. CBS Home Entertainment, 2014. Blu-ray.
Smith, David C. *H. G. Wells: Desperately Mortal.* New Haven: Yale University Press, 1986. Print.
Smyth, Steve. "What Would Happen to the Star Trek Storyline If Spock Successfully Underwent Kohlinar Instead of Being Interrupted?" Quora.com. Quora, 10 Feb. 2018. Web. 24 Dec. 2018.
Soper, Taylor. "Q&A: Star Trek's Data on Autism, Space Travel, and the Link Between Humanity and Technology." GeekWire.com. GeekWire, 30 May 2013. Web. 30 Aug. 2018.
Spelling, Ian. "Leader of the Next Generation." *Starlog* Dec. 1991: 39–43, 65. Print.
_____. "Voyage of Discovery: It's Been a Long Road." *Star Trek: Discovery the Official Collector's Edition.* Ed. Christopher Cooper. London: Titan, 2017. 6–9. Print.
Star Trek: Discovery the Official Companion. Ed. Nick Jones. London: Titan, 2018. Print.
Star Trek: First Contact. Writ. Brannon Braga, Ronald D. Moore. Dir. Jonathan Frakes. Prod. Rick Berman. Paramount Pictures, 1996. Film.
Star Trek: The Motion Picture. Writ. Harold Livingston. Dir. Robert Wise. Prod. Gene Roddenberry. Los Angeles: Paramount Pictures, 1979. Film.
Star Trek: Nemesis. Writ. John Logan, Rick Berman, Brent Spiner. Dir. Stuart Baird. Prod. Rick Berman. Paramount Pictures, 2002. Film.
"*Star Trek: The Next Generation*, Inside the Writers Room." *Star Trek: The Next Generation* Season Three. Dir. Roger Lay, Jr. Writ./Prod. Roger Lay, Jr., Robert Meyer Burnett. CBS Home Entertainment, 2013. Blu-ray.
Star Trek II: The Wrath of Khan. Writ. Jack B. Sowards. Dir. Nicholas Meyer. Prod. Harve Bennett. Paramount Pictures, 1982. Film.
"Starship Mine." Writ. Morgan Gendel. Dir. Cliff Bole. Exec. Prod. Rick Berman, Michael Piller. *Star Trek: The Next Generation.* Paramount Television. 27 Mar. 1993. Television.
"Steve Jobs Must Be a Star Trek Fan—Captain Picard Has an iPad." AppAdvice.com. AppAdvice, 1 Apr. 2010. Web. 14 Apr. 2012.
"Sub Rosa." Writ. Brannon Braga. Dir. Jonathan Frakes. Exec. Prod. Rick Berman, Michael Piller, Jeri Taylor. *Star Trek: The Next Generation.* Paramount Television. 29 Jan. 1994. Television.
Suber, Howard. Liner Notes. *2001: A Space Odyssey.* Writ. Stanley Kubrick, Arthur C. Clarke. Dir. Stanley Kubrick. Prod. Stanley Kubrick. Los Angeles: Metro-Goldwyn-Mayer, 1968. The Voyager Company, CC1160L, 1988. Laserdisc.
"Suddenly Human." Writ. John Whelpley, Jeri Taylor. Dir. Gabrielle Beaumont. Exec. Prod. Gene Roddenberry, Rick Berman. *Star Trek: The Next Generation.* Paramount Television. 13 Oct. 1990. Television.
"Symbiosis." Writ. Robert Lewin, Richard Manning, Hans Beimler. Dir. Win Phelps. Exec.

Prod. Gene Roddenberry. *Star Trek: The Next Generation.* Paramount Television. 16 Apr. 1988. Television.
Szalay, Jeff. "Gene Roddenberry: The Years Between, the Years Ahead." *Starlog* Oct. 1981: 36, 40–42, 60. Print.
"Tapestry." Writ. Ronald D. Moore. Dir. Les Landau. Exec. Prod. Rick Berman, Michael Piller. *Star Trek: The Next Generation.* Paramount Television. 13 Feb. 1993. Television.
Taylor, Jeri. Personal Interview. 9 Mar. 1995.
Thompson, Keith, ed. *To Be a Man: In Search of the Deep Masculine.* Los Angeles: Jeremy P. Tarcher, 1991. Print.
"Time's Arrow." Writ. Joe Menosky, Michael Piller. Dir. Les Landau. Exec. Prod. Gene Roddenberry, Rick Berman, Michael Piller. *Star Trek: The Next Generation.* Paramount Television. 13 June 1992. Television.
"Time's Arrow, Part II." Writ. Jeri Taylor, Joe Menosky. Dir. Les Landau. Exec. Prod. Rick Berman, Michael Piller. *Star Trek: The Next Generation.* Paramount Television. 19 Sep. 1992. Television.
Tonks, Paul. Rev. of *Star Trek: The Next Generation: The Complete Series.* Amazon.com. Amazon, 2 Oct. 2007 Web. 9 Apr. 2012.
Trimble, Bjo. "Ideas About Ideas." *Starlog* Nov. 1980: 21, 61. Print.
_____. "My Part in the Second *Star Trek* Film." *Starlog* June 1982: 46–7. Print.
_____. *Star Trek Concordance.* New York: Ballantine Books, 1976. Print.
Tulloch, John. *Television Drama: Agency, Audience and Myth.* London: Routledge, 1990. Print.
"TV Market List." *The Journal* Apr. 1995: 50–1. Print.
"TV Programs of the Year 2005." AFI.com. American Film Institute, 4 Feb. 2006. Web. 31 Dec. 2018.
"Unification I." Writ. Jeri Taylor. Dir. Les Landau. Exec. Prod. Gene Roddenberry, Rick Berman, Michael Piller. *Star Trek: The Next Generation.* Paramount Television. 2 Nov. 1991. Television.
"Unification II." Writ. Michael Piller. Dir. Cliff Bole. Exec. Prod. Gene Roddenberry, Rick Berman, Michael Piller. *Star Trek: The Next Generation.* Paramount Television. 9 Nov. 1991. Television.
"Up the Long Ladder." Writ. Melinda M. Snodgrass. Dir. Winrich Kolbe. Exec. Prod. Gene Roddenberry. *Star Trek: The Next Generation.* Paramount Television. 20 May 1989. Television.
"Vaulting Ambition." Writ. Jordon Narvino. Dir. Hanelle M. Culpepper. *Star Trek: Discovery.* CBS All Access. 21 Jan. 2018. Television.
Verne, Jules. *From the Earth to the Moon.* 1865. New York: Scholastic Book Services, 1972. Print.
"Violations." Writ. Pamela Gray, Jeri Taylor. Dir. Robert Wiemer. Exec. Prod. Gene Roddenberry, Rick Berman, Michael Piller. *Star Trek: The Next Generation.* Paramount Television. 1 Feb. 1992. Television.
"The Void." Writ. Raf Green, James Kahn, Kenneth Biller. Dir. Michael Vejar. Exec Prod. Rick Berman, Brannon Braga. *Star Trek: Voyager.* UPN. WWOR, New York. 14 Feb. 2001. Television.
"The Vulcan Hello." Writ. Bryan Fuller, Akiva Goldsman, Alex Kurtzman. Dir. David Semel. *Star Trek: Discovery.* CBS All Access. 24 Sept. 2017. Television.
Wainer, Alex. Personal Interview. 9 Apr. 2012.
Walsh, Michael. "The Torch Has Passed Off-Camera, Too." *Time* 28 Nov. 1994: 76–7. Print.
"The War Without, the War Within." Writ. Lisa Randolph. Dir. David Solomon. *Star Trek: Discovery.* CBS All Access. 4 Feb. 2018. Television.
Warrick, Patricia. "The Man-Machine Intelligence Relationship." *Many Futures, Many Worlds.* Ed. Thomas D. Clareson. Kent, OH: Kent State University Press, 1977. 182–223. Print.

"WATCH: Creative Arts Emmy Award Video Honoring Trek." StarTrek.com. CBS Entertainment, 16 Sept. 2018. Web. 18 Sep. 2018.
Weick, Karl E. *The Social Psychology of Organizing.* Reading: Addison-Wesley, 1969. Print.
Welch, Claude Emerson. *Anatomy of Rebellion.* Albany: State University of New York Press, 1980. Print.
Werts, Diane. "The Bold and the Beautiful." *TV Guide—Star Trek: Four Generations* Spring 1995: 22–5. Print.
"Where No Fan Has Gone Before..." *Previews* May 1995: 279. Print.
"Where No One Has Gone Before." Writ. Diane Duane, Michael Reeves. Dir. Rob Bowman. Exec. Prod. Gene Roddenberry. *Star Trek: The Next Generation.* Paramount Television. 24 Oct. 1987. Television.
"Where Silence Has Lease." Writ. Jack B. Sowards. Dir. Winrich Kolbe. Exec Prod. Gene Roddenberry. *Star Trek: The Next Generation.* Paramount Television. 26 Nov. 1988. Television.
Whitfield, Stephen E., and Gene Roddenberry. *The Making of Star Trek.* New York: Ballantine Books, 1969. Print.
"Who Watches the Watchers." Writ. Richard Manning, Hans Beimler. Dir. Robert Wiemer. Exec. Prod. Gene Roddenberry, Rick Berman. *Star Trek: The Next Generation.* Paramount Television. 14 Oct. 1989. Television.
Wilkerson, Ronald, and Jean Louise Matthias. Personal Interview. 1 Dec. 1994.
Wilmot, William W. *Dyadic Communication.* 2d ed. Reading: Addison-Wesley, 1979. Print.
"The Wolf Inside." Writ. Lisa Randolph. Dir. T.J. Scott. *Star Trek: Discovery.* CBS All Access. 14 Jan. 2018. Television.
Wood, Julia T. *Communication Theories in Action.* Belmont: Wadsworth, 1997. Print.
Worland, Rick. "Captain Kirk: Cold Warrior." *Journal of Popular Film and Television* 16 (1988): 109–17. Print.
Yuhas, Alan. "Who Owns Klingon? Lawsuit Draws Battle Over Invented Languages into Court." theguardian.com. The Guardian, 30 Apr. 2016. Web. 28 Apr. 2018.
Zoglin, Richard. "Trekking Onward." *Time* 28 Nov. 94: 72–9. Print.
Zyber, Joshua. "Review: *Star Trek: The Next Generation—The Next Level.*" highdefdigest.com. High-Def Digest, 21 Feb. 2012. Web. 28 Feb. 2012.

Index

Abrams, J.J. 32, 164
Adam (biblical account) 35
Adama, Capt. Lee "Apollo" 142
The Adventures of Captain Proton 138
Africa 119
African American 29, 63
Age of Ascension 54
Ahab, Capt. 8, 47
Ain't It Cool News 152
Air and Space Museum 89
Akritirian government 139
Aldiss, Brian W. 10, 11, 12, 13, 14
Alexander, David 2, 15, 16, 17, 20, 21, 22, 23, 24, 25, 27, 28, 45, 52, 56, 63, 93, 101, 105, 112, 123, 124, 125, 163, 164, 167, 168
Alice's Adventures in Wonderland 130
"All Good Things..." 42, 79, 81, 83, 105
All-Story 11
"Allegiance" 78, 158
Alpha Quadrant 141
Altman, Mark A. 28, 29, 30, 31, 46, 47, 48, 49, 50, 51, 53, 55, 56, 57, 58, 59, 60, 61, 62, 63, 67, 68, 76, 77, 78, 79, 80, 81, 82, 87, 88, 89, 91, 94, 98, 102, 103, 104, 106, 108, 111, 117, 126, 146, 147, 148, 149, 164, 165, 166, 167
Altman and Taylor 37
Amazing Stories 12
Amazon 32
American(s) 3, 8, 15, 20, 83, 105, 134
American Gods 154
American literature 71
American Revolution 8
American Science Fiction Film and Television 151
American West (aka Old West) 57, 59, 153

Analog 12, 13
"Analysis of a Modern Myth" 38, 86–87
Anatomy of Rebellion 143
Anderson, Craig 4, 24
android 44, 45, 46, 47, 48, 49, 50, 51, 71, 73, 83
"Angel One" 57, 80, 157, 166
Anglo-Saxon culture 96
Animal House 27
AppAdvice 152
Apple, Inc. 152
An Approach to Literature 42
Archer, Capt. Jonathan 147
Aristotle 104
Arizona State University 143
Arnold, Richard 125
"The Arsenal of Freedom" 78, 157
Arthurian folklore 155
Asherman, Allan 1, 4, 17, 18, 20, 22, 24
Asia 119
Asians 127
Asimov, Isaac 13, 163
Asperger syndrome 118
Aster, Jeremy 55
Astounding Science Fiction 12
Astounding Stories 12
Athena 67
"Attached" 62, 79, 159
audience-artifact relationship 33, 41, 100, 145, 149
Aufderheide, Pat 85
Auntie Mame 53, 58
Australia 119
Autism (Spectrum Disorder) 118

B-17 bomber 15
B, William 144
Babylon 5 154

185

Index

Bader, Hilary 154
Badlands 144
Bajor 29, 103
Bajoran(s) 29, 103, 106, 119
"Balance of Terror" 101, 163
Ballard, J.G. 5
Banks, Jane 4
Bantam Books 123, 125
Barclay, Lt. Reginald 50, 56, 161
Barrett, Majel 16, 18, 19, 53, 163
Batman Beyond 154
Battle of Hampton Roads 8
Battle of Wolf 359 97
Battlestar Galactica 15, 142, 153, 154
Beasts (*The Island of Dr. Moreau*) 10
Beata, Mistress (Elected One) 80
Bechdel, Alison 72
Bechdel Test 72
Behr, Ira Steven 5, 29, 145, 154
Beimler, Hans 154
Bennett, Harve 25, 26, 27
Bentham, Jeremy 111
Berman, Rick 28, 29, 30, 31, 58–59, 62, 78, 94, 95, 103, 121, 122, 146, 166
"The Best of Both Worlds" 61, 62, 73, 91, 107, 108, 158, 167
"The Best of Both Worlds, Part II" 61, 62, 72, 74, 90, 91, 97, 107, 108, 158, 167
Betazoid 55, 57, 80, 164, 165
"The Big Goodbye" 78, 157
Biller, Kenneth 5
"Birthright, Part I" 51, 159, 164
Black, Chris 146, 147, 149
The Black Hole 15
Blade Runner 14, 15, 85, 86
Blair, Karin 36, 52, 74, 84, 118
Blish, James 123
Bloch, Robert 42, 96, 164
"Blood Fever" 140
Bloom, Melanie M. 35, 36
Bluhdorn, Charlie 25
Bly, Robert 67
"The Board and the Art of the Pitch" 126
Bochco, Steven 87, 88
"The Bonding" 56, 68, 158, 168
Bonds, Martha J. 26
Boreth 104
Borg 30, 61, 72, 73, 86, 90, 97, 98, 107, 137, 144, 151, 153, 158, 167
Bradbury, Ray 8
Braga, Brannon 31, 46, 51, 62, 82, 147, 148, 153, 165

Brandt, Dr. Andrea 129
"Bread and Circuses" 104
Bridges, Lloyd 18
A Brief History of Time 118
British television series 88
"Broccoli" (nickname) 56
"Broken Bow" 31, 147
Brooks, Avery 29
Brooks, Cleanth 42
Brooks, Mel 118
"Brothers" 48, 158
Brown, Chris 151
Brown, Eric Renner 133, 135
Buber, Martin 47
Buck Rogers 13, 44
Bumppo, Natty 71
Burnham, Cmdr. Michael 128, 129, 130, 131, 132, 133, 134, 135, 136, 149
Burroughs, Edgar Rice 11
Burton, LeVar 63, 71
Bush, President George W. 147
Bustle website 133
Butler, Robert 16

"The Cage" 17, 18, 19, 30, 163
Cairn 54
California State University Channel Islands 116
Camelot 94
Cameron, James 85
Campbell, John W. 12, 13, 164
Čapek, Karel 45
"Captain Kirk: Cold Warrior" 41, 92
Captain Video 15
"Captain's Holiday" 78, 158
Cardassia 103, 144
Cardassian(s) 29, 69, 103, 143, 144, 165
"Caretaker" 30, 138
Carnivalè 154
Carpenter, John 14, 85
Carren, David 88, 117
Carroll, Larry 88
Carson of Venus 11
Casey, Kathryn 123
Cassidy, Marsha F. 36, 60
Castle 153
Cawelti, John G. 43, 122
CBS 16, 17, 32, 146, 152, 163
CBS All Access 3, 32, 155
cbs.com 132
Changeling 145
Chapel, Nurse Christine 19, 52
Chavers, Alexander 29
Chekhov, Ens. Pavel 19, 86

Index 187

Chicago Tribune 20
"The Child" 57, 80, 81, 157
Chinese (Red) 92
Chingachgook 71
Chris-Craft Industries 30
Christenson, Gary D. 2, 28
Christianity 9, 105
"The Chute" 139
Cinefantastique magazine 126
Cipriani, Casey 133, 134
Civil War 8
Civil Wars (television series) 94
Clareson, Thomas D. 7, 10, 11
Clarke, Arthur C. 13, 99, 163
Cleveland, OH 19
Clinton, President Bill 67
Clinton, Chelsea 67
Clinton, Hillary R. 67
A Clockwork Orange 85
Close Encounters of the Third Kind 15, 24
"The Cloud" 138, 140
Cold War 92, 93
"Coming of Age" 68, 157
"The Committee" 20
Communication Theories in Action 129
"Comparing the Captains" 89
Conan Doyle, Sir Arthur 11, 50
"The Concept of Artistic Matrices" 43, 122
Conn 66, 70
"Conundrum" 80, 158, 167
convention(s) 19, 22, 28, 43, 81, 112, 113, 114, 117, 118, 119, 120, 122, 127, 155
Conway, James L. 31
Coon, Gene L. 21
Copleston, Frederick 104, 111, 167
Cornwell, Vice Adm. Katrina 136
"Cost of Living" 53, 58, 82, 158
Coste, Didier 33, 101, 112, 122
Coto, Manny 31, 148
Cranny-Francis, Anne 36, 52, 93, 124
Crash (television series) 154
Creator (religion) 10
Critelli, Joseph W. 38, 86
"Critical Methods: Speculative Fiction" 10
Cronbach coefficient 114, 115
Crosby, Denise 52, 105, 167
Crusher, Dr. Beverly 47, 50, 51, 59, 62, 65, 66, 67, 69, 71, 72, 74, 75, 76, 77, 78, 79, 90, 95, 97, 139, 160, 161, 164, 165, 166
Crusher, Lt. Cmdr. Jack R. 67, 68, 79

Crusher, Leslie 66
Crusher, Wesley 51, 65, 66, 67, 68, 69, 74, 82, 102, 103, 111, 139, 160, 165
Crystalline Entity 47
CSI: Crime Scene Investigation 146, 154
Cult 154
The CW 31

"*Dallas* Refigured" 36, 60
Danar, Roga 56
Daniels, Marc 16
Daren, Lt. Cmdr. Nella 77, 166
"Dark Page" 53, 54, 81, 159
"Darmok" 42, 102
Darwin, Charles 9, 10
Data, Lt. Cmdr. 36, 44, 45, 46, 47, 48, 49, 50, 51, 55, 59, 63, 67, 69, 70, 71, 73, 74, 83, 87, 90, 91, 97, 98, 106, 107, 118, 129, 136, 138, 153, 157, 158, 161, 164, 165, 167
"Datalore" 46, 48, 157
"Data's Day" 62, 158
Dathon, Capt. 102
Davis, Erik 127
Dawson, Roxann 139, 141
Dax symbiont 136, 143, 145
"Day of Honor" 140
The Day the Earth Stood Still 13
Decker, Cmdr. William 24, 79
Deep Space 9 (space station) 29, 30, 138, 143, 144
The Deerslayer 71
"The Defector" 50, 158
"Defiant" 144, 166
Defiant (starship) 144
Delany, Samuel R. 10, 12
Delta Quadrant 30
Demilitarized Zone 142, 144
Descartes, René 102
"Descent" 48, 159, 167
Desilu Studios 16, 17, 19, 21
"Despite Yourself" 132, 133
Dewey, John 38
Dillard, J.M. 18, 20, 21, 22, 26, 163
Diller, Barry 23, 25
"Disaster" 57, 158
Discovery (starship) 32, 131, 132, 133
Disney+ 15
The District 154
Doctari Alpha 129
Dr. Kildare 15
Doohan, James 18, 152, 168
Dorn, Michael 55, 59, 81, 120, 166
Dorvan V 142

"Drive" 141
"The Drumhead" 91, 95, 158
D'Sora, Lt. j.g. Jenna 46, 71
Dukat, Gul 144
Dune 14
Duras 55, 75, 110, 164
dyad(s) 37, 43, 65, 66, 67, 69, 70, 75, 83, 84, 91, 114, 136, 137, 138, 139, 165
Dyadic Communication 65, 70
dyadic theory 36, 37, 65, 83, 113

Earth 5, 31, 92, 104, 141, 142, 144, 148
Earth 2 6
Ebert, Roger 14
Echevarria, René 77, 152, 153
Eddington, Lt. Cmdr. Michael 144, 145
Eddy, Cheryl 132
Eisner, Michael 23, 24, 25
Elderkin, Beth 29
"Elementary, Dear Data" 50, 71, 153, 157
Ellington, Jane Elizabeth 38, 86
Ellison, Harlan 14, 15, 20, 25, 163, 164
Ellul, Jacques 63
Eloi 10
"Emergence" 50, 159
"Emissary" 95
"The Emissary" 75, 157, 165
Emmy Award(s) 1, 22, 32, 150
"Encounter at Farpoint" 45, 66, 77, 80, 152, 157, 168
"Endgame" 31, 141
"The Enduring Appeal of *Star Trek*" 94
England 155
English(man) 102, 135
"Ensign Ro" 29, 158
"The Ensigns of Command" 46, 48, 158, 166
Enterprise (starship) 3, 4, 17, 19, 21, 23, 24, 26, 27, 32, 44, 63, 74, 87, 92, 93, 109, 117, 118, 122, 128
Enterprise-D (starship) 29, 30, 41, 45, 46, 49, 50, 54, 57, 58, 60, 61, 63, 66, 69, 70, 75, 77, 80, 81, 83, 86, 88, 94, 96, 97, 98, 102, 106, 107, 108, 139, 151, 152, 153, 161, 165
Entertainment Weekly magazine 133
Erdmann, Terry J. 142, 143, 145
Erikson, Erik 35
Eros 130, 131, 132
Escape from New York 85
E.T.: The Extra-Terrestrial 15
"Ethics" 42, 58, 62, 82, 158, 166
Europe 119
ew.com 135

The Expanse 154
"The Expanse" 147
"Extreme Risk" 141
"Eye of the Beholder" 83, 159

"Face of the Enemy" 57, 159
Fajo, Kivas 46
Falling Skies 154
"Family" 67, 107, 158, 164
Fan, Mary 71, 131
Farrand, Phil 74, 75
Farscape 154
Federation (United Federation of Planets) 55, 57, 73, 92, 93, 94, 95, 97, 103, 109, 110, 131, 135, 136, 143, 144, 145, 146, 150, 165
Feinberg, Paul D. 101, 102, 104, 107, 109, 110, 111
Ferengi 80, 119, 151
Filmation Associates 22
"Filmmaker's Visions of Tomorrow" 85
"Final Mission" 68, 158
Finn, Huckleberry 71
First Contact protocols 135, 140
"The First Duty" 68, 69, 111, 158
A First Look at Communication Theory 35, 44
"Firstborn" 58, 59, 159
Fisher, B. Aubrey 38, 39, 41, 89, 90
"A Fistful of Datas" 57, 58, 59, 82, 153, 159
Flash Gordon 13, 44
Florida 8
Fontana, Dorothy (D.C.) 16, 20, 22
Foote, Stephanie 95
"For the Cause" 144
"For the Uniform" 145
Forbidden Planet 13, 45
"Force of Nature" 71, 159
Forester, C.S. 16
Fort Laramie 142
The 4400 154
Foss, Sonja 32
Foster, Alan Dean 123
The Four Loves 128, 129, 130, 134
Fox (television network) 30
Frakes, Jonathan 59, 61, 77, 79, 80, 118, 165, 166, 167
"Frame of Mind" 50, 51, 159
Frankenstein 7, 45, 48
Frankenstein, Victor 7,10
Frazetti, Dr. Daryl G. 116, 117, 121
Fredericks, S.C. 10
Free World 93

Freiberger, Fred 21, 164
French 143
Freudian (psychology) 86
From the Earth to the Moon 8
Frost, Robert 146
Fuller, Bryan 32, 154
Furillo, Capt. Frank 88

"The Garden in the Machine" 118
Geisler, Norman L. 101, 102, 104, 107, 109, 110, 111
gender differences (identity) 35, 36, 52, 53, 56, 58, 59, 63
Gene Roddenberry: Star Trek and Beyond 84
Genesis (biblical book) 35
Genesis Project 93
Georgiou, Empress 131
Georgiou, Capt. Philippa 129, 130, 131, 132, 134, 135
Geraghty, Lincoln 151, 154
Gernsback, Hugo 12
Gerrold, David 3, 4, 5, 22, 25, 26, 51, 56, 66, 121, 148, 165, 166, 168
Gianetti, Louis 14
Gilgamesh 102
Gilligan, Carol 35, 36, 53, 54, 56
GLAAD 76
God 7, 8, 9, 10, 104, 105, 106, 130
"The God Thing" 23
Goldberg, Whoopi 46, 84, 166
Golden Age (of Science Fiction) 11, 13, 42
Good (philosophy) 109
Gorbachev, President Mikhail 94
Gordon, Steven 147, 148
Gore, Vice President Al 61
Gowron, Chancellor 55, 104
Grant, Lou 88
Graves, Dr. Ira 48
Grayson, Amanda 129, 130
Great America 119
Great Bird of the Galaxy 43
Greek 67, 130
Greenberg, Harvey R. 36, 51
Griffin, Em 33, 35, 38, 39, 40, 41, 44, 96, 97, 164
Grimm 154
group communication 33, 38, 39, 40, 41, 84, 100, 116
Guinan 46, 47, 72, 73, 74, 84, 90, 97, 98, 161, 166
Gulf War 89
Gulliver's Travels 100

Haggard, H. Rider 11
HAL 9000 computer 45
"Half a Life" 53, 158
Hall, Stuart 146
Halliway, Capt. Thomas 107
Hannibal (television series) 154
Harberts, Aaron 132
Hark, Ina Rae 112
Harris, Mel 1, 2, 27
"Haven" 53, 80, 157
Hawking, Dr. Stephen 118, 167
"Heart of Glory" 54, 157, 164
Heinlein, Robert A. 4, 5, 13, 163
Henderson, Mary 89, 90
Henry IV, Part II 72
Henry V 50
Herculean 123
Hercules: The Legendary Journeys 154
"Hero Worship" 45, 46, 158
Hetrick, Jennifer 77
Hetzel, Pierre-Jules 8
High Council (Klingon) 55
High-Def Digest 3
"The High Ground" 78, 158
Highway Patrol 15
Hill, Dixon 153
Hill Street Blues 87, 88
Hispanics 127
Hoffman, Jordan 134, 136
"Hollow Pursuits" 56, 158
Holloway, Daniel 29
Hollywood, CA 16, 168
Holmes, Sherlock 50, 138, 152, 153
holodeck 47, 50, 54, 56, 57, 59, 63, 70, 71, 75, 78, 82, 138, 140, 151, 152, 153
Homer 67
Hornblower, Horatio 16, 26
Horton, Donald 42, 100, 112, 113
"The Host" 76, 158
Houske, Marta 27
Huckleberry Finn 71
Hudson, Lt. Cmdr. Calvin 143, 144, 145
Hughes, Wendy 77
Hugo Awards 150
Hulu 32
Hunley 8
"The Hunted" 56, 158
Hunter, Jeffrey 18
"Hunters" 139
Hurley, Maurice 86
Hyperspace 108

I & Thou 47
"I, Borg" 73, 97, 98, 158

Index

"'I Have Been, and Ever Shall Be, Your Friend'" 38, 71
"The Icarus Factor" 61, 157, 165
Ilia, Lt. 24, 79
Illich, Ivan 45
"Imagination and Modern Social Criticism" 96
IMDb 137, 151
In a Different Voice 35, 36, 53, 56
"In Search of Spock" 36, 51
"In the Hands of the Prophets" 103
"In the Pale Moonlight" 145
"In Theory" 45, 46, 71, 158
"In Thy Image" 2, 24
The Incredible Shrinking Man 13
Industrial Revolution 45
Infinite (religion) 105
Infinite Diversity in Infinite Combinations 41, 95, 105, 109, 121
information systems approach 40, 41, 96
"Inheritance" 49, 159
"The Inner Light" 61, 77, 158
interact system model 38, 41, 89, 90
interacts 38, 39
"Interface" 71, 159
interpersonal communication 33, 36, 38, 40, 41, 42, 45, 46, 64, 65, 84, 100, 112, 136, 149
intrapersonal communication 33, 37, 38, 40, 41, 42, 44, 53, 65, 100, 128, 129, 130, 149
Introduction to Philosophy 101
Invasion of the Body Snatchers 13
io9 website 29, 132
iPad 152
Isenberg, Jerry 23
Ishmael 71
The Island of Dr. Moreau 9–10
Ithacan 67

Jammer's Reviews 144
Janeway, Capt. Kathryn 30, 136, 137, 138, 141
Japan 94, 104
Javert, Inspector 145
Jenkins, Henry III 6, 33, 116, 117, 118, 123, 124, 125, 127
Jesuit priest 105
Jesus 104, 105
Jim (literary character) 71
J'naii 76
John Carter, Warlord of Mars 11
Johnson, Diane 7
Jones, Dorothy 123
Jono (aka Jeremiah Rossa) 109, 110
"Journey's End" 69, 103, 142, 159
Judeo-Christian 9, 112
Jung, Carl (archetypes) 51, 87, 118

Kahless the Unforgettable 104
Kaku, Michio 108
Kaluza-Klein theory 108
Kandel, Stephen 18
Kant, Immanuel 111
Kassing, Dr. Jeffrey 143
Kataan 61, 166
Katz, Oscar 16, 17
Katzenberg, Jeffrey 25
Kaufman, Philip 23
K'Ehleyr 58, 75, 110, 164, 165
Kelley, DeForest 19, 163
Kemper, David 154
Kennedy, President John F. 89, 94
Kenny, Anthony 102, 111
Khan Noonian Singh 26
Khitomer 54, 55
Kiley, Dr. Dan 140
Kim, Ens. Harry 136, 138, 139, 140
Kincaid, Buster 138
King Lear 55
Kirk, Capt. James T. 18, 26, 31, 32, 41, 52, 61, 63, 71, 74, 83, 86, 87, 88, 89, 92, 93, 95, 104, 109, 116, 124, 128, 136, 138, 150, 151
Klingon(s) 51, 54, 55, 58, 59, 70, 75, 92, 93, 94, 95, 104, 110, 119, 120, 129, 131, 133, 134, 135, 140, 141, 150, 166
Klingon Assault Group 119
Klingon Fan Clubs and Groups website 119
Klingon Legion of Assault Warriors 120
Koenig, Walter 16, 19, 22
Kohlberg, Lawrence 35
Kolbe, Winrich 51
Kolinahr 128
Koste, Elaine 112
Krishna, Swapna 141
Kruge, Cmdr. 93
Kubrick, Stanley 13, 14, 45, 85
Kurn 54
Kurtzman, Alex 32
Kutzera, Dale 48, 49, 51, 69, 71, 79, 88

L.A. Law 87, 94
La Forge, Lt. Cmdr. Geordi 47, 50, 58, 59, 62, 63, 70, 71, 73, 74, 83, 89, 90, 97, 98, 106, 136, 138, 165, 166

La Forge, George 63
Lal 49
Landau, Les 53
Landis, David R. 51, 55, 56, 57, 61, 63, 75, 76, 77, 83, 98, 103, 104, 107, 108, 166, 167
Landry, Cmdr. Ellen 131
Laren, Ens. Ro 57, 80, 106
Las Vegas, NV 120, 137, 155, 167
Law and Order 146
Law and Order: Special Victims Unit 146
"Legacy" 45, 158, 166
Le Guin, Ursula K. 98
Lemay, John 120, 121
"Lessons" 61, 77, 159, 166
"Let That Be Your Last Battlefield" 101, 164
"Lethe" 129, 130, 133
Lever, Janet 36
Lewin, Robert 78
Lewis, C.S. 11, 13, 129, 130, 131, 134
The Lieutenant 15, 16, 19
"Lieutenant Mary Sue" stories 124, 125
"Lineage" 141
Littlejohn, Stephen W. 33, 34, 39, 40
"'Live Long and Prosper'" 94
Lobi crystals 138
Locke, John 102
Lockwood, Gary 15, 16
Logan's Run 85
The Long Hunt of April Savage 18
Lorca, Capt. Gabriel 131, 132
Lord, Jack 18
Lore (android) 47, 48
Los Angeles, CA 28, 118, 119
Los Angeles Times 22
Los Angeles Tribune (fictitious newspaper) 88
"The Loss" 57, 80, 158
Lost in Space 17, 163
Lou Grant 87, 89
"Lower Decks" 88, 159
L'Rell 133
Lucas, George 14, 15
Lynch, Lawrence 7, 8, 9
Lynch, Timothy W. 88, 106, 107

Macdonald, Dr. Erin 137
Machiavellian 109
Machinac, Mindy 85
Maddox, Cmdr. Bruce 49
Maddox, David 119, 121
"Magic to Make the Sanest Man Go Mad" 133

Make It So 155
The Making of Star Trek: Deep Space Nine 126, 127
Making Star Trek: Enterprise Even Better 147
A Man Called Hawk 29
"Man of the People" 57, 159, 167
Mancini, Marc 14
The Mandalorian 15
"Manhunt" 53, 157, 164
Manning, Richard 154
Maquis 30, 137, 141, 142, 143, 144, 145, 149
"The Maquis, Part I" 143, 144
Marin, Rick 89
Marr, Dr. Kila 47
Marseilles, France 138
The Mary Tyler Moore Show 87
mass communication 33, 41, 99, 100, 112, 116, 126
"Mass Communication and Para-Social Interaction" 42, 100, 112
Master of the World 15
"Mata Haris" 74
Matthias, Jean Louise 88, 117
Mazza, Tom 30
McCarthy, Sen. Joseph 91
McConnell, Frank 94
McCoy, Dr. Leonard 19, 86, 87, 90, 91, 151
McFadden, Gates 62, 66, 78, 79, 121
McMillan, Graeme 31, 146, 147, 148
McNeill, Robert Duncan 138, 139
Mead, George Herbert 33, 34, 35, 36, 45, 47, 49, 50, 51
Meaney, Colm 29
"The Measure of a Man" 49, 73, 157
Medeiros, Mark 119
Medium (television series) 153
Medium (website) 29
Megatrends 64
Melrose Avenue 27
Melville, Herman 8
"Ménage à Troi" 23, 53, 68, 80, 158
Menosky, Joe 102
Mentor 67
metanarrative 32, 33, 122
Metaphysics 104, 167
Metropolis 13
Meyer, Nicholas 26
Meyers-Briggs 87
MGM 16
Mill, John Stuart 111
Miller, Kevin 119, 121, 127

192 Index

Miller, Wyatt 80
Mind, Self, & Society 33, 45
Mintaka III 105
"Mirror, Mirror" 133
Mirror Universe 131, 132, 133, 134
Les Misérables 145
Moby Dick 47, 71
A Modern Utopia 9
USS *Monitor* 8
Monkees 19
"Monty Cristo" 152
Mooney, Darren 31, 145, 147, 148
Moore, Ronald D. 48, 58, 62, 66, 68, 69, 75, 81, 82, 94, 111, 142, 153, 164, 165, 167, 168
Morbius, Dr. 45
Moreau 10
Moriarty, Prof. James 50, 152
Morlock 10
"The Most Toys" 45, 46, 48, 158
Mozart, Wolfgang Amadeus 68, 69
Mudd, Harry 133
"Mudd's Women" 18
Mulan 154
Muldaur, Diana 78
Mulgrew, Kate 137
Murphy Brown 94
Muzak 8
"My Appointment with the *Enterprise*" 98

Naisbitt, John 63
Naked City 15
"The Naked Now" 46, 77, 157
Narrative as Communication 101, 122
NASA 3, 23
Native American Indians 69, 103
NATO 41, 93
Nautilus 8
NBC 1, 6, 17, 18, 19, 20, 21, 22, 28, 146, 163, 164
Nemecek, Larry 2, 27, 46, 49, 55, 56, 57, 61, 62, 66, 67, 71, 74, 76, 78, 80, 87, 91, 102, 110, 155, 165
Netflix 32
"The Neutral Zone" 85, 151, 157
New Age (spirituality) 103
The New Batman Adventures 154
"New Ground" 58, 158
New World Order 94
New York, NY 22
New York Times 2, 3, 23
Newscorp 30
Newton, Sir Isaac 122, 167

"The Next Phase" 106, 158
Nichols, Nichelle 16, 19
Nietzsche, Friedrich 10
Nimoy, Leonard 16, 18, 24, 44, 164
9/11 terrorist attacks 147, 148, 155
The Nitpicker's Guide for Next Generation Trekkers 74
Nobel laureates 108
North America 119
Northwestern University 36
Nuclear Nuances (bar) 27
Number One 17, 18, 52, 79, 153
Nye, Bill 1

Obligatory Scene 136
O'Brien, Chief Miles 29
Odan, Ambassador 76
Odo, Constable 129
The Odyssey 67
Odyssey 5 154
"The Offspring" 49, 158, 168
"The Omega Glory" 18
Omni magazine 94
"On Science Fiction" 11
Ops 70
O'Quinn, Kerry 2, 28
organizational communication 33, 40, 41, 84, 85, 86, 92, 96, 97, 98, 100, 115, 116, 124, 142, 143, 149
Otterson, Joe 29, 155
"The Outcast" 76, 158
The Outer Limits 15
Outlander 153, 154
An Outline of History 10
"The Outrageous Okona" 47, 157
Oxford Dictionaries 138

PADD(s) 152
Paglia, Camille 45
Pahvo (Pahvan) 133, 135
Palm Beach Atlantic University 151
"Parallels" 82, 83, 108, 159, 165, 166
Paramount Communications 125
Paramount Network 24
Paramount Parks 119
Paramount Pictures 1, 2, 3, 4, 21, 22, 23, 24, 25, 26, 27, 28, 30, 31, 118, 120, 121, 125, 127, 150, 152, 163, 166, 168
parasocial interaction(s) 6, 42, 100, 112, 115, 137
Parham, Thom 43, 113, 114, 167
Paris, France 8
Paris, Miral 141
Paris, Lt. j.g. Tom 136, 138, 139, 140, 141

Paris in the 20th Century 8
Peabody Award 150
Peeples, Samuel A. 18, 22
Pellucidar 11
The Peter Pan Syndrome 140
"Phantasms" 51, 159
Phillips, Michelle 77
Piaget, Jean 35, 36
Picard, Capt. Jean-Luc 41, 42, 49, 50, 55, 59, 60, 61, 62, 63, 65, 67, 68, 69, 70, 72, 73, 74, 75, 77, 78, 79, 83, 85, 87, 88, 89, 90, 92, 95, 97, 98, 102, 105, 106, 107, 108, 109, 110, 111, 113, 114, 115, 150, 151, 152, 153, 154, 155, 160, 161, 165, 166, 167, 168
Picard, Robert 107
Pidgeon, Walter 45
Pike, Capt. Christopher 18, 52, 163
Pike, Christopher 94
Pike, John 27
Piller, Michael 28, 29, 30, 46, 60, 61, 62, 82, 86, 90, 91, 95, 102, 103, 106, 110, 111, 126, 143, 153, 166
Pinocchio 45
Piscopo, Joe 47
Planet of the Apes 85
Plato 60, 111, 152
"Plato's Stepchildren" 52
Pocahontas 154
Pocket Books 125
Poe, Edgar Allan 11
Police Story 18, 163
Post, Stephen G. 135
Potemkin (starship) 81
Powell, Gen. Colin 118
"Power Play" 57, 106, 158, 167
"The Price" 72, 158
Prime Directive (Starfleet General Order #1) 41, 93, 95, 109, 135
The Prince of Egypt 154
A Princess of Mars 11
Priority One podcast 119
Profiler 154
Prophets (Bajoran) 103
Proton, Capt. 138
Psychiatry magazine 42, 100, 112
Psychology Today magazine 129
Pulaski, Dr. Katherine 78, 91, 161, 164
Purser, John Thibaut 42
Pushing Daisies 32, 154

Q 30, 42, 106, 107, 151
Qo'noS 136
"Qpid" 78, 153, 158

Quark 138
Quarton, Janet 2, 27
Quayle, Vice President Dan 61
QueeQueg 71
Questor 45
Quora 128

Ral, Devinoni 72
Rand, Yeoman Janice 19
Randazza, Marc 120
Reality (philosophy) 104
Reception Theory 145, 146, 148
"Redemption, Part I" 55, 105, 158
"Redemption, Part II" 48, 55, 105, 158
Reed, Donna 66
Reed, Lt. Malcom 147
Reeves-Stevens, Judith and Garfield 29, 126, 142
"Relics" 63, 152, 159, 168
"Remember Me" 67, 78, 103, 158
"Reunion" 55, 75, 110, 158
Rhetorical Criticism 32
Rice, Lt. William 15–16
The Rifleman 28
Right (philosophy) 109, 167
"Rightful Heir" 104, 159
Riker, Lt. Thomas 62, 72, 80, 81, 144, 166
Riker, Cmdr. William T. 45, 51, 57, 58, 59, 61, 62, 65, 68, 72, 74, 75, 76, 77, 79, 80, 81, 83, 87, 89, 90, 91, 97, 118, 144, 160, 161, 165, 166, 167
Robby the Robot 45
Roberts, Dr. Wes 155
Robin Hood 153
robot(s) 13, 20, 45
Roddenberry, Gene 1, 2, 6, 15, 16, 17, 18, 19, 20, 21, 22, 23, 24, 25, 26, 27, 28, 29, 30, 43, 44, 45, 50, 52, 57, 63, 64, 66, 70, 78, 79, 83, 84, 85, 86, 87, 91, 93, 94, 95, 96, 98, 100, 101, 102, 103, 104, 105, 109, 112, 117, 121, 123, 124, 125, 127, 139, 142, 143, 149, 150, 151, 155, 163, 164, 165, 166, 167, 168
Roman Empire 104
"Romances of the Future" 10
Romanticism 5, 7
Romper Room 58
Romulan(s) 54, 55, 57, 86, 92, 95, 105, 106, 119, 164
Romulus 60
Ronin 72
Ross, Bill 155
Roth, Dany 73, 74

Royal Navy 138
Rozhenko, Alexander 53–54, 58, 59, 66, 75, 82, 139, 165
Rozhenko, Helena 54, 58, 164
Rozhenko, Nikolai 54, 164
Rozhenko, Sergey 54, 164
Rubenstein, Josh 151, 152
Ruditis, Paul 30, 137, 138, 139
R.U.R. (play) 45
Russell, Dr. Toby 62, 165
Russian(s) 19
Ryan, Maureen 32, 129, 131

Sackett, Susan 23
Sacks, Dr. Oliver 118
St. Eligius Hospital 88
St. Elsewhere 87
"*St. Elsewhere* and the Evolution of the Ensemble Series" 41, 87
"Samaritan Snare" 68, 157
San Diego Comic-Con 32
San Francisco Chronicle 23
San Jose, CA 119
Sandríne's bar (aka Chez Sandríne) 138, 140
Sarek, Ambassador 129, 130, 133, 134, 136
Saru, Cmdr. 135
Satie, Rear Adm. Norah 91, 92, 95
Saturday Night Live 116
Saturn 5 15
Schatz, Thomas 41, 87, 88, 89
"The Schizoid Man" 48, 157, 167
Schmidt, Stanley 13
Sci-Fi Channel 142
"Science as Fiction" 4
Science Fiction Encylopedia 4
Science Fiction Films of the Seventies 24
"Scorpion, Part II" 137
Scott, Lt. Cmdr. Montgomery 18, 63, 86, 87, 152, 168
Scott, Ridley 85
Sea Daddy 138
seaQuest 2032 154
"Second Chances" 62, 72, 80, 81, 159
Second Coming (religion) 104
Sela, Cmdr. 55, 105
Selly, April 38, 71
"The Sentinel" 13
Serling, Rod 15
Seven of Nine 129, 136, 137, 138
"Sex and *Star Trek*" 36, 52, 74, 84
"Sex Differences in Ethical Systems" 35
"Sexuality and Sex-Role Stereotyping in *Star Trek*" 36, 52, 93

Seymour, Carolyn 57
"Shades of Gray" 80, 157
Shakespeare, William 50, 55, 70, 72, 154
Shankar, Naren 153, 154
Shatner, William 15, 16, 17, 18, 19, 21, 22, 23, 116
Shelby, Lt. Cmdr. 90, 91
Shelley, Mary 7, 8, 10, 45, 48
Shenzhou (starship) 130
"Ship in a Bottle" 42, 50, 138, 152, 159
"Si Vis Pacem, Para Bellum" 133, 135
"Silicon Avatar" 45, 46, 47, 158
Simon & Schuster publishing 125
Simonds, P.K. 6
"Sins of the Father" 54, 75, 94, 158, 168
Sirtis, Marina 53, 56, 57, 81, 165, 166
Sisko, Capt. Benjamin Sisko 29, 95, 103, 136, 143, 144, 145
"Skin of Evil" 56, 60, 80, 83, 105, 154, 157
Sliders 154
Smith, Cecil 22
Smith, David C. 9, 10
Smithsonian Institution 23
Smyth, Steve 128
Snodgrass, Melinda 48, 49, 51, 94, 164
The Social Psychology of Organizing 40, 96
Son of God (religion) 105
Soong, Dr. Noonian 47, 48, 51
Soong, Juliana 49
Soper, Taylor 118, 119
Soren 76, 77, 166
South America 119
Soviet Union (Soviets) 19, 92
Sowards, Jack B. 26
Space: 1999 46, 64
space opera 5, 6, 12, 13, 14, 15, 18, 25, 44, 98, 100, 112, 124, 142
"Space Seed" 26
space shuttle 3, 4, 23, 163
Spelling, Ian 32, 121
Spenser for Hire 29
Spielberg, Steven 24
Spiner, Brent 44, 51, 118, 119
Spirit of St. Louis 23
Spock, Cmdr. 17, 18, 19, 21, 24, 44, 51, 52, 71, 83, 86, 87, 88, 90, 91, 109, 124, 128, 129, 130, 136, 138, 150, 151, 164
Spock Must Die 123
"Spock's Brain" 21
"Squire of Gothos" 151
Stamets, Lt. Paul 133
Stapf, David 32

Index

Star Trek (Original Series) 1, 2, 3, 4, 16, 17, 19, 20, 21, 22, 23, 25, 26, 28, 43, 52, 63, 71, 74, 83, 86, 87, 89, 91, 92, 93, 94, 101, 104, 108, 112, 114, 117, 124, 125, 133, 136, 142, 146, 148, 161, 163, 164, 167
Star Trek (2009 film) 32, 152
"*Star Trek* and Television's Moral Universe" 112
The Star Trek Concordance 123
Star Trek Creator 123
Star Trek: Deep Space Nine 5, 28, 29, 31, 32, 95, 103, 114, 119, 126, 127, 128, 129, 136, 142, 143, 144, 149, 151, 153, 154, 161, 163, 165, 166, 168
Star Trek: Deep Space Nine Companion 145
Star Trek: Deep Space Nine Writers Bible 142
Star Trek: Discovery 3, 31, 32, 128, 129, 132, 134, 135, 136, 149, 154, 155
Star Trek Encyclopedia 143, 167
Star Trek: Enterprise 31, 128, 129, 145, 146, 147, 148, 149, 153
Star Trek: First Contact 31, 142, 159
Star Trek Generations 3, 47, 61, 142
Star Trek II: The Wrath of Khan 2, 26, 58, 109, 129
Star Trek III: The Search for Spock 27, 93
Star Trek IV: The Voyage Home 27
"*Star Trek* Mail Call" 20
Star Trek Movie Memories 21, 22
Star Trek: Nemesis 81, 121, 159
Star Trek: Phase II 2, 24, 79
Star Trek: Picard 155
"*Star Trek* Rerun, Reread, Rewritten" 33, 123
Star Trek: The Motion Picture 2, 24, 25, 52, 79, 128, 129, 149, 168
Star Trek: The New Voyages 125
Star Trek: The Next Generation 1, 2, 3, 5, 6, 27, 28, 29, 30, 31, 33, 41, 42, 128, 129, 136, 138, 139, 142, 146, 148, 149, 150, 151, 152, 153, 154, 155, 157, 161, 165, 166, 167, 168
Star Trek: The Next Generation Companion 49
Star Trek: The Next Generation Companion (rev. ed.) 155
Star Trek: The Next Generation Episode Guide 51, 55, 56, 57, 61, 63, 75, 76, 77, 83, 88, 89, 98, 103, 104, 106, 107, 108, 165, 166, 167
Star Trek: The Next Generation Writers/Directors Guide 70, 79
Star Trek: The Next Generation Writers/Directors Guide 2d. ed. 91
Star Trek VI: The Undiscovered Country 26
Star Trek: Voyager 5, 30, 31, 32, 52, 65, 101, 119, 127, 128, 129, 136, 137, 138, 141, 142, 143, 144, 145, 146, 149, 153, 163, 165, 168
Star Trek: Voyager Bible 140
Star Trek: Voyager Companion 137
Star Wars 14, 15, 24, 85, 168
Starfleet 26, 27, 29, 30, 41, 49, 52, 54, 55, 56, 61, 66, 70, 86, 92, 93, 94, 95, 96, 98, 109, 110, 111, 117, 120, 124, 130, 134, 135, 136, 137, 139, 142, 143, 144, 145, 146
Starfleet Academy 54, 57, 68, 69, 111, 134, 161
Starfleet Medical Reference Manual 123
Starfleet Technical Manual 123
Starlog magazine 2, 25, 26, 28, 86, 126
starship(s) 2, 4, 16, 17, 28, 29, 30, 31, 48, 55, 63, 66, 72, 81, 131, 132, 133, 135, 137, 139, 141, 142, 144, 165
"Starship Mine" 60, 159
Statler-Hilton hotel 22
Stellar Sciences 77
"Steve Jobs Must Be a *Star Trek* Fan" 152
Stevenson, Robert Louis 11
Stewart, Sir Patrick 51, 59, 60, 61, 77, 78, 154, 167
The Strain 154
"Sub Rosa" 62, 72, 106, 159, 167
"Suddenly Human" 109, 110, 158
Sulu, Lt. Hikaru 18, 86
Sumerian legend 102
Superboy 154
Superman: The Animated Series 154
Supreme Being (religion) 104, 105
Sweeney, Terrance 105
"Symbiosis" 95, 157
symbolic interactionism 33, 36, 44, 45

Takei, George 18
Tal Shiar 57
Talarians 110
Tamarian 102
Tankel, Jonathan David 4
"Tapestry" 106, 107, 159
Tartikoff, Brandon 28
Tarzan at the Earth's Core 11
Tarzan of the Apes 11

Taurik, Ens. 89
Taylor, Jeri 31, 47, 48, 52, 57, 62, 65, 69, 76, 77, 79, 80, 91, 92, 101, 109, 110, 112, 143, 153, 166
Teen Wolf 153
TekWar 154
Telemachus 67
Television Academy 1
Television Drama: Agency, Audience, and Myth 5
The Tempest 50
Ten Forward 72, 73, 88
Terminator 85
"Terra Nova" 147
Terran 51, 128
Terran Empire 131, 133, 134, 136
Them! 13
"Thine Own Self" 48, 58, 159
The Thing 14, 163
Things to Come 13
Third of Five (aka "Hugh") 73, 98
Third World 92
Thompson, Bradley 154, 168
Thompson, Gregory 139, 140
Thrace, Lt. Kara "Starbuck" 142
Tilly, Cadet Sylvia 130, 131, 132
The Time Machine 9, 10
Time magazine 100
"Time's Arrow" 72, 73, 158
"Time's Arrow, Part II" 72, 73, 159
T'Kuvma 135
Tom Corbett: Space Cadet 15
Tonks, Paul 152, 153
Tools for Conviviality 44–45
Tormé, Tracy 90, 154, 164
Torres, Lt. j.g. B'Elanna 136, 139, 140, 141
T'Pol 129
"The Tradition of Agape" 135
The Traveler 68, 69, 102, 103
Trekkers 2, 28, 29, 31, 89, 95, 99, 115, 129
Trekkie(s) 117, 118
"Trekking Onward" 100
Trelayne 151
Trillian 76
Trimble, Bjo 2, 21, 26, 43, 123
Trimble, John 21, 123
Troi, Counselor Deanna 36, 51, 52, 53, 54, 55, 56, 57, 58, 59, 63, 65, 66, 68, 71, 72, 74, 75, 77, 79, 80, 81, 82, 83, 90, 97, 108, 161, 165
Troi, Kestra 54
Troi, Lwaxana 53, 54, 58, 66, 68, 80, 81, 82, 166

Trojan Wars 67
"The Trouble with Tribbles" 25, 121, 148
Trump-era politics 134
Tulloch, John 5
The Tunnel 13
"Turnabout Intruder" 21, 63
TV Guide magazine 2, 28, 89, 95
"TV Market List" 126
24 153
20,000 Leagues Under the Sea 8
The Twilight Zone (1959) 15
The Twilight Zone (2002) 154
2001: A Space Odyssey 13, 14, 45, 85
Tyler, Lt. Ash 132, 133, 134

Uhura, Lt. Nyota 19, 52, 86, 104
Ulysses 67
"Under the Moons of Mars" 11
"Unification" 60, 105, 158
United Nations 92
United States 2, 4, 19
United States Navy 138
University of Chicago 33
UPN (United Paramount Network) 30, 31, 136, 154
Upstairs, Downstairs 88

Variety magazine 1, 19, 29, 32, 129
Vash 78
Verne, Jules 7, 8, 9, 11, 12, 163
V'ger 103, 128, 129
Viacom 119
Victorian (period) 5, 10
Vietnam 15
Vikings 58
"Violations" 80, 158
CSS *Virginia* 8
Virginia Beach, VA 42, 113
VISOR 70
Voq 134
Vorik, Ens. 140
Voyager (starship) 30, 137, 139
Voyager 6 (space probe) 129
Vulcan (s) 21, 24, 44, 109, 118, 119, 123, 128, 129, 130, 132, 133, 135, 147

Wagon Train 142
Wainer, Alex 43, 113, 114, 151, 167
Walsh, Michael 122
Wang, Garrett 138, 139
The War of the Worlds 9
War on Terror 147
Warner Bros. 30
Warren, Robert Penn 42

Washington, D.C. 89
Watergate 15
"The Way to Eden" 21
The WB 30, 31
"We Have Met the Enemy and It Is" 95
Weddle, David 154, 168
Weick, Karl 40, 41, 96, 97, 98
Welch, Claude Emerson 143
Wells, Herbert George (H.G.) 9, 10, 11, 12, 163
Werner, Mort 17
Werts, Diane 60, 74, 75
Western society 93
Westerns (genre media) 93, 98
Westphall, Dr. Donald 88
Wheaton, Wil 68, 165
Wheel of Fortune 3
When Calls the Heart 154
"Where No Man Has Gone Before" 18, 20
"Where No One Has Gone Before" 68, 69, 102, 157
"Where Silence Has Lease" 105–106, 157
Whitfield, Stephen 17, 19
Whitney, Grace Lee 19
"Who Watches the Watchers" 56, 103, 105, 158, 166
"Why Discovery Should Drop Burnham's Romantic Subplot" 133
Wilkerson, Ronald 88
Williams, Robin 118
Wilmot, William W. 36, 37, 65, 70

Wired magazine 31, 146, 147, 148
Wisdom (philosophy) 104
Wise, Robert 24, 164
Wohl, R. Richard 42, 100, 112, 113
Wolfe, Sheila 20
Wood, Julia T. 129
Worf, Lt. 36, 51, 52, 53, 54, 55, 56, 57, 58, 59, 62, 63, 66, 67, 69, 70, 74, 75, 81, 82, 83, 90, 92, 94, 97, 104, 108, 110, 120, 139, 161, 164, 165, 166
Worland, Rick 41, 92, 93
World Science Fiction Convention 19
World War II 15, 96, 143
Wright, Herb 90, 166
Writers Guild of America 5, 164, 165
Writers Guild's *Journal* 126

Xena: Warrior Princess 154
Xindi 148
Xon, Lt. 24

Yar, Ishara 46
Yar, Lt. Tasha 46, 52, 55, 80, 83, 105, 154, 161
Yates, Capt. Kasidy 144
Yeltsin, President Boris 94
Yeoh, Michelle 130
"Yesterday's Enterprise" 55, 105, 158
Young Sheldon 150

Zoglin, Richard 100, 112, 116, 118, 122, 125, 150
Zyber, Joshua 3

www.ingramcontent.com/pod-product-compliance
Lightning Source LLC
Chambersburg PA
CBHW032044300426
44117CB00009B/1191